A
Better
Place
to Live

A Better Place to Live

Reshaping the American Suburb

PHILIP LANGDON

The University of Massachusetts Press

Amherst

Copyright © 1994 by Philip Langdon
All rights reserved
Printed in the United States of America
LC 93-42348   ISBN 0-87023-914-7
Designed by Mary Mendell
Set in Melior by Keystone Typesetting, Inc.
Printed and bound by Thomson-Shore, Inc.
Library of Congress Cataloging-in-Publication Data
Langdon, Philip.
A better place to live : reshaping the American suburb /
Philip Langdon.
p.   cm.
Includes bibliographical references and index.
ISBN 0–87023–914–7 (alk. paper)
1. Suburbs—United States—Planning.   I. Title.
HT352.U6L36   1994
307.1′214′0973—dc20   93–42348 CIP

British Library Cataloguing in Publication data are available.
Portions of this book were published in a different form as
"A Good Place to Live" in the *Atlantic Monthly* (March 1988).

To Paul A.
Knights,
a generous
and diligent
teacher

Contents

When I began crisscrossing the nation ten years ago writing architectural articles and books, I was frequently shown America's newest and supposedly best-designed suburban residential developments. In these developments, the builders or realtors or architects who served as my tour guides liked to point out that the bad old days of postwar tract development were over. "Look at all the trees we save," they boasted. "We set aside land for parks and open space. We provide amenities like tennis courts and clubhouses. We choose a *theme* for the architecture." The individuals guiding these developments assured me, "This is what people want." For the most part, I listened respectfully. Their success at selling what they produced seemed to indicate that the places I was seeing probably *were* what people wanted.

Yet the highly touted new developments — and many other new suburban projects built on leaner budgets with fewer luxuries — left me with doubts. In almost every case, something important seemed to be missing. What was it?

From each of these trips I returned home to a New Haven neighborhood that had been developed between 1905 and 1920. Invariably I felt happier in this old neighborhood, which I'd adopted as my own in 1983, than in the new places I visited. For a while I thought that it was mainly the artificial materials and perfunctory craftsmanship of the newly built houses that made the new places seem unsatisfying. Certainly those elements were part of the trouble. Old houses I've known have tended to have hardwood floors, thick moldings, substantial window casings, and other weighty features. Accurately or not, they convey a sense of solidity and strength that is much harder to discern in many new houses.

But as I continued traveling, other kinds of contrasts between the new and the old occupied my attention. It became evident that house construction was only one of the differences between the new suburban areas and the older places I was familiar with. More important than construction details of the dwellings was the community layout and the pattern of daily life it fostered. In Greenville, Pennsylvania, where I was born in 1947, I recalled that I walked innumerable times to stores that were situated on mostly residential streets within a few blocks of home, there to buy candy bars, comic books, and other childhood treats. My parents relied on me to make frequent trips to the diminutive East End Bakery, bringing back soft, floury potato rolls and other fresh baked goods. Greenville, with its 9,000 inhabitants, was a place that a child or an adult could get around in by foot or bicycle. Some of the men in the neighborhood walked the three blocks to their jobs at Greenville Steel Car Company, which man- ufactured railroad cars and was one of the town's major employ- ers. My father did not; he was a newspaperman for the local *Record-Argus* and worked each day in a second-floor office in Greenville's small, busy downtown. Yet even though our family didn't get a paycheck from "the Steel Car," as it was commonly called, the fact that the street from our middle-class block led right past the company's factory and office made me conscious, from an early age, of where many of the townspeople earned a living and what they produced. The street network provided the beginnings of an education. Good streets introduce a person to the community and provide an opportunity to begin thinking about its character and well-being. A sense of civic responsibility may spring from such exposure.

As a consequence of my father's unexpected early death and my mother's remarriage, we left Greenville when I was eleven and I spent my high school years in Wesleyville, Pennsylvania, a compact little community near Lake Erie, next to the city of Erie, which then had a population of about 130,000. Wesleyville, orga- nized by religious folk who in 1823 named the settlement for John Wesley, the founder of Methodism, evolved in the twentieth century into a suburb, but one that harbored its own distinct local spirit. With 3,300 people in a single square mile, it was, like Greenville, a pedestrian-scale town. Residents could walk in a few minutes to any of four churches, perhaps two dozen stores, the bank, the post office, the borough hall, a few eating and drink- ing places, doctors' and dentists' offices, and other establishments, most of which were located on the town's principal thoroughfare, Buffalo Road, U.S. Route 20.

The third community in which I spent a stretch of several years was East Aurora, New York, a village of 7,500 that was founded in the first decade of the 1800s and was gradually pulled into the suburban orbit of Buffalo, about fifteen miles to the northwest. Except for the headquarters and hometown factory of Fisher-Price Toys and a few smaller employers, East Aurora was an automobile commuter village. I drove five days a week to my job at a newspaper in downtown Buffalo; my wife worked in the city too. Because East Aurora had been laid out long ago, it was still compact and walkable. It was a refreshing place to come home to. Stores, churches, restaurants, offices, and civic buildings were strung along pleasant, maple-shaded Main Street, which was connected at each block to the surrounding residential streets. Nearly everything the inhabitants needed, except a full range of employment, was close to home. East Aurora, because it was so nearly complete, maintained a strong sense of its own identity.

When my wife and I, searching for better work, eventually moved from East Aurora, we found similar patterns in our New Haven neighborhood: dry cleaners, dentists, haircutters, mom-and-pop grocery stores, taverns, churches, pizza joints, parks, softball diamonds, child care centers, and much else lay within walking or biking distance. Our neighborhood, though it benefited from having Yale University in the vicinity, was not terribly out of the ordinary. This was how most American communities used to take shape.

Few of the new suburban developments I have been introduced to around the country follow anything like these patterns. They adhere to the modern notion of segregation of land use. Offices are kept separate from retailing. Retailing is kept separate from housing. The housing frequently is divided into mutually exclusive tracts. Detached houses are built in one tract, townhouses in a second tract, garden apartments in a third, with further subdivision by economic status. Manufacturing, no matter how clean and quiet—today's industries are rarely the noisy, smoke-belching mills of urban memory—is kept away from residential areas or excluded from the community entirely. Street layouts in new developments enforce apartness. To unlock the rigid geographic segregation, an individual needs to obtain a key—which is a motor vehicle. For obvious reasons these keys are not issued to those under sixteen, the very segment of the population for which the suburbs are supposedly most intended. These keys are also denied to some of the elderly who can no longer drive. These keys to overcoming acute geographic segregation are denied, as well, to residents who cannot afford a car or who do not have a vehicle at their disposal all the time. When contrasted against the patterns of old communities, the development patterns of modern suburbs make for an inconvenient way of living, one that generates a variety of troubles for their residents and for society as a whole.

So I became engrossed with the thought of exploring whether suburbs today could be designed differently. It struck me that earlier forms of community building, many of which had been cast aside in the rush toward being as "modern" as possible, might supply useful ideas for our time. Recognizing that there was much I didn't know, I decided to see many different kinds of places that had developed during a long span of American history, from eighteenth-century Savannah, with its elegantly ordered streets and squares, to postwar towns in southern California. I visited streetcar suburbs, railroad suburbs, automobile suburbs, garden suburbs, urban neighborhoods, small towns, company towns, greenbelt towns, 1960s New Towns, newly constructed suburban "villages," planned-unit developments, and much anonymous suburban development. I observed how things worked. I tried to talk with all kinds of people, "experts" and nonexperts alike. In five years' time I traveled to eighteen states. Many of the suburban residents I met told me about their frustrations with today's development formulas; they were less pleased than the marketing specialists and sales records had suggested.

I was not the first person to embark on such investigations. A spate of suburban studies, some of them excellent, appeared in the 1950s and 1960s, petering out by the 1970s. In the past few years, as the suburbs have gained a dominant position in American life, studying the suburbs has again become a compelling activity for journalists, academics, planners, and designers. Not only have people increasingly been talking and writing about the suburbs; a small number of designers, developers, and planners in different parts of the country, most of them on the East, West, and Gulf coasts, also have been creating communities aimed at overcoming the defects of postwar suburban growth. I wrote about two of the leaders of this effort, Andres Duany and Elizabeth Plater-Zyberk, in a cover article in the *Atlantic Monthly* in March 1988 and have broadened my search since then.

Suburbs, I believe, need to break free of the crippling limitations imposed on them since approximately the 1940s. We need to develop suburbs that foster neighborhood and public life rather than squelch it. This requires designing suburbs so that public areas throughout the community are enjoyable to occupy. Comprehensive networks of sidewalks are essential. Sidewalks and streets should be organized so that people will have incentives to explore their neighborhoods. Houses need to treat the public areas as important, congenial places. Instead of glorifying interior and private spaces while leaving the public environment dominated by uncommunicative facades and garage doors, we need to reorient houses so that they dignify and enliven the places where neighbors and strangers come in contact with one another.

We need to rethink our planning ideas so that neighborhood stores, neighborhood institutions, neighborhood gathering places will have a better chance of coming into being and giving heart to the community. Neighborhood gathering places will not fare well unless communities are designed and regulated differently from what has been customary in the past fifty years.

We need to think about achieving a broader mixture of housing, so that communities can become more nearly complete, interdependent societies, containing people of varied ages and incomes. We need to consider increasing the density of some suburbs. Rather than reflexively favoring houses on big lots, we ought to ponder the advantages of creating enough concentration to nurture a vigorous community spirit and to support stores and institutions within walking distance of homes. If we do this, many of the vexations of our current way of living might begin to diminish.

We need to tame the transportation departments, few of which have recognized how their standards and practices make modern suburbs unsatisfying.

Modern times have tended to adopt a hostile attitude toward the relevance of the past. One of the widespread assumptions of the last several decades has been that modern conditions differ so radically from those of earlier times that they render historical practices obsolete. The notion that today we inhabit a wholly new epoch, with no need for the physical forms and social connections upon which people previously depended, has flattered the modern soul tremendously. It has given modern designers heroic conceptions of their powers. It has promised to liberate people from age-old constraints. But this antitraditional way of thinking has also led to the abandonment of much that is valuable, much that we cannot healthily do without. The fact is, humanity's basic needs change extremely slowly, if at all. Technology may leap forward and as it does the economy may undergo spasms of change, but we are foolhardy if we base the nature of our communities on the latest technological and economic innovations while blinding ourselves to innate human needs.

When I started writing about architecture nearly twenty years ago, the architectural profession was, on the whole, antagonistic toward all popular suggestions that new buildings should look and behave much like old buildings. It took the determination of the historic preservation movement—made up largely of citizen activists, not architects—to move the architectural profession toward acknowledging the many virtues of traditional buildings. Today it's not uncommon for new buildings to draw from tradition. Some new buildings do so in faddish, superficial ways, oblivious to the true strengths of historic buildings. But quite a few new buildings successfully incorporate the real virtues of the old—healing the breach between late twentieth-century construction practices and our cultural underpinnings. They contribute to a more satisfying environment. Genuine improvements have occurred.

A similar campaign has to take place at the level of community design. Today's critical task is to understand how modern methods of planning and design have led us astray and to identify elements of the past that more fully encompass human needs. In this book I look with an appreciative eye at traditional ways of designing communities—ways that I believe have in many instances served people well. I attempt to encourage those who plan, design, build, and inhabit the suburbs to recognize qualities of traditional design that could be employed for society's benefit. In some cases practices from the past can be revived intact. In other instances they must be adapted to changed circumstances. The point is not that today's world should in every respect mimic the past. It is that historic communities embodied many important understandings about human nature, about what contributes to a satisfying individual and family life and a healthy society. The past possesses an accumulation of wisdom which we ignore at our peril.

Those who recognize that the modern American suburb is mired in serious difficulties should be searching for ways of creating a better place to live. That search is what this book is about.

Acknowl-

edgments

I wish to thank the Graham Foundation for Advanced Studies in the Fine Arts for a grant that enabled me to begin research for this book. I am grateful to the National Endowment for the Arts for a USA Fellowship, which enabled me to travel extensively and complete the project.

Many people, more than I can name here, provided valuable help. During three years of illuminating meetings, Patrick Pinnell shared his knowledge and suggested many beneficial changes in the manuscript. Anton Nelessen read the manuscript and offered useful suggestions. Portions of the manuscript were also reviewed by Philip B. Herr, Mark Hinshaw, James Krohe, Jr., Walter Kulash, Dennis McClendon, Joe McElroy, Evan McKenzie, Ray Oldenburg, Elizabeth Plater-Zyberk, Ethan Seltzer, Richard Untermann, James Wentling, and David B. Wolfe. Their suggestions greatly improved the text. Any flaws in the text are my own.

I am grateful to Kris Allen and her students at Upland High School for essays the students wrote about Euclid Avenue at my request. Thanks to the many people and institutions who helped with illustrations, particularly Denise Van and the Village of Oak Park, Illinois, and Duany and Plater-Zyberk, Architects. I also wish to express appreciation to Randall Arendt, David J. Baab, Jonathan Barnett, Michael Brill, Robert Bruegmann, Patricia Butler, Richard Calderon, Peter Calthorpe, Daniel Cary, Rick Chellman, John A. Clark, Robert S. Davis, Chris and Mike Dodd, Bob and Marilyn Dorfman, Andres Duany, Keller Easterling, Michael Ebner, John Fairfield, Thomas Fisher, William Fulton, Mark Gottdiener, Samuel M. Hamill, Jr., Douglas Pegues Harvey, Morrell and Barbara Heald, Xavier Iglesias, Douglas M. Kleine, Ruth Eckdish Knack, Alex Krieger, Randall Lewis, J. Carson Looney, Zane Miller, Buz and Roz Paaswell, Frank S. Palen, Mitchell

Rouda, Jennifer Shakespeare, Daniel Solomon, Douglas L. Stern, Ed Straka, Robert Teska, Henry Turley, Janet Warburton, Alan Ward, Mike Watkins, Robert Yaro, and Reuel Young.

Thanks to Bill Whitworth, editor of the *Atlantic Monthly,* for sending me on the magazine assignments that whetted my appetite for this subject. Thanks to Kit Ward, my agent, and Bruce Wilcox, director of the University of Massachusetts Press, for so enthusiastically shepherding the manuscript to publication. Finally, I am grateful to my wife, Maryann Langdon, for her patient support during what turned out to be a very long undertaking.

A
Better
Place
to Live

ONE

America's Failing Suburbs

The United States has become a predominantly suburban nation, but not a very happy one. Today more than three-quarters of the American people live in metropolitan areas, and more than two-thirds of those live in suburbs. Each year development pushes out across more than a million acres, yet the expansion of highways, housing tracts, and other suburban construction rouses fewer cheers than at any time in the past. The problem is not simply that a sensible person can no longer believe in the rightness of turning huge expanses of farmland, forest, desert, and other rural landscapes into additional suburbs. The problem is that the suburbs we build are fostering an unhealthy way of life.

In this book I try to show how the prevailing methods of planning, building, marketing and regulating the suburbs have fostered frustration—not for everyone, at least not yet, but for so many that the subject can no longer be safely ignored. It is no coincidence that at the moment when the United States has become a predominantly suburban nation, the country has suffered a bitter harvest of individual trauma, family distress, and civic decay. There is a strong connection between the ills we exhibit as a people and the suburban "communities" (to use a much-abused word) that we inhabit. How much responsibility the suburbs bear for today's widespread ills is difficult to say with precision, just as it is difficult to judge whether a person who came down with lung cancer got it solely from living in a house full of cigarette smoke. It could be that the person with cancer got it from breathing the heavy pollution that pervades the entire town. It could be that the disease arose from exposure to other noxious substances or because of some weakness in the person's own biology. It could be a combination of all of these. Cause and effect are often not as clear as we would like; they are especially murky when the subject is rampant social ills. So I should be clear: The late twentieth-century suburbs are not the only thing making us sick. But the suburbs are implicated in the downward spiral. After spending much of the last several years exploring the workings of suburbs, I have come to the conclusion that suburban ways of living—in particular, the ways of living associated with the suburbs we have been building since World War II—have been bad for us as individuals and as a society.

We are being injured in two ways—one from the defects of the suburbs themselves, the other from the more general contaminants in our society, contaminants that a well-designed community might enable us to fight, just as the body's immune system enables us to fight all manner of diseases and infections. The contaminants, or agents of distress, affect virtually the whole body of society. Though not new, the contaminants or agents of distress have reached high levels in recent years. They include:

—The economy, many of whose jobs are unfulfilling.
—The costliness of American life and the presumption that a person who does not obtain expensive material goods is a failure. This presumption is perhaps a little more subtle than my one-sentence summary of it, but its effects come down to this: only the winners of the economy's Superbowl of material rewards are encouraged to feel truly good about themselves. A physician who spends much of her social time with affluent professionals recently told me, "Everybody I know thinks they're not making enough money or not living as well as they should be." America seems to have devised a Superbowl in which even the Most Valuable Players are unhappy with their performance. This, of course, serves the interests of businesses that fill the exaggerated wants.
—The insecurity of work and pay. Many companies in recent years have upset their employees by fiercely cutting staff, shutting offices and factories, moving out of state or out of the country, and demonstrating in other ways that conscientiously doing one's job does not guarantee a future. With labor unions weakened, pensions questionable, and governments unwilling or unable to protect individuals from the roller-coaster ride of the economy, people at all income levels are uneasy. Robert Hodges, an executive of Sampson, Neill & Wilkins, a management recruiting firm, told the *New York Times,* "Stress used to

be noticeable around age 55, but now we find it at earlier and earlier ages."

—The influence of marketing and advertising in American life. Since mastering the basics of psychology in the 1920s, the marketing profession has spent several decades honing its ability to manipulate our apprehensions about our attractiveness, social status, and other attributes. The latent worries are stirred by seductive commercial messages whose underlying theme is: Buy or be incomplete.

—A barrage of distressing news and information from near and far. As custodians of the global village, the mass media administer a daily shock treatment that makes even the occupants of the most comfortable family room feel involved in the worst calamities the world has to offer.

—An entertainment industry that depends on shock value as a way of competing for audiences and earnings. There is a ceaseless push for performances that test the bounds of taste or morality, with the result that standards are uncertain and the more conservative part of the populace is in a nearly constant state of being offended by popular culture.

Every reader can add to this list of the forces that keep people off balance, forces that encourage them to feel they have little control over their lives and their society.

Many of the forces I have cited have existed for a long time. What is notable is how pervasive many of them have become in recent years. For example, there have long been purveyors of mass culture—newspapers, magazines, radio—but in their video incarnation the instruments of mass culture possess more potency than ever. The larger and more lifelike the video images become, the greater their capacity to disturb. Television makes it easy for the world's tensions and a commercial outlook about what is important in life to penetrate the home several hours a day. In a typical American household, the TV is turned on for seven hours daily; the tone and the content of life in its most intimate setting cannot help but be influenced by it.

These forces would be potentially unhealthy under any circumstances. The great virtue of a well-designed community is its ability to offset some of the debilitating effects and to offer compensating sources of satisfaction. A good community counteracts the forces that when unchecked tend to break down individuals and societies.

3

One way that suburbs traditionally have accomplished this is by supplying contact with nature. Being close to plant and animal life—trees, gardens, birds, wildlife—has always been restorative for people burdened by urban and social pressures. The presence of nature connects people with what is authentic and what is beautiful. Any worthwhile suburb preserves elements of nature so that individuals can refresh their spirit.

A healthy suburb, however, should do much more than offer contact with nature. A healthy suburb ought to foster a balanced way of living; it should nurture avenues of behavior that improve the chances for attaining satisfaction. It should enhance our ability to steer a wise course and avoid becoming mired in modern life's man-made swamps.

The suburbs built since the Second World War have instead made people more vulnerable to the pressures of modern life. They have narrowed the opportunities for attaining important kinds of satisfaction. This is so both because of problems or defects in the suburbs themselves and because of troubles in the society at large—troubles that a better-designed suburb could counteract.

The first of these involves time—specifically, the scarcity of it. Increasingly suburbanites are pressed for time to spend with their families, time to devote to individual pursuits, time to involve themselves in social and community affairs, time to keep the household functioning.

Time is being eaten up in at least three ways. First, the workweek has stopped shrinking; for many Americans, the number of hours spent on the job has begun to expand. Because of deep cutbacks in the work force at many companies, the employees who remain are under pressure to work longer hours. Junior corporate managers whom William H. Whyte studied in the early 1950s for his book *The Organization Man* were shown, in a classic photograph, departing the 4:51 train they had taken from downtown Chicago to Park Forest, a new suburb south of the city. The message of the black-and-white photo seemed to be what a herdlike existence these men lead. But today the message is less single-minded. What emerges now is the relative ease of their schedule. They left work so early! They arrived home with several hours of the day still to enjoy. They had time to spend with their families. They had time to spend in what seems by today's standards a whirlwind of neighborhood and community activity. They had time to spend in other pursuits. Time outside of work

Even in 1953 a day at the office took a lot out of a person. But the commuters just off the 4:51 train from downtown Chicago to the new suburb of Park Forest still had plenty of time left in the day, and they spent much of it socializing with neighbors.

became tantalizingly generous for many people in the 1950s. Predictions of a three-day workweek began to be heard. Such forecasts have since fallen into oblivion. Harvard University economist Juliet Schor reports that the average American works 163 hours more per year than his or her counterpart did in 1970. Measured in forty-hour workweeks, the portion of the year spent working has grown by four weeks. Measured in time lost per day (assuming the individual works five days a week, fifty weeks a year), thirty-nine minutes have disappeared from each day's leisure. Today people are being told to expect to work longer or harder or both.

A second component of the time problem is that most women today run on a kind of double treadmill. They continue to be responsible for the bulk of the work at home, the Big C's—cleaning, cooking, and child care. Men are helping with these duties more than they used to, but the burdens are still split unevenly between husbands and wives, and there seems little reason to believe that a fifty-fifty division of domestic duties will arrive soon, if at all. Despite this, women, even those with young children, go out to earn paychecks, something most of them did not need to do thirty years ago. Nearly 60 percent of married women hold paid jobs. More than half the married women with preschool children are in the workforce. The opening of employment opportunities to women is an extension of justice and ought be safeguarded, but it is also a reflection of a stressful increase in material expectations, which makes suburban life harder. The practical reality is that day-to-day life has become more hectic both for women and for the men they marry.

A third component of the time problem is that the inhabitants of some suburbs in the largest metropolitan areas are having to devote punishing amounts of time to commuting to and from work. The minority of suburbanites who find themselves in this situation are affected by it enormously. "Around New York City, the new growth has taken place along a ring roughly 60 miles from Manhattan," John Herbers reported in 1985. Since then development of housing has continued moving outward. A growing number of people travel between jobs in New York City or nearby suburbs and homes in western New Jersey or eastern Pennsylvania. Workers in the Boston area, with its population of 4.2 million, commute from homes as distant as Cape Cod. The Cape is the most rapidly suburbanizing part of the state; its population has nearly tripled since 1960, and it is not uncommon for the commuters who live there to have a daily round trip of 100 to 120 miles. Suburbanization in the Los Angeles region, with its 14.5 million people, has leaped northward over the San Gabriel Mountains and penetrated the Mojave Desert. Simultaneously it has extended eastward beyond Riverside and San Bernardino.

Journalists have coined a new term—"the boomdocks"—to describe some of the outer suburbs that combine remoteness and rapid growth. One swelling corner of the boomdocks is Moreno Valley. Moreno Valley is the fastest-growing municipality in

Moreno Valley, California, where commutes of sometimes four hours a day erode family and neighborhood life.

Riverside County, which in turn is the fastest-growing county in California. Mainly a bedroom community, Moreno Valley sits in a 1,600-foot-high basin surrounded by low, brown mountains, twenty miles east of the Los Angeles County border. From 28,000 in 1980, Moreno Valley's population exploded to 116,000 in 1990. By the year 2000 it is expected to reach 170,000.

Early in the mornings a multitude of Moreno Valley residents crowd onto Highway 60 to drive through a pass in the mountains and then onto the 91 Freeway for forty-five-mile trips to jobs in Orange County. Those working in Los Angeles travel still farther. The resulting traffic congestion is becoming legendary. "A lot of people put in about four hours a day on the freeway," says former mayor Judith A. Nieburger. (Four hours a day of commuting is also common for residents of Mojave Desert towns who work in or near Los Angeles.) "It's getting worse," Nieburger says. "Around here at 4:30 or 5 o'clock in the morning it's amazing how busy it is on the road. Those with campers or motor homes go in and sleep in the parking lot before work."

The average freeway speed in southern California dropped from more than 50 miles an hour in the mid-1970s to 47 miles an hour in 1984, and it is expected to plummet to 24 miles an hour by 2010 unless new transportation facilities are built. Once celebrated for their ability to connect a huge metropolis with ease, the freeways now spawn what sound like tall tales—except that they are true. The *Wall Street Journal* told about a man called "The Owl" who lingers around his office at a defense contracting firm in El Segundo until others have departed. Then he eats a brown-bag supper, writes letters, reads, and practices his golf swing. At the end of the evening, he goes to the company parking lot and spends the night in a sleeping bag in his car. He does this several nights a week rather than endure the four-hour, 110-mile round trip to his four-bedroom house in Yorba Linda. "My wife just hates it," he said, adding that he worries about whether he will be available to help his wife, who is pregnant, when she has to be taken to the hospital. "People just aren't meant to live like this," he said. The Owl blames himself for his predicament. "The biggest mistake I ever made," he said, "was not learning a skill I could use in a place like Montana, where you can really enjoy the time you've got on earth."

In Santa Ana, in Orange County, I visited Howard and Anne, who live with their twins—a boy and a girl—in an attractive two-bedroom house in a neighborhood of tree-lined streets built in the 1950s. Howard is a lean, athletic man in his forties with a wry sense of humor. If his high school class in Pennsylvania had picked anyone as "most likely to succeed," Howard would have been the one. He excelled in both sports and academics, eventually getting a doctorate in economics after a stint as an aerospace engineer. Now he is an economist for a large financial institution. Anne, a former schoolteacher, works as a manager for a pharmaceutical company. They are both successful in their careers; they are intensely pressed for time. Anne begins her days by dropping the five-year-olds at preschool and then driving to her job in a nearby suburb. Howard spends an hour and twenty-five minutes en route to his office in Los Angeles. At the end of the afternoon, commuting eats up nearly an hour and a half. Anne arrives at work at 8:00 A.M. She leaves in the afternoon at 5:55 P.M. "I drive like hell to make it to pre-school by 6:00 P.M., as the fine is $5 per minute per kid after six o'clock," she says. "Howard is not home to help until 6:50 or 7:00."

Occasionally Howard thinks of his father, who had a ten-minute drive between a suburban home and his job as a factory foreman. In the fall Howard's father would stop after work to watch him practice as quarterback of the high school football team. In the spring his dad would stop to watch him play with the tennis team. Unless something changes drastically, Howard will have no opportunity to lavish such attention on his own children. By the time he gets within range of home and school, the day's athletic workouts and other extracurricular activities will have been dismissed.

The sacrifice of everyday pleasures and responsibilities weighs

similarly on people in northern California. The San Francisco–San Jose–Oakland region, home to 5.9 million people, is developing long-distance commuting patterns increasingly like those of Los Angeles. The Bay area has generated suburbs as far away as the Central Valley. Karen Palmer works as a financial manager in San Francisco and lives in Antioch, a fast-growing suburb fifty-three miles to the east. Her household chores frequently pile up, and she often feels exhausted. The commute leaves her little time to spend with her daughter. "When she was little," Mrs. Palmer told a newspaper reporter, "I had this fear [that she wouldn't] recognize me."

For most workers with long-distance commutes, evenings and weekends revolve around hurried attempts at child care, shopping, cooking, cleaning, yard maintenance, auto servicing, and other duties. Is shopping an enjoyable break from home? Not when time is scarce. Sixty-three percent of the people surveyed in a *Business Week* poll in 1989 said shopping was drudgery or worse. This is one reason for the 60 percent increase since 1983 in the number of people who do some of their shopping by mail or phone. The fact remains that shopping by catalog cannot make up for more than a small portion of the time spent in transit. Time lost is gone forever. In the words of former mayor Nieburger, the loss of time through commuting "kills family life."

These cases are worse than the norm. Most people in the

United States commute for fifty-five to seventy minutes a day, according to Elizabeth Deakin of the University of California at Berkeley. The majority of residents of the newest suburbs do not commute into the old central business district. Some of the jobs are moving out toward the hinterland, closer to where the new suburbanites live. But the spreading out of metropolitan regions and the reliance on increasingly clogged highways do not bode well for the future.

The second defect or problem in which the suburbs are involved is money—specifically, the large amount of it needed to maintain a suburban mode of life. At the remote edges of metropolitan area, houses are cheaper than they are close in. This is the biggest reason why people settle in distant suburbs like Antioch and Moreno Valley. Yet suburban life, even in the boomdocks, is anything but cheap. When each working adult needs a car and when teenagers need vehicles too, transportation devours a substantial portion of household income. The strain of automobile ownership is evident in car loans, which have stretched from two- to three-year terms in the past to the now-common four- and five-year duration. On top of the purchase price and financing are piled a series of other automotive expenses: insurance, gasoline, oil, inspections, maintenance, repairs, licensing, parking, tolls, and, in some jurisdictions, property taxes. The American Automobile Association calculates that in 1991 an average mid-sized car cost 43.6 cents a mile to own and operate. Assuming that the car is driven 10,000 miles per year, this means that a suburban family spends $4,360 to keep a car at its disposal. But it's a rare suburban family that gets by with just one vehicle. In the suburbs built since World War II, homes have been deliberately placed away from work and stores; public transportation in these communities is scant, there being no efficient way to serve such dispersed houses, workplaces, and shopping areas, even if the demand for public transportation were strong. So the average suburban household has a car for each of its adults. If we look at the typical family, there are two cars, not one. The annual cost of vehicles, then, is likely to double, to $8,720. How much of a crimp does this put in the family budget?

The Census Bureau says that in 1991 the mean income of households outside central cities but inside metropolitan areas was $44,103. In that year, the average household nationally paid $5,901 in federal income taxes and $2,807 in federal payroll taxes, for a total federal tax bill of $8,708. If we subtract the federal taxes from the $44,103 annual income, the mean after-tax income comes out to $35,395. Transportation expenditures of $8,720 thus consume 24.6 percent of the household's income after federal taxes. If these figures are a fair representation of the suburban families' finances, this means that suburban families are working ninety days of each year just to pay for transportation. They work from January 1 through March 31 to support their cars. To recognize the cost of suburban living, we could designate April 1 as Auto Freedom Day. On April 1 people begin earning money for food, shelter, education, clothing, recreation, household furnishings, and so on. Up to April 1 all their after-tax money is going to buy transportation.

If these figures err, they probably err on the conservative side. If, rather than *mean* household income, I had used *median* household income (the income figure that half the nation's households exceed and half the households fall below), the figure for gross suburban household income would have been considerably lower: $36,590. By that calculation, the family would have had a good deal less money—$7,513 less—to start with. Transportation would then have consumed closer to 27 percent of the family income. The AAA figures on which I've relied could be criticized for assuming that the family buys new mid-sized cars and trades them in every four years. Some families pay less for transportation because they drive cars that are older and cheaper. But if the AAA figures overestimate costs by assuming that everyone starts out with a new car, they underestimate costs in other respects. To cite two examples, they assume that no car goes more than ten miles to work, which is unrealistic, and they assume that there are no young drivers in the household. In most suburban households with children over sixteen years old, the children drive, so the insurance costs are much higher than in the AAA calculations. Many teenagers also decide they need a car of their own, so many suburban families end up with a third vehicle, which further boosts their transportation costs.

The postwar suburban style of life is predicated on unlimited access to automobiles. This generates a number of costs that are not reflected in my estimate that suburbanites work ninety days a year to support their vehicles. Suburban households nearly always have driveways and garages. These occupy a sizable portion of the property. A two-car garage is bigger than the typical living room or family room. The cost of the land needed for the driveway and a two-car garage and the cost of constructing the

Facades are a blank parade of garage doors in this subdivision in the Newport Hills area southeast of Seattle.

garage increase the cost of housing. The AAA estimate also omits the substantial indirect costs of building entire metropolitan areas to accommodate near-total reliance on private vehicles. The automobile is the aristocrat of American development. A car would no more be expected to make do with a single place to park than a Rockefeller would be expected to make do with only one home. A car, under present standards, requires multiple parking places—one at home, one at work, one at the store—all of them off the public street, no matter how costly metropolitan land happens to be. Enabling the automobile to move about is an enormously expensive system of streets and roads. According to the Federal Highway Administration, construction of a metropolitan interstate highway costs $39 million a mile. The Miami architect Andres Duany observes, "Nobody ever says, 'Let's build a cheap road.'" To these vehicle-related costs might be added the expense of building many extra miles of water and sewer pipe, electrical lines, gas lines, and other infrastructure to serve the spread-out automobile community. The full cost, both public and private, of designing communities around maximum use of private vehicles is immense. As one person has remarked, for the first time in human history we can drive ourselves to the poorhouse.

People feel the brunt of suburban costliness in a variety of ways. In the San Ramon Valley—a rapidly developing valley well east of the San Francisco Bay, over the hills from Oakland and other East Bay communities—I talked with Mark and Linda, who live in a suburb called San Ramon. Mark, the general manager of a cellular telephone business, welcomed me into a several-year-old tract house where he and Linda, a schoolteacher, were bringing up two sons and a daughter. They had bought their house, with its four bedrooms and its three-car garage, a year before my visit. Mark was still astonished by the price. "You know, you're sitting in a half-million-dollar house!" he exclaimed as I lowered myself into the family room sofa.

Mark had stayed with the same company for twenty-two years, moving nine times as he advanced up the corporate ladder. Linda had taught in a succession of schools; California was the fifth state in which she had earned a teaching certificate. The main financial reward for their work was their not particularly well-built subdivision house, which dominated its lot, just as the other two-story houses on the cul-de-sac dominated the other lots. Neither Mark nor Linda complained about the hurdles they had jumped to get where they were now. They spoke enthusiastically about experiencing life in a variety of places, including Ohio, Pennsylvania, Tennessee, Connecticut, Texas, and now California. Their children seemed to have taken the moves well. Their older son, Aaron, had become an Eagle Scout at fifteen, working at it with the goal (as he told Mark and Linda afterward) of making Eagle Scout at a younger age than Mark himself had done.

Yet even with two salaries, Mark and Linda's finances felt the strain of their suburban way of life. "We're on a budget," Mark said. "We have to watch our pennies." Housing was the most noticeable expense, but hardly the only one. School costs could unexpectedly throw the family budget out of whack. The local school district had stopped supporting many extracurricular activities; if the students or their parents wanted extracurricular activities, the students or parents had to pay extra for them. When Aaron, muscular and confident, won a spot on the high school football team. Mark and Linda had to pay for uniforms and equipment and for Aaron's share of the coach's salary. Class sizes, too, were increasingly being left to the paying abilities of parents. Parents who wanted a low student-teacher ratio in an important college preparatory class had to raise the money among themselves each semester to pay for the extra teacher. Linda said, "Some of the people around here are struggling."

A dispersed, automobile-dependent suburban development is expensive to build and maintain. Governments have coped with the public costs—such as streets and roads—by shifting some of those costs to developers, who in turn charge higher prices for the housing they produce. Institutions such as school districts have cut back on other services once paid for with tax dollars. In the end, the residents are stuck with the costs in more than one way, as Mark and Linda and their neighbors had learned. The suburban ways of developing are costly.

If financial burdens and a shortage of time for enjoyment are two of the chief problems suburbanites encounter, a third problem is a sense of fragmentation and disconnection. Linda had the good luck to get a teaching job near their home, but Mark's office is in Hayward, over the range of hills to the west. It is far enough away that Mark rarely found opportunities to relax with people from work. Mark had felt a sense of disconnection recurrently in his career. When he and Linda lived in Connecticut, he faced a nearly fifty-mile round trip between his home in Trumbull and his job in Stamford. Because of the distances, Mark said, "there was no overlap between work and home. The people I'd see at work I would never see at church or other activities in Trumbull." The realms of work and home failed to reinforce each other.

Disconnection or fragmentation undermines the social ties that give individuals pleasure and invigorate community life. In southern California, Howard the economist says the people he knows at work do not go out together for a drink or recreation at the end of the afternoon. They have to make wheels turn for the long journey home. Nor do they see one another in the evenings after dinner. "We all live in different directions," he says. When they arrive at their remote homes, they find constraints there; neighborhood sociability is limited. Howard arrives home late. The neighbors have commutes of their own. The prospect of relaxing with those who live in the vicinity is slim.

People tend to endure fragmentation stoically. Compared with how readily suburbanites talk about financial strain and a hurried schedule, they talk much less freely about their disappointment with the lack of a daily social life outside of work and home. It may be that they have a hard time finding the right words. Or they may feel embarrassed, as if their longing for a more sociable community marked them as weak. Many people undoubtedly assume that a scarcity of daily contact with fellow inhabitants of their community is a fact of contemporary life beyond their control. In the *Atlantic,* Nicholas Lemann compared Park Forest, Illinois, in the 1950s with the newer suburb of Naperville, Illinois, in 1989 and concluded: "In Naperville it seems much more possible not to know your neighbors." Talk about "family values" during the past couple of decades may have nourished the idea that each family should take care of its own emotional and other needs, independent of neighbors or community. Builders have placed great emphasis on making the interior of the house as lavishly equipped as possible.

The overemphasis on the home and family—and the concurrent neglect of the usefulness of regular socializing with others in the neighborhood—puts marriage under more stress. Many psychologists believe that marriages function better when the demands placed on them are less all-encompassing. Relying for one's well-being solely on home and work is like trying to sit on a two-legged stool. It can be done—but for how long and with how much strain? *Homo sapiens* is a social animal. He, or she, stands a better chance of contentment when avenues for acting on social impulses are plentiful.

In *The Great Good Place,* sociologist Ray Oldenburg argues that people need a "third place," outside of work and home, where they can make contact with others. In Britain, the pub is one such third place. People often take a short walk in the evening to a neighborhood pub. It gets them out of the house, provides a change of pace, and nourishes their ties with other people from the neighborhood. There are no dues to pay at the pub and no rigid schedule to adhere to. People arrive when they wish and leave when they please. People typically depart the pub feeling better about their day, their neighborhood, and their lot in life.

In France, many people spend part of the day at a cafe. In Scandinavia, they enjoy others' company while soaking in a sauna. In Russia people go to bathhouses in search of companionship as much as cleansing. Through the centuries, societies have spawned informal gathering places where the stresses of work and home can be left behind for a while. The companionship of others is an important balm. It is instinctive to human nature; we deny it at our peril.

But it is denied in most of the suburbs built in the past fifty years. Oldenburg calls them "the sterilized and purified suburbs." The tavern, the cafe, the coffee shop, the neighborhood store—these and other potential gathering places have been zoned out of residential areas. Few are the neighborhood places where people can go in hopes of striking up a conversation with

others who have a little time on their hands. As informal gathering places have been banished, many opportunities for making friendships and pursuing common interests have disappeared.

Jim is an investment analyst who works in Chicago's Loop. When I visited him at his home in Lisle, Illinois, one of the city's western suburbs, he said his biggest disappointment with his subdivision was the difficulty of developing lasting friendships. He and his family moved into a subdivision ten years ago when it was new. Like most new neighborhoods, it started with an exuberant pioneering spirit. Neighbors organized progressive dinners. They got to know one another. That spirit faded as years went by and houses changed hands. Households became more withdrawn from one another. For a while Jim worked to make friends with the newest arrivals in the subdivision. The area contained many corporate transferees, however, and no sooner would a friendship solidify than the friend would move away. Some houses changed hands four times in ten years. "I'm more reluctant to try to make friends now," Jim said. "It takes a lot of time and effort to make a friend."

The difficulty he has experienced is chronic in high-turnover neighborhoods. Each year in the United States approximately a fifth of the population changes addresses. Neighbors are continually moving away. Conventional suburbs leave someone like Jim with sharply restricted possibilities. The most likely course is to become a member of formal institutions—a church, for instance, or a country club. Jim has done a little joining. He has discovered, however, that formal organizations are not a wholly satisfactory answer. The church he goes to has a limited, fixed schedule, and like many churches, it's not located where it can serve as a gathering place for people in his neighborhood. Jim and his wife cannot walk to their church; it's in Naperville, the next town to the west. Nor can they walk to a country club.

They cannot walk to a neighborhood gathering spot for the simple reason that there *are* no neighborhood gathering spots. "For a while, the people in the subdivision used to get together to take care of the sign at the subdivision entrance and the landscaping around it," Jim said. "Then the house next to the entrance changed hands, and the new owners started taking care of it themselves. That was pretty much the end of organized neighborhood activity." No one—neither the designer nor the developer nor local officials—thought to create gathering spots or to make it easy for such places to come into being after the subdivision was occupied.

Jim is not an outwardly unhappy man. But as he talked, it became evident that suburban life has not satisfied him as much as he would have liked. A great many suburbanites are in the same situation as Jim.

A community center under construction, barely connected to the subdivision it serves in Lincoln, Nebraska.

The lack of neighborhood connection is unmistakable in a subdivision I visited in Crofton, Maryland, south of Baltimore and east of the nation's capital. A couple I spent time with in Crofton, Frank and Beverly, have a comfortable house with three bedrooms, two cars, one dog, no children, and a dearth of neighborhood life. They have lived in their subdivision nearly ten years. A couple of years ago they got involved in a program of the Naval Academy in nearby Annapolis which encourages families to welcome midshipmen into their homes for a couple of hours to a couple of days at a time. On some weekdays and most weekends Frank and Beverly have one or more students from the academy over for meals, sports on TV, studying, and other activities. At Christmas as many as six young guests gather around the dining room table. The academy's visitor program improves the social life not only of students (which is its goal) but also of the host families.

But no matter how rewarding, a program with young people who live a dozen or more miles away cannot compensate entirely for the lack of vigorous community life in one's own neighborhood. "We both feel there's something missing," Frank said of life in Crofton. When they retire—which is several years in the future—they are thinking of moving back to the small town in Ohio where Frank grew up. All their years in Crofton have failed to bond them to their neighborhood.

The frequency with which Americans move from one town to another or one part of the country to another has been celebrated as an expression of freedom and opportunity. But it is also something very different—a reflection of the shallowness of the places they leave behind. People hop from suburb to suburb or from one part of the country to another because few suburbs are compelling enough to command their affection. The typical modern suburb is a temporary stopping place. It does not offer rewards strong enough to make people insist on staying. This is exactly the opposite of many urban ethnic neighborhoods, where people will put up with old buildings, antiquated interiors, tight parking, noise, and mediocre public services because they get so much stimulation and contentment from their surroundings, particularly the people around them.

A sense of isolation is always close to the surface in suburbs where there are no handy gathering places. One night when I was in Frank and Beverly's house, screaming pierced the quiet atmosphere outside. In the darkness the screaming continued for some time. The rest of the neighborhood remained silent. No one responded. It was as if everyone was pretending that nothing disturbing was happening. I learned that the screams were coming from a house across the road where an alcoholic woman lived alone. The screaming in the night was not unusual; it occurred periodically.

There is more distress in the suburbs than people like to admit. And there is far too little capacity for responding to it. Frank and Beverly were unhappy about the misery across the street but were unsure what to do. A natural reaction in such a situation is to want to do something, yet to feel unauthorized to intervene. The people who live in Frank and Beverly's vicinity do not gather regularly. They know one another superficially, if at all, and they remain inexperienced in how to reach an informal consensus on issues that concern them. A lone household will usually not solve a neighborhood problem. Solutions are much more likely when there exists a genuine society of neighbors—people who know one another, who are in the habit of getting together as a group, and who therefore feel empowered to act in the neighborhood's interest.

Murray Bookchin argues in *The Rise of Urbanization and the Decline of Citizenship* that individuals isolated from one another are powerless. By contrast, individuals who form an active local society gain the ability to influence conditions. People coming together—discussing their concerns, exchanging ideas, noticing how the others respond—learn how to handle many delicate situations. They map strategies that are sometimes remarkably complex. When they stay apart, with no gathering places and little informal mixing, they are often impotent to handle even the most elementary annoyances. In Hamden, Connecticut, a suburb near my home, once or twice a week I bike through a residential area that includes a large undeveloped property continually strewn with trash and broken trees. The people who live in the vicinity seem unable to get the owner or the town to clean it up—and seem incapable of organizing to clean it up themselves. When I bike past the area (I once stopped and collected the returnable bottles and cans myself; there were a couple of dollars' worth), it occurs to me that this is not a neighborhood; it is only a collection of unconnected individuals. Unfortunately, America has devoted most of the past fifty years to building neighborhoods that foster just such individualistic impotence.

Let it be said that modern America does contain a staggering number of organizations. There are associations, federations, institutes, coalitions, clubs, and leagues galore. Block clubs, neighborhood associations, and similar organizations serve important purposes. Most of America's organizations, however, operate with severe limitations. The most politically influential organizations work mainly at a regional, state, or national level, where they become caught up in pursuing generalized solutions to problems that have occurred in numerous places. In their search for broad themes and common solutions, they lose sight of the distinctiveness and nuances of local situations. A problem that occurs in only one community will fail to register on the consciousness of a regional or state organization. A second flaw is that many organizations pursue narrow interests. When Americans divide up into separate groups with narrow concerns, it becomes difficult for the community as a whole to reach a consensus. Suburbanites have displayed a poor capacity for bringing together people with varied interests at the municipal or neighborhood level so that they can act on local or neighborhood concerns. Americans would have better luck at resolving problems if they were more frequently in contact with other members of their neighborhood or municipality. Regular local activity is a key to influencing local life.

Return for a moment to the woman screaming in the night in the subdivision in Crofton, Maryland. When distress like this forces its way into public notice, many Americans respond with an individualistic point of view: the distress is the result of the weakness or foolish behavior of the person in pain. But each of us is weak in one way or another. The composition of our households and the design of our neighborhoods magnify the weaknesses.

Edward Shorter, a medical historian, has found that people in the United States and Canada today have more medical complaints than they did a few decades ago, especially complaints that doctors consider psychological in origin. He believes that one reason for the increase in psychological complaints is the decline in the number of individuals per household. When people lived in bigger households, they had contact with more people daily in their homes. Because of this, they tended not to dwell so much on their maladies. If they did complain about an ailment, the listener knew enough about their personality and habits to provide reasonably effective reassurance. Regular social contact often prevented small problems from developing into large ones. In today's small households, contacts are fewer, and problems can fester. The average household size has declined to 3.17 persons. Roughly a quarter of American households consist of a solitary person. Some 23 million Americans, like the woman in Crofton, live with no companions.

With so many small households, it is more essential than ever that people have opportunities for social contact. They need opportunities to form a network of relationships, fending off the dangers of excessive isolation. Some of today's distress either stems from, or is exacerbated by, America's scarcity of everyday mechanisms for dissipating trouble. Individuals suffer from being isolated from potential friends and contacts. Neighborhoods suffer from being ill equipped to ease residents' troubles and address mutual concerns. Social scientist Amitai Etzioni says, "The consensus of sociological and psychological work supports the basic notion that isolation—whether the product of urbanization, mass society or other phenomena—erodes the mental stability necessary for individuals to form their own judgments and resist undue external pressure and influence. Thus, individuals require community; without it, they are diminished if not incapacitated." Etzioni further states, "A basic observation of sociology and psychology is that *the individual and the community 'make' one another,* and that individuals are not able to function effectively without deep links to others, to community."

It is not that suburbs are devoid of places where people cross paths with one another. One such place is the shopping mall, which is frequently described as today's community center. Dr. Judith Coady, a sociologist at the University of Connecticut, studied American shopping malls for five years. "I expected to find the mall as some kind of new community, particularly for suburbia," she told the *New York Times*. "But I found that the mall is not a community at all. . . . There was the appearance of community, but the interaction was truncated if there was any at all. The focus is on consumption, on the pleasure of just being there. The issues that are part of our everyday community are not discussed there, so it doesn't function as a community." In observing some mall-goers, Coady discovered a particular style of walking, which she calls the mall walk. "It's primarily a slower walk to the rhythm of music in the mall," she said. "The eyes are unfocused. Generally speaking, there's a kind of glaze on the eyes and a benign stare on the face. The mall brings it on."

The mall gives people an erroneous impression of community life, Coady said. "There is a feeling that you have participated in the community, when you have merely wandered in the presence of other wanderers." Meanwhile, she observed, "The community problems get worse, because while people are dallying in malls, the problems remain hidden and out of sight."

Other places where people cross paths in the suburbs include the gyms, swimming pools, tennis courts, and other facilities that developers have provided in some of the more lavish residential developments. These provide the setting for a certain amount of shared activity. But these are often expensive and are tailored to those with specific, usually athletic, interests. More important, they are often not situated within walking distance of homes, so they do not necessarily function well as community gathering places. Ideally gathering places would be inexpensive—allowing people to use them regardless of their finances—and they would be at least partly informal, so that people can come and go at will, and located within an enjoyable walk of the homes of their clientele.

For centuries, informal gathering places helped people to find out what was on their neighbors' minds and begin to form a consensus on issues that needed to be tackled. On the basis of informal discussions, people sometimes decided how to handle problems—without requiring the involvement of government agencies and other formal institutions. In small towns, many problems have customarily been handled in an informal way, by people who know who is out of work or whose children are making trouble or which park could use some sprucing up. Not every problem needs to be forced onto the agenda of a town council or referred to a department of social services. When problems do require decisions by governments or other organized bodies, the existence of a vigorous informal community life helps ensure that the problem and the possible solutions will be thoroughly understood. A place that lacks an informal community life is like a ladder with a rung missing. The formal institutions will serve their purposes poorly when everyday connections in the neighborhood are lacking. One of the prerequisites is a place where those connections can flourish.

In the neighborhood where I live, the favorite gathering place is a park where many people take their dogs to run during the late afternoons. People arrive individually and leave individually, but from 4:30 to 5:30 in the winter, later in the summer, there is nearly always a cluster of people talking with one another while trying to keep the dogs out of mischief. Participants gradually learn a set of implicit ground rules: An individual should refrain from drawing too much attention to what he or she does for a living. An individual should keep the social atmosphere casual. Sometimes a dog owner in the park for the first time tries to introduce himself by shaking hands with everyone and giving his full name. The last time I saw this happen, a woman member of the group remarked in a cheerful manner that "we don't know each others' last names." She was warding off a cocktail-party decorum that none of the park regulars wants.

Sometimes an intense two-person conversation develops. There is an unspoken understanding, however, that private conversations are less appropriate than talk that anybody can join in. A number of the dog owners instinctively steer the group toward topics of common interest. In the last three months these have included the weather, dogs, the condition of the park, good local pizza, books, movies, auto racing, home improvements, trips, musicians, computers, atrium hotels, youthful rebellion in the 1950s, the deterioration of the local newspaper, and a newly divorced member's extended visit from a Frenchman. An individual can gripe now and then, but if so, the griping should be done concisely or—even better—entertainingly. Humor is guaranteed an appreciative response. The group frequently and boisterously criticizes a fastidious local garden club that has been campaigning to restore the park to a landscape plan drawn up in 1909, a campaign that includes cutting down trees that have grown up where the plan did not specify them. The group of dog owners finds joy—and humor—in opposing the starchy garden club. For a circle of people who hang out together, there is a delicious pleasure in having a villain, especially a villain which, it is agreed by the circle of friends, lacks common sense. Perhaps because the park regulars have many differences, they savor their common bonds.

Most of the park regulars stay for a half-hour to three-quarters of an hour and then leave. Rarely do these get-togethers lead to visits to one another's homes. People enjoy a privilege Jane Jacobs identifies in *The Death and Life of Great American Cities*— that of being able to talk with other individuals without worrying about whether they are compatible enough to invite home.

It is doubtful that anyone became a member of the loose park group out of a desire to influence the neighborhood, the local government, or the world. Yet in thinking back on recent sessions, I realize that the loosely formed group of dog owners frequently discusses more than private concerns. In the past three months the late-afternoon talk has also touched on whether a nearby gas station should be allowed to expand into a convenience store, whether increases in teachers' pay have improved the schools, what crimes have taken place in the area, how to rid the park of a suspected drug dealer, how to fix the national economy, why black teenagers are shooting one another so often, whether Interstate 95 should be widened, and so on.

Those who gather in the park become a little better equipped to handle local and neighborhood concerns and to understand matters of all kinds. People take what they've learned back to their homes to entertain and inform others. The local news and opinion ripples outward; residents get a sense of how the neighborhood is faring. Neighborhood consciousness reaches a higher pitch. At other points in the day the members of the group are exposed to TV, radio, newspapers, and the rest of commercial and bureaucratic civilization. Those mass influences provide many benefits. But they do not make a full or balanced life. It is in the local gathering place that people often get a useful perspective on what matters and what is ephemeral—frequently at odds with the prevailing official or commercial messages. Hannah Arendt wrote insightfully about this. "However much we are affected by the things of the world, however deeply they may stir and stimulate us, they become human for us only when we can discuss them with our fellows," she said. "We humanize what is going on in the world and in ourselves only by speaking of it, and in the course of speaking of it we learn to be human." In the park the regulars get the heartening feeling of being part of a community. For those who have had a hard day or who have had little face-to-face contact with others, the visit to the park is a high point of the day. It is an important social ritual. But this is not provided for in the designs of most suburban subdivisions built since World War II.

In conventional opinion, what the suburbs are mainly meant for is bringing up children. People move to the suburbs because they think they're healthier environments for children. But are they? Children end up suffering from the imbalances and disconnection of the suburbs, just as adults do. Myrna Blyth, editor of the *Ladies' Home Journal,* said she sometimes imagines suburban neighborhoods after school hours as places where, in each solitary house, a solitary child sits gazing at a TV set. Things are not going well for many children. The incidence of psychological problems in children indicates that something is wrong. A study by psychologist Nicholas Zill found that 10 percent of children between the ages of twelve and sixteen were frequently lonely. Loneliness soars during the teenage years. Suburbs do not cause all of children's problems, but many suburbs make some conditions worse.

Parents have ensconced their children in strictly residential subdivisions—removed from stores, offices, workplaces—on the assumption that this will make the children's lives safer. It may—for a while—but at the cost of impeding children's education, maturity, and independence.

When Mark, the suburban father in San Ramon, was growing up in a small community on the Great Lakes, he got an after-school job in a hardware store. His father had died, leaving Mark as the oldest of four children his mother had to care for. The after-school job was possible because the store was only three blocks from home and three blocks from school. He could walk to it in five minutes. (His mother also took a job—in the municipal office a block beyond the hardware store.) The proximity of residential streets to stores and to employment enabled Mark to earn some money. But in addition, Mark was being initiated into the world of work. In the hardware store—the personal kind of store, once common, where customers asked employees for however many tenpenny nails they wanted and had them scooped out and weighed on a metal scale—Mark worked side by side with three or four adult men. It was a maturing experience. In a good community, youngsters can obtain maturing experiences. They are not kept in the dark about workplaces and the world of adults.

On television nowadays, it's common to hear lofty exhortations directed at young people. "Be the best." "Pursue your dream." A little girl in a TV commercial sits at a computer, and the computer screen tells us that her ambition is "to be the best writer ever." It's hard for many adolescents to know what to make of impossibly high-sounding injunctions. Do they disbelieve them and turn cynical? Do they accept them and then feel ashamed because they are not yet the "best" (whatever that means)? Suicides among Americans fifteen to nineteen years old quadrupled from 1950 to 1988. One wonders how many of these deaths were prompted by difficulties in dealing with the pressure to excel, or loneliness, or the effects of an impersonal, fragmented way of life. For Mark, who lived in a community that was part suburb, part small town, with businesses within easy reach of homes, there were opportunities to ground his ambitions in paid work and to see how adults actually dealt with their jobs and their lives. He had recourse to something other than home and school. The availability of the adult world of work opened up a greater understanding of his place in society. Mark was able to begin what is, for many people, the lifelong project of reconciling ambition and reality, idealism and necessity. In most suburbs today youngsters get a surfeit of words and a scarcity of useful experience.

To sum up: the costliness of the suburbs, the scarcity of time, and the disconnection and fragmentation of the community have serious consequences. They harm children and adults alike. They raise hurdles to human happiness. Individuals suffer the repercussions, and so do communities. If we are to overcome this disconnection, we must rethink some of our attitudes and we must begin to lay out our suburbs on different principles. In the remainder of this book I will be developing ideas about how the suburbs have failed and the concrete steps we can take to improve them.

TWO

Streets and Where They Lead Us

The communities that Americans have built since the Second World War lack many of the satisfactions found in older suburban areas. This lack stems from many reasons, one of the most important of which is a change in the street and road system. Streets and roads mold a community's character. They enliven daily life or deaden it. They foster human contact or frustrate it. They broaden people's choices or limit them to a narrow range of experiences. In this chapter I will be moving back and forth between old suburbs and relatively new ones in an attempt to show how the streets and roads affect the well-being of individuals, families, and communities.

Let's start by looking at a typical recently developed suburb. I'll call this suburb Car Town because the layout of its streets and roads encourages and, more than that, *requires* extensive travel, almost always by private motor vehicle. Car Town, like most newer suburbs, has what traffic engineers term a street *hierarchy,* which is a fancy way of saying that each street or road is designed to serve a specific purpose, ranging from high-speed travel across the region to shorter, slower trips within a subdivision. At the top of Car Town's hierarchy is a *limited-access highway,* which carries vehicles toward destinations throughout the metropolitan area. When plans for construction of the limited-access highway were announced some years ago, Car Town residents were enthusiastic—the new route promised quick, effortless movement to distant places. But today people in Car Town grumble about the fact that the smooth new highway is congested much of the time. The original four lanes were widened to six lanes, which eased the backups for a while, but now congestion again is intensifying, and there's no room for further expansion. Bulldozers scraped away the bushes and trees that had been planted when

Traffic engineers concentrate much of the motor traffic onto a limited number of large roads, which businesses promptly turn into unpleasant commercial strips like this one in East Haven, Connecticut.

the highway was only four lanes; at the perimeter of the enlarged road the state transportation department has erected tall concrete walls to shield the nearby homes from traffic noise. No teenagers have yet spray-painted their names on the walls. That will be the next offense.

The people who inhabit Car Town are mainly commuters. When they return from their jobs in other suburbs or in the distant city, they drive the limited-access highway and then exit onto the second rung of the street hierarchy—one of the *arterial roads,* designed to carry traffic throughout town at fifty miles per hour. The arterials are several lanes wide and equipped with synchronized signals, so they operate at close to full speed—part of the time. But businesses knew that with as many as 50,000 drivers a day on the arterials, properties along these routes would be unbeatable locations for Wal-Marts, Home Depots, Radio Shacks, Midas Mufflers, Burger Kings, Pizza Huts, and other retailers and their asphalt parking lots. The burgeoning commerce has altered driving conditions dramatically. Now traffic darts in and out of businesses' driveways much of the day, making the arterials chancy. During rush periods the traffic is stop-and-go.

At intervals along the arterials there are *collector roads,* which lead off into residential subdivisions. These roads carry a large number of vehicles too, especially during rush periods, because

A collector road in Oviedo, Florida. Even with a perimeter of neatly trimmed grass, a road like this is not enticing to travel. Walls between road and subdivision make the transportation corridor a land of nowhere. Pedestrians, recognizing dullness when they see it, leave the sidewalks uninhabited.

the typical subdivision has only one or two of them—the sole access routes from the arterial to homes in the subdivisions. A vehicle entering or leaving a subdivision in Car Town has no choice but to travel the same collector road that many other vehicles are using.

Some collector roads have houses along them, but with the entire subdivision's traffic hurrying past, these are hardly ideal locations for residential life. Most Car Towners prefer to live on *minor streets,* which branch off from the collector. It's along the minor streets, free of through traffic, that the great majority of Car Town's houses are located. Some minor streets are loops, which pass two or three dozen houses and then curve around to rejoin the collector road. Others are cul-de-sacs.

Most of the suburbs built in the United States in the past few decades are laid out like Car Town. Their details vary, but the underlying principle remains consistent: Big, theoretically fast roads deliver their traffic onto moderately large roads, which distribute their traffic onto still-smaller streets, which ultimately lead to the minor streets. Every time a person wants to go somewhere, he or she must travel up or down the hierarchy. Since at least the 1950s, traffic engineers have widely embraced this system. They have considered it superior to the extensively inter-

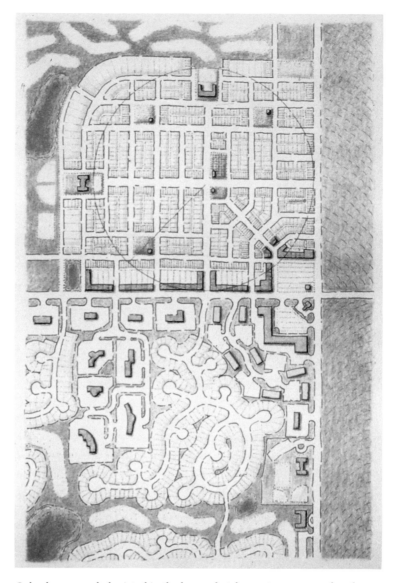

Suburban sprawl, depicted in the lower sketch, creates a geography of separation. Stores, offices, and housing are deliberately kept apart, forcing people to drive to every destination. Traditional neighborhood design, by contrast, ties a community's elements into a network of streets that provides many choices of how to get from one point to another—on foot, on a bicycle, or in a motor vehicle.

connected streets of older communities. Older street networks such as grid plans, commonly used in development until the Second World War, have been dismissed by traffic engineers because their many intersections allow traffic of all kinds to flow on minor streets as well as major thoroughfares. The new street hierarchy—called a *sparse hierarchy* by some because it severely limits the number of through routes—promises more order and efficiency.

But the beliefs that have prevailed since the Second World War are coming in for close scrutiny, and it is now clear that modern traffic engineers have erred in important ways. One of the few professional studies of how the modern traffic hierarchy compares with a more traditional network of streets, such as a grid, was conducted in 1990 by Walter Kulash, a transportation engineer at Glatting Jackson Kercher Anglin Lopez Rinehart, a community planning firm in Orlando, Florida; William J. Anglin, Jr., an urban designer at Glatting Jackson; and David Marks, a real estate analyst at Real Estate Research Consultants in Orlando. Their conclusion: Motorists and pedestrians obtain less satisfaction in the modern system of arterials, collectors, and minor streets than in the older style of street network. Traveling is less pleasurable and in many respects less efficient in a modern hierarchy than it is in street networks like those of older suburbs and older urban neighborhoods.

Kulash says the modern hierarchy suited the mental outlook of traffic engineers because it possessed an orderly structure much like the systems that other engineers have designed for delivering public utilities. The public water supply, for example, may flow through sixteen-inch-diameter transmission mains, divide into a series of eight-inch distribution mains, and finally enter an individual house through a one-inch service line. The water lines make up a sparse hierarchy. Similarly, sewer lines make up a hierarchy. Wastes flow out of the house in four-inch pipes, which feed into eight-inch collectors, which discharge into twelve-inch mains on their way to sewage treatment plants. Similarly, too, there is a sparse hierarchy for the delivery of electrical power. A big transmission line carrying electricity long distances steps down to lower-voltage distribution lines when it reaches the local areas it serves; it steps down again, to 240-volt lines, when it enters the customers' houses. But, Kulash says, the same logic does not fit transportation needs. People do not behave, or want to behave, like water or electricity, following a single path, day after day, between a large, distant point and the individual household. Human behavior is markedly different from public utility engineering. People have many purposes and desires, and for most of these there is likely to be a different destination, which is best reached by following a different route. People want to go in many directions. It makes little sense to try to funnel them into the kind of structure used for transporting water or electricity. It will be useful to keep Kulash's observation in mind as we move on to examine suburbs around the country.

Some communities have displayed extraordinary devotion to the modern street and road hierarchy. Prominent among these communities is Irvine, California, a "New Town" that was begun in the early 1960s and that earned a reputation as one of the premier examples of modern community planning in the western United States. Irvine is an instructive place to ask about the results of the modern street system.

Irvine occupies forty-three square miles on what was once the Irvine Ranch in west-central Orange County, between Los Angeles and San Diego. Orange County, where thousands of acres of orange groves blossomed on huge ranchos originally established by Spanish colonialists, was a largely rural area for the first half of the twentieth century. That was bound to change as population migrated to California. With its beautiful hills overlooking the Pacific, with its benign climate, and most of all with its proximity to Los Angeles, it was destined to attract development. After the Second World War, the northern and western portions of the county, closest to Los Angeles, were transformed into suburbs in just a few years. Northern and western communities such as Anaheim, Garden Grove, and Santa Ana, arranged mostly on a continuous grid of streets, propelled the county's population from 220,000 in 1950 to 704,000 in 1960. Rapid development was clearly going to continue. The prospect of continued expansion (which boosted the county's population another 1.6 million between 1960 and 1990) caused developers in the 1960s to rethink how communities should be laid out. The planners of Irvine scoffed at extending the grid. "Do you do it two hundred miles long?" asked Raymond Watson, who became the first planning chief of the Irvine Company in 1960. "The grid," Watson said, "is a throwback to when the total area of urbanization was smaller."

To get away from the grid, Watson said, Irvine's planners

Part of Irvine, California, a "New Town" begun in the 1960s, now home to a population that has surpassed 100,000 and continues growing.

"went into the 'village' idea." Irvine "villages" vary in size. On average they contain 1.4 square miles and a population of 9,000. Each village has its own shopping area, its own schools, its own identity. The street system is used to heighten that identity. Freeways or arterial roads, sometimes running straight, sometimes curving, define each village's edges. In between the arterials, Irvine's planners have designed circuitous streets, with many cul-de-sacs. The planners wanted to prevent crosstown traffic from intruding on residential neighborhoods. This they have generally succeeded in doing. However, after thirty years of this form of development, other effects have also manifested themselves. One of these is grossly inefficient traffic patterns. The older, gridded suburbs were, and are, easy to get around in; plenty of uncomplicated routes go in all directions. Arterials in the gridded suburbs occur at frequent intervals. In between the many arterials there is an abundance of continuous two-lane residential streets that allow local people to reach their destinations by traveling through pleasant neighborhoods. By contrast, continuous residential streets are few in Irvine. Arterials are not as numerous as in the older, gridded suburbs. To go from one part of Irvine to another there is often little choice but to make one's way to a freeway or a major arterial. Many residents resent this. "It's irritating to have to go out to an arterial," an Irvine urban planning consultant admitted. It's especially irritating when arterials are clogged with traffic, which is not uncommon. The street hierarchy aggravates traffic jams. "Irvine has worse congestion than most other places in the country," says geographer Peter O. Muller. "The irony is that Irvine was designed specifically to *avoid* congestion."

Part of the problem is that the Irvine Company developed business and industrial areas with tens of thousands of jobs but developed far too little housing that moderate-income workers could afford—thus causing workers to find homes in distant communities and make long commutes to their jobs in Irvine. As if to exacerbate the mismatch of jobs and housing, the Irvine Company paid little heed to county planning officials, who years ago foresaw traffic congestion and urged the company to consider building mass transit facilities in the villages. Those factors account for some of Irvine's current difficulties. But the modern street and road system must bear its portion of the blame. The system adopted in Irvine and most other new communities gives people few choices of how to go from one point to another. The street layout stretches out nearly every trip a person takes—particularly local trips, which have to find their way through a collector-arterial maze instead of using direct routes like those in older grid-planned communities. As the modern street hierarchy has spread, distances traveled have grown. The average licensed driver in the United States now drives thirty-two miles a day.

The love of automobiles, which once reached fever pitch in California, has cooled as traffic has become vexing. Nobody records popular songs anymore about the pleasures of "little deuce coupes" and "little GTOs," as they did with outstanding success in the 1960s. Walter Kulash and his fellow researchers in Orlando attribute part of the growing discontent to the modern street system's channeling of drivers onto big roads, which are generally unappealing places to spend time.

What's wrong with big roads?

First, there is an irritatingly large number of vehicles struggling for space on them. For any given size of development, the volume of traffic on arterial roads is greater in a modern street hierarchy than in a traditional street pattern, according to the Orlando study.

Second, drivers have little ability to alter their route to bypass accidents or traffic jams. The vulnerability of modern arterials was made evident to me one evening when I was driving to a restaurant in a suburban section of Lake Worth, Florida. I noticed flashing lights in the road ahead. There had been an auto accident, and the police had temporarily closed the road. Not far

Modern road systems guarantee that drivers will spend much of their time at large intersections amid pavement, traffic lights, and parking lots.

beyond the collision stood the restaurant. But because Lake Worth's newer neighborhoods had been laid out with cul-de-sacs, loops, and collector roads, there was no way to detour easily around the police barricade. I had to reverse direction on the arterial and travel nearly a half-mile west, then a half-mile south on another arterial, then a half-mile east on a third arterial, and finally nearly a half-mile north on a fourth arterial, all to reach a destination a fraction of that distance away. When a community is designed with a hierarchy of this sort, anything that shuts down a through road—an accident, road repairs, utility work, flooding, fallen trees—has the potential to disrupt traffic. "It's a traffic heart attack," says Patrick Pinnell of the Yale University School of Architecture.

Third, big suburban arterials are unpleasant because there are long waits at traffic lights—longer than at traffic signals in traditional grid networks of local streets. The stop signal lasts longer, and on modern arterials it's necessary to have special left-turn lanes with their own time to go, during which all other vehicles sit idling. When motorists have been asked how long the wait is at these signals, they overestimate, Kulash says, by about 30 percent. The time spent at a conventional suburban intersection seems longer than it really is. It seems overly long because these roads possess a fourth unappealing feature: the surroundings are ugly or boring. Travelers are stuck viewing highway pavement and businesses that have established themselves along the arterials. This particular business environment, the commercial

35

strip, was designed, you'll recall, to attract customers who might be driving past at fifty miles an hour. So it is by nature a place of simplified, pared-down communication. Kulash compares the roadside business environment to a newspaper headline; it imparts basic information about the businesses, and that's all. Yet the poor suburbanite is forced by the street and road hierarchy to use the same route over and over, so he or she sees this same simple, newspaper-headline-style environment hundreds of times a year. It dulls the senses.

Businesses behave as the road system has encouraged them to do. Douglas Pegues Harvey, a San Antonio architect, points out that retail enterprises need to be situated where a sufficient number of customers can reach them. Even if zoning allowed, few stores could survive in a modern subdivision. The scarcity of connections among the streets—hobbled by all those movement-stopping cul-de-sacs—would prevent potential customers from reaching them. The collector road channels the customers to the arterial and helps to make the arterial the suburb's one vital business location. Because the arterial is virtually the only place where retailers can prosper, property prices along the arterial rise—a process that favors businesses with deep pockets, such as national chains and franchise organizations, from McDonald's to K-Mart. Irvine, because its land was owned by a single company with a strong vision of how it wanted to guide development, has managed to keep its arterials free of most commercial clutter. Much of Irvine's retailing has been concentrated in "village" shopping centers. But this is not what happens in Car Towns with dispersed property ownership and a less powerful planning apparatus. The typical Car Town is overwhelmed by landowners, speculators, and retailers who want to place businesses along the arterials. Kulash calls an arterial street with 50,000 drivers a day "a gift-wrapped, gold-plated, irresistible invitation to develop strip commercial." The arterial becomes, Kulash says, a "sellscape." Most suburbanites are dismayed by this. In visual preference studies, people have shown that their satisfaction with what they see during their car trips starts out high in residential neighborhoods, declines on collector roads, and sinks to deeply negative ratings on the arterials.

It is not only the commercial segments of the arterials that draw negative reactions. Increasingly, residential areas along arterials are unappealing to look at, too. Since there is much more traffic on a modern suburban arterial than on an arterial in a

These privacy walls along a road in Sun City West, Arizona, are supposed to enhance living conditions for occupants of the houses hidden behind them. But the walls make every trip a more tedious one for those residents and for everyone else.

neighborhood with extensively interconnected streets, developers orient the houses to face away from the busy arterial. What's visible to passersby on the arterial is the houses' backs and back yards. Even those are often obscured by six-foot-high fences or privacy walls between the road and the perimeter of the subdivision. In California the most common privacy wall is "slumpstone," an inelegantly named concrete block that has a bulging face. Some developers, like the Irvine Company, decided, after experience with it, that slumpstone looks unpresentable, so they have substituted other materials, such as smooth stucco or split-face (uneven-surfaced) concrete block. In some Irvine neighborhoods, vines have grown up and covered the walls, creating an attractive surface. But few suburbs have vine-covered walls like Irvine's. Most walls are bleak. And when continued for more than a short distance, even walls that are well planted exert a dulling effect. Travelers sense that they have been shut out of the community, consigned to a zone that in architectural and human terms is dead.

For the motorist, the final affront is the confusion generated by the modern street hierarchy. The arterial-collector-minor street organization is clear in concept, but it rarely looks clear to people trying to find their way amid streets that curve and curl and twist

Mount Auburn Cemetery in Cambridge, Massachusetts, birthplace of the curvilinear style that was later to conquer the suburbs. A map of Mount Auburn Cemetery published in 1835, four years after the picturesque "rural" cemetery was founded. Its planning began in the 1820s.

and bend. Strangers and residents alike lose their way because of the disorienting curvilinear street layout. When residents of modern suburbs want out-of-town friends to come visit, they have to send them maps. The mystifying curvilinear style has made a fortune for Rand-McNally.

The idea of curving, irregular streets was a long time in gestation. Historian John W. Reps says the inspiration for it took hold during the first half of the nineteenth century with the design of new cemeteries at the edges of American cities. "Rural cemeteries," as they were called because of their winding lanes and irregular topography, offered relief from dense, congested nineteenth-century cities. Cemeteries such as Mount Auburn, which was planned in the 1820s for Cambridge, Massachusetts, and Laurel Hill, which was planned in 1836 for Philadelphia, attracted thousands of strollers, picnickers, and courting couples each year. The sylvan refuges were substitutes for parks, which few cities had yet developed to any significant extent.

By the 1850s, curving roads set in picturesque or pastoral landscapes became part of suburban planning. In 1851 the civil engineer Robert C. Phillips laid out what has been described as the nation's first planned curvilinear suburb, Glendale, Ohio, north of Cincinnati. In 1853 the architect Andrew Jackson Davis planned Llewellyn Park in the Watchung Mountains of West Orange, New Jersey. In 1856 David Hotchkiss laid out Lake Forest, Illinois, on mildly undulating terrain along Lake Michigan north of Chicago. In 1869 Frederick Law Olmsted, the founder of American landscape architecture, planned the best-known curvilinear suburb of the nineteenth century, the Illinois town of Riverside. Some seven decades later, in the 1930s, curvilinear suburbs appeared in the New Deal's greenbelt towns, which were intended as displays of up-to-date planning. The Federal Housing Administration, which came into being at roughly the same time as the greenbelt towns, ultimately put the government seal of approval on curvilinear streets. In the 1950s and 1960s they appeared everywhere.

Olmsted's Riverside, a two-square-mile Chicago suburb with 8,760 inhabitants, prefigured the problems of today's omnipresent curvilinear streets. When Olmsted and his partner, Calvert Vaux, were hired to lay out Riverside on flat land ten miles southwest of downtown Chicago, Olmsted insisted that straight streets were inappropriate because they suggested "eagerness to press forward, without looking to the right hand or to the left." Curved lines, Olmsted said, suggested "leisure, contemplativeness, and happy tranquility." Enough of Olmsted and Vaux's design was carried out so that Riverside reflected their aesthetic vision. The curvilinear layout, the large front lawns, and the profusion of flowers, shrubbery, and trees do convey tranquility. The town feels as if it were meant for people who never have to hurry, people who got around at the clip-clop pace of a horse-drawn carriage in the nineteenth century and who have no need to move faster today. However, the pastoral curves, one looking much like another, make it hard for anyone except an established resident to maintain a sense of orientation. Tradesmen assigned to work in Riverside are known to leave a job site at lunchtime and be unable to find their way back half an hour later. "If you ask anyone in Chicago whether he's been to Riverside, he'll say, 'Once—I got lost,'" says Edward Straka, a Riverside architect. "For the first six months people get lost," Straka says. "You can never completely conceive the plan."

And so it is that in modern American suburbs the collector streets curve one way and another. Major roads start off in one direction and unexpectedly arc off in another. Clarity vanishes.

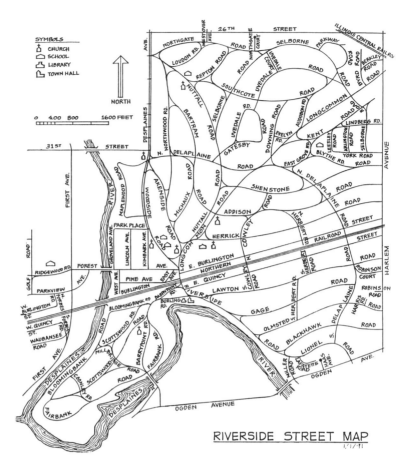

A map of Riverside, Illinois, where visitors and residents have something in common: All lose their way in a confusing collection of curving streets.

RIVERSIDE STREET MAP

In the place where the curvilinear approach first captured the American public's imagination—Mount Auburn Cemetery in Cambridge—the problem has been recognized. Painted down the middle of the main drive is a dotted green line; people follow the dotted line through the mounds and meandering hills, secure in the knowledge that it will lead them back to the entrance gate. Modern suburbs, in contrast, go on sowing confusion. In a nation of huge mobility, where people change their address an average of once every five years everyone at one time or another is bound to be disoriented.

Until now we have been looking at the modern street system's impact on motorists—its inefficiency, its congestion, its lengthening of trips, its frequent unpleasantness, its confusion. These are all important concerns, but there is another perspective which I believe is still more significant, namely, the effects on residents when they are out of their vehicles.

In Kenmore, New York, a Buffalo suburb that developed in the early twentieth century, William Flynn had trouble sleeping in the house that he and his wife Noreen bought after moving from a newer suburban-style area of Annapolis, Maryland. The Flynns' Kenmore house was a spacious, solidly built clapboard dwelling from the 1920s, but it was located at the intersection of two streets, one of them a busy suburban arterial. At night a motorcycle would rev its engine or a loud car would speed through a traffic light, and Bill would snap awake. "It took quite a while to get used to traffic noise," Flynn said. "It was so quiet where we lived in Maryland. We didn't hear traffic."

In Annapolis the Flynns had lived in a 1960s house facing a paved semicircle. The semicircle sheltered a group of houses from a through street. It gave the Flynns and their neighbors a quiet atmosphere, a degree of noise protection that suburbanites more commonly obtain from living on cul-de-sacs. On a cul-de-sac, shielded from through traffic, quiet nights are expected.

Traffic noise affects neighborhood behavior. In studying streets in San Francisco, Donald Appleyard found that traffic profoundly influenced socializing. On a street with light traffic (200 vehicles an hour at its peak), people were much more likely to know who lived next door than they were if they lived on a heavily traveled street. Activities like talking to neighbors were common on a lightly traveled street. "I feel my home extends to the whole block," said one resident. "I feel a sense of responsibility; I planted trees in front of my house and keep the property and sidewalk clean," said another. "There are warm people on this street," said a third. "I don't feel alone." Yet another noted that "people on their way somewhere always drop in." The heavily traveled street, with a peak of 1,900 vehicles an hour, was a different world. "It's not a friendly street," one resident said. "No one offers help." People regarded only their building or their apartment, not the block, as their home territory. Inhabitants of the lightly traveled street had three times as many local friends and twice as many acquaintances as those on the heavily trafficked street. When traffic volume was small, friendships and neighborhood spirit blossomed.

Cul-de-sacs, by eliminating through traffic, foster certain kinds of neighborhood life. Radburn, a development begun in 1929 in Fair Lawn, New Jersey, is credited with popularizing the cul-de-sac. In Radburn, cul-de-sacs were short, narrow, straight paved streets intended for deliveries. Children were expected to play in the small yards or the grassy common meadow behind the houses; actually, children often chose to play in the cul-de-sac, where there were hard surfaces that were better for bouncing a ball or riding a tricycle and where contact with the outside world made for a more stimulating atmosphere. After the Second World War an increasing proportion of suburban developments adopted cul-de-sacs, which became longer and wider, terminating in a broad circle. They generally did without Radburn's common meadow, to cut land costs.

For young children a cul-de-sac is a natural gathering place. The circle of pavement is a safe place to roller-skate, play hopscotch, or learn to ride a bike. In some subdivisions the cul-de-sac with the largest number of children living around it becomes a magnet for youngsters from other streets. When children play in the cul-de-sac, parents close by are drawn outward, into conversation with their neighbors. In especially successful cul-de-sac developments, families get to know one another well. Some cul-de-sacs encourage the development of neighborhood events or stimulate daily social routines. In the era when most married women spent their days at home, it became common for them to gather near the throat of the cul-de-sac in late afternoon. There they would talk with their neighbors while keeping an eye on the children at play. The grapevine would be nourished until the arrival of vehicles bearing husbands signaled it was time for the women to disperse to their homes and start preparing dinner. The movie *Edward Scissorhands* sweetly parodies this social ritual.

A cul-de-sac loses much of its drawing power once children enter their teenage years. Residents look into the cul-de-sac and, instead of seeing children playing, view empty pavement. On the far side of the circle the vista is closed in by the neighbors' houses. In a twenty-year-old subdivision in Fairfax County, Virginia, I noticed that one resident, Carol Frost (not her real name), repeatedly spoke antagonistically about a couple that lived on the other side of her cul-de-sac. "The Kansans love to sit on their lawn chairs," Mrs. Frost said, looking out the kitchen window toward a middle-aged couple who sat for long periods, impassive, at the top of their driveway. "Kansans" dropped from her tongue as if being from Kansas were a character defect. Mrs. Frost seemed to know a great deal about the couple from Kansas, and for reasons never fully articulated, the Kansans bothered her. Probably one source of irritation was the Kansans' view; from where they sat they could gaze at Mrs. Frost's house and catch glimpses of her every time she went to the kitchen sink or stepped out the side door. She could not enter the carport or retrieve the mail without being observed.

Cul-de-sacs enforce familiarity to a degree beyond that of ordinary streets. On a straight block of houses people may see what the neighbors across the street are doing, but people do not feel so tightly entwined with one another. A circle, however, is an emotive shape. When pioneers feared attack from Indians, they gathered their wagons into a circle. When teachers want to break down passivity and force students to speak up, they gather chairs into a circle. A debate in which people toss around ideas in a collegial manner is called a roundtable discussion. The circle is relied upon frequently by psychotherapy groups.

A circle is appropriate for people who have a common goal or a shared outlook. But this is often not the case for suburbanites. Their common bonds are few, and yet the cul-de-sac suggests that the neighbors should form and perpetuate a close relationship, even when no one wants that. The shape of the surroundings suggests who one's friends should be. In such a situation it's natural that many people would retreat to the privacy of their houses or their back yards, leaving the cul-de-sac empty—except for stalwarts like the Kansans.

The group-mindedness embodied in the cul-de-sac seems to be based on a simple "just-folks" conviction that no matter who moves into the cul-de-sac, the little society of neighbors will get along famously. This is a foolishly optimistic assumption. Environmental psychologists have repeatedly shown that people are happiest not only when their surroundings offer opportunities for contact with others but also when the surroundings allow them to *avoid unwanted contact.* The cul-de-sac often seems to promote more contact than is desired, especially in a polyglot, individualistic society like the United States.

How does a person gracefully come and go when living in a cul-de-sac? If one drives an automobile, it's simple enough. The car is a shield against all but the most superficial human contact. But if you're a child, you must walk or bike past the neighbors. At one time or another, children have trouble with neighbors and bullies. There are situations in which it is best to deal with the difficult neighbor or confront the bully. At other times, however, avoidance is the wiser course. This the cul-de-sac makes nearly impossible; there is only one way in and out.

Cul-de-sacs limit the social contacts of many elderly or shy residents. According to psychologist Philip G. Zimbardo, approximately 40 percent of the population consider themselves shy. If neighbors on the cul-de-sac do not want to become friendly with them or do not have time for socializing, the shy man or woman ends up more isolated than ever. It's a rare outsider who ventures into a cul-de-sac uninvited. In someone else's cul-de-sac, an outsider always feels like an intruder. The Kansans can sit on their lawn chairs all day without seeing anyone from the surrounding blocks. They are like the lone figure in an Edward Hopper painting, gazing on a scene of haunting stillness, as if waiting for activity that never comes. America has growing numbers of people who live alone, who work at home, who have retired early, or who are unable to find full-time jobs. Unless these people have a network of friends or organizations, they may find the modern suburb a lonely place. There is much isolation in the suburbs.

Cul-de-sacs do not encourage walking and biking. The ability to choose a route best-suited to the destination and to countless other considerations is what makes walking and biking rewarding. In an extensively interconnected street network, such as a grid, a person's choices multiply at every intersection. At the first intersection, one can go right, left, or straight ahead. A block later one gets a second set of choices, and with each additional block, the freedom of mobility continues to expand. The result, in a grid network, is that one's route can take on a huge number of variations, and one can choose from many potential experiences. The rich possibility for movement and experience is eloquently described in Jane Jacobs's *Death and Life of Great American Cities*. It is missing from subdivisions made up of dead ends.

The cul-de-sacs and loops in Irvine illustrate the difficulty of walking in communities built since the Second World War. Let's say that a Mrs. Deering lives on Timberline in Irvine's village of El Camino Real. Suppose she wants to visit a friend, Mrs. Forest, who lives on Caraway in the village of Woodbridge. (The women's names are fictitious; the street and neighborhood names are real.) As the crow flies, it's about a quarter-mile from Timberline to Caraway. In a grid network it would be a short walk. But in Irvine, with its cul-de-sacs, loops, collectors, and arterials, the route is extraordinarily complicated. Mrs. Deering lives at the end of a cul-de-sac. To go toward Caraway, which lies to the southwest, she does not walk in that direction. She must first go *east* on Timberline. Then she turns onto a collector road called Deerwood, which takes her *north.* From Deerwood she turns east onto Deer Creek. Then she turns onto Deerfield, following it to the southeast. Next she turns onto Yale Avenue, a larger connector, which follows to the southwest—through an intersection with an arterial—for almost half a mile. She turns right at West Yale Loop and follows the Loop northwest for three-eighths of a mile. At Woodhollow she turns to the northeast. Then she turns right—southeast—onto Oakdale for two short blocks. She walks left briefly, then right onto Thistledown. A block later she turns left again, northeastward. She has at last arrived at her destination: Caraway. This is not the longest route she could have taken; actually it is the shortest.

Mrs. Deering, who by now has worked up a sweat, knocks on Mrs. Forest's door and asks her why she hasn't dropped by lately. Mrs. Forest feels embarrassed by the question. "Oh dear," she says, "I keep meaning to stop over. But I've been feeling sort of seedy." Someone with a bird's eye view of Irvine might have a different answer: It is a chore to get through the maze of streets. The layout has stretched a distance of a quarter-mile into a trip of a mile and a quarter over ten different streets, aiming toward every point on the compass. The modern street system drastically complicates access to friends and acquaintances.

The mobility problem is especially acute for suburban adolescents. When sociologist Herbert Gans lived in Levittown (now Willingboro), New Jersey, from 1958 to 1960, he discovered that Levittown's most dissatisfied residents were its adolescents. They were living on the outskirts of the fourth-largest metropolitan area in the United States—Greater Philadelphia, a region bursting with activities—yet they had little access to attractions other than those of Levittown itself. For many suburban youths the hemmed-in feeling has not changed. In a modern suburb, adolescents can go few places under their own power. They need wheels—four of them. After they turn sixteen they can drive, but only if they or their parents can afford a vehicle, gasoline, insurance, and maintenance. This sets up a situation fraught with tension. At the very moment when adolescents are trying to establish a degree of independence from their parents, they are made dependent on them for a car or the money to operate it.

For younger children the situation is also far from ideal. In old suburbs with fully connected networks of streets, children can go many places on foot or bicycle. Most old suburbs have a number of local stores on streets where traffic is light enough to allow them to be reached by bicycle. Parents feel secure in sending their children on errands. When youngsters make trips to the bakery or the grocery store or the post office at their parents' request, they contribute to the family's well-being. Youngsters get satisfaction from this; they may also get a little cash or a treat for their efforts. In newer suburbs, children are less useful. How many parents are willing to send their children to a convenience store on a busy, multilane arterial throbbing with 50,000 vehicles a day? The newer suburbs are laid out in such a way that children cannot safely go on their own to many destinations. Parents run the errands while Junior sits watching TV and complaining of boredom. The modern street system apportions leisure and responsibilities among members of the family in peculiarly unrewarding ways.

Mothers become chauffeurs for their children. Mary Cahill, a mother of two teen-agers in Ellicott City, Maryland, was so ensnared by chauffeur duties that she wrote a book entitled *Carpool: A Novel of Suburban Frustration.* Cahill told the *New York Times* that with her responsibility for transporting a son and daughter around suburban Baltimore, "I was driving every morning and after school, and there were activities beyond that, into the darkness. And in between there were doctors' appointments, and I had to make dinner." Carpooling—transporting her own and other families' children—is, in Cahill's view, "the dark underside of suburbia. It is like a subculture. There are times when you feel you are wasting your life."

The misshaping of modern suburbs causes problems even for residents of old suburban neighborhoods with well-connected streets. After settling in the old, grid-planned part of Herndon, Virginia, Michael and Christine Dodd discovered that their movement was hindered by the newer cul-de-sac developments on the community's edge. Their dead ends made it difficult for the Dodds to drive their daughter Annie directly to the field at the edge of town where she plays soccer. The soccer field is a little under a mile from the Dodds' home, but since the cul-de-sacs eliminate straightforward routes, much of Herndon's traffic is funneled onto the town's main drag, Elden Street. The Dodds' trip becomes a journey of two and a half or three miles indirectly across Herndon by car. On weekends, when working parents run errands and carpool their children to soccer and other activities, traffic crawls through the stoplights. Eventually a major arterial called Herndon Parkway is to be completed, circling the center of town. This may alleviate congestion on Elden Street, but it will carry so many cars and trucks that parents will not want their children bicycling or walking along the new road. The fundamental problem—the dependence of children on adults and automobiles for getting to routine local destinations—will persist.

Modern American street systems create insurmountable problems for some of the nation's elderly. Daniel M. Cary tells of an episode that took place in Stuart, Florida. His wife was standing in line at a supermarket checkout when she noticed that the elderly woman in front of her seemed upset. The elderly woman fumbled with her purse and dropped her keys. When Mrs. Cary offered to help, it was as if an emotional dam broke loose. The elderly woman let out that she was nervous because tomorrow she had to take a test to have her driver's license renewed. "If I fail, I don't know what I'm going to do," the woman said. "I won't even be able to drive to the grocery store. My husband died several years ago. I've been living in the same house for twenty years. I don't want to move." The woman's independence and ability to remain in familiar surroundings were in jeopardy.

To Daniel Cary, who is the executive director of the Treasure Coast Regional Planning Council, overseeing planning in Palm Beach, Martin, St. Lucie, and Indian River counties, that exchange indicates some of the costs of the current method of laying out communities. Cary thinks the elderly suffer some of the worst consequences of current development patterns. "A lot of people in Florida actually retire twice," Cary says. "In their first retirement, they quit working and move to Florida. It's a pleasant life. They're healthy and they get around easily." Then, says Cary, "they age fifteen or twenty years. They can't drive anymore, so they have to retire a second time. The second retirement isn't so nice." This second retirement is a removal—often reluctant—from the home and community they had grown accustomed to. "They may get warehoused in places like Century Village," Cary says. Century Villages, of which South Florida has several, are huge retirement complexes containing thousands of old people, separated from the surrounding areas by long walls.

The issue that Cary identifies is most pronounced in Florida, but it exists nationwide. Modern suburbs impose cruel choices on people in their declining years. On the one hand, when people lose their ability to drive, they can move to someplace where services are readily accessible, giving up their homes and familiar surroundings. Some die from the shock of such uprooting. On the other hand, they can stay where they've lived for years and depend on others for transportation. In recent years many governments and social service agencies have established van services that collect elderly or infirm people at their homes and transport them around town. These are valuable programs, but not all elderly people are comfortable with them. Many are not eager to be made the objects of special programs, which imply that they are in some sense "handicapped." It would be less demeaning to have regular public bus or rail transportation available; it is futile to wish for buses, however, let alone trains, in suburbs made up of low-density cul-de-sacs—it would cost too much for the government or for the passengers. Another solution would be to have stores and services right in the neighborhood. But as we have already seen, it is rare that stores can survive in cul-de-sac subdivisions.

For a large proportion of the population, then, the modern system is frustrating. Elderly people, children, adolescents, working parents, and people who cannot drive or who do not have enough money to afford an automobile all face major obstacles in the suburbs built in the past few decades. Anyone who settles in the modern suburbs will be seriously held back during one or more periods of life.

Teaching the young is one of the important functions that a community performs. Childhood is a time when a boy or girl gradually increases his or her knowledge and mastery of the world. Much childhood education occurs not in school but in experiences throughout the community. Although children benefit from the safety of the cul-de-sac subdivision when they are small, they cannot live whole lives there. They have to extend themselves. In older suburbs with fully connected networks of streets, youngsters can get to know their own block, then the block around the corner, then another, and so on. They can test the environment incrementally, ranging steadily farther from home. Mostly they can accomplish this while avoiding dangerously heavy car traffic. Older communities distribute most of their traffic over scores of two-lane streets rather than concentrating massive volumes on hazardous collector roads and multi-lane arterials. So youngsters can go many places by bike. Trips to stores, churches, schools, and sports events can be made on local streets, opening fresh observations on each journey. People gather much of their knowledge not in a formal, planned way but as a spin-off of some other activity. Youngsters riding their bikes through town see how a variety of people conduct themselves, mull their observations over, and form insights, all because of exposure to the surrounding areas. The traditional street system draws youngsters out, pretty much at their own pace. The world beckons as an interesting place. Depending on how far they venture and the degree of risk they want to take, they may eventually acquire what is known as street smarts.

There is no corresponding term for intelligence in modern suburbs. As San Francisco architect Daniel Solomon observes, no one speaks of "cul-de-sac smarts." Youngsters in the cul-de-sac have a hard time getting to know their community or the communities that lie beyond. The shift from minor street to collector to arterial is too abrupt. Obstacles interfere with the acquisition of a widening fund of knowledge. Children of course get to know certain points well—the home block, the school grounds, the lobby of the multiscreen cinema, the concourse and food court of the shopping mall—but many areas in between these points are rarely experienced and never adequately conceptualized. Ours is an age overflowing with knowledge, but most of it is knowledge collected, digested, and transmitted by a business or institution with its own agenda. There are countless things that schools, movies, television, advertising, and shopping malls do not or cannot tell children about the world. For a full connection to one's society and surroundings, there is no substitute for direct experience. Yet this is sharply limited by the layout of the recent suburbs. A modern subdivision is an instrument for making people stupid.

Modern suburbs are not known as satisfying hometowns. This failing is particularly damning, given that suburban parents usually explain their choice of community by saying it's a good place "for the kids." Journalist Steve Coll was reared in subdivisions near the Rockville Pike, one of the main arterials of Montgomery County, Maryland, north of Washington. In "Growing Up Suburban" he writes that "the trouble with remembering a youth in Montgomery County, even one as recent as the mid-1970s, when I graduated from high school, is that many of the landmarks of my experience have already been plowed under and rebuilt in a way that denies the past."

After finishing high school Coll spent several years in California and then moved back to Montgomery County. "It was a mistake," Coll writes. "For days I drove aimlessly up and down the Pike, stopping at the malls, examining store signs, searching for even the slightest epiphany, the vaguest sense that I was home. But I felt only dread. In eight years the entire Pike seemed to have been obliterated and rebuilt."

Coll had spent many hours of his adolescence working or hanging out along the Rockville Pike, but few of the places in which he had invested his loyalty and affection survived. "On the Pike," Coll writes, "stores and owners changed each season as new mini-malls were built, discount chains went bankrupt, and fast-food franchises swapped their brightly colored signs, competing for prime turf." Coll says he wanted "to find some solid ground after years in California." Solid ground eluded him. In prosperous metropolitan areas, the buildings, places, and institutions that anchor daily life are swept away with stunning swiftness, replaced by something new, which in turn soon disappears. The modern economy is merciless in destroying and transforming the man-made environment. The title of a book by Marshall Berman about the modern experience captures that truth in seven words: *All That Is Solid Melts into Air.* Such evanescence is exacerbated by the modern system of streets and roads, which concentrates enormous volumes of energy, traffic, and money on a relatively few busy arterials like the Rockville Pike. On these arterials, hurricanes of development sweep through, allowing little to stand for long.

Designing the road system differently will not undo the ruthlessness of the modern economy, but it might moderate some of its effects. It might allow suburbs to retain a recognizable character even while allowing progress. I will conclude this chapter by showing how traditional well-connected street networks accomplish that in two older suburbs—Oak Park, Illinois, and Upland, California. In Oak Park and Upland the streets themselves deliver many forms of satisfaction.

Oak Park is the older of the two suburbs. Located on Chicago's western border, eight miles from the Loop, Oak Park developed after the great Chicago fire of 1871, its streets laid out on an irregular grid. By the Great Depression, Oak Park's four and a half square miles were almost completely built up. Members of Chicago's business and professional elite constructed homes in the northern part of the village, where Frank Lloyd Wright lived from

Four views of Oak Park, Illinois. Top, *a couple strolling on Elizabeth Court, one of Oak Park's few curving streets.* Second from top, *people gather at Petersen's restaurant and ice cream shop on Chicago Avenue, one of several neighborhood business districts.* Next, *the Lake Theatre, a landmark in downtown Oak Park.* Bottom, *a station on a rapid transit line that takes Oak Parkers to jobs in Chicago.*

1889 to 1909, where Ernest Hemingway was born in 1899, and where Edgar Rice Burroughs wrote some of his Tarzan novels. Families of more modest standing settled mainly in the southern part of town. Today Oak Park contains 53,000 people.

Almost all the streets in Oak Park run in straight lines, occasionally jogging at intersections. Most blocks are between 500 and 600 feet long and about half as wide. Since, on average, people walk a half-mile (2,640 feet) in about ten minutes, it takes only about two minutes to walk the length of the typical Oak Park block. Pedestrians get a sense of making rapid progress. Intersections come at frequent intervals, presenting a succession of choices and points of interest. Minor streets are only thirty feet wide, allowing even children and the elderly to cross them safely with minimal effort. Between sidewalk and curb, mature trees stand, creating a shady, soft, green atmosphere that appeals to pedestrians and motorists alike. Stretching back from the sidewalks in the northern part of town are large front lawns belonging to houses built in Italianate, Gothic, Queen Anne, Prairie, and other styles.

Some of the streets are one-way to limit vehicular traffic and noise, and a few have been converted into dead ends in the past twenty-five years, but even the dead-end streets have sidewalks that let people on foot or bicycle continue on through. From the Wright studio, which has been preserved as a museum on leafy Chicago Avenue, it is an easy walk past two- and three-story houses and three- to six-story apartment buildings to Oak Park's business district on Lake Street, one of the town's principal east-west thoroughfares. Some of the retailers who used to be on Lake Street are gone, done in by shopping malls in newer suburbs. But in the face of intense regional competition, Lake Street still contains bookstores, clothing stores, restaurants, optometrists, banks, dry cleaners, travel agents, a drug store, a supermarket, a health club, and the four-screen Lake Theatre. These are augmented by civic and religious institutions, including a well-stocked public library, a post office, Unity Temple (designed by Wright for Oak Park's prominent Unitarians), and the grounds of the Oak Park–River Forest High School. The street and sidewalks remain active well into the evening. Oak Park's population density of 11,000 per square mile—high by today's suburban standards, yet remarkably uncrowded in appearance, thanks to the spacious lawns and the many trees—partly accounts for the downtown's remaining vitality.

Those who walk a block south from Lake Street arrive at two of the three commuter rail lines that together carry more than 15,000 Oak Parkers each workday to downtown Chicago, the University of Illinois Chicago campus, and other destinations in the city. Although most Oak Park inhabitants own cars, the commuter transit lines are critically important; the ease of traveling to and from work on them has done much to maintain the desirability of Oak Park. The grid of streets and sidewalks meshes well with the rail transit system, making it convenient for people to go between their homes and eight transit stations in Oak Park over a variety of routes. The grid also provides plentiful access to buses that connect Oak Park to suburbs to the south and west.

Commerce is not limited to Lake Street. Pleasant, tree-lined streets also lead Oak Parkers to several neighborhood business districts scattered through the town. In these business districts, with their small stores and pedestrian pace, people from the surrounding neighborhoods find many of the goods and services upon which daily life depends. The Oak Park writer James Krohe, Jr., notes that a 2½-block stretch of Chicago Avenue near the Wright studio houses more than two dozen enterprises. Those who live in the vicinity buy groceries at Villager Foods, a small supermarket. On their way to work, they drop clothing off at O'Connor's or the Oak River Cleaners. During the day or after work they get meals and ice cream cones at Petersen's Emporium, a fixture of Oak Park since 1919. They pick up pizzas at Giordano's. They buy bikes at the Oak Park Cyclery. Neighborhood identity and social life coalesce around the small business districts like the one on Chicago Avenue, Krohe observes.

These business districts possess what Steve Coll missed along suburban Maryland's Rockville Pike—a sense of permanence, an enduring community center. Small neighborhood centers, tied to the surrounding residential areas by a network of streets and sidewalks, can generate a powerful sense of attachment. These neighborhood centers represent Oldenburg's third places. It can be profoundly satisfying to have a place where yours is a familiar face, known and greeted by others. After an absence of years, a person could return to Chicago Avenue, unlike the Rockville Pike, and feel heartened. The returning person might even be remembered, something that is unlikely on a commercial arterial with its rapidly changing chain enterprises. Many of the admirable qualities of Oak Park emanate from its extensively connected, pedestrian-oriented street network.

One traditional street that is absent from Oak Park is a long, grand boulevard. For that we travel to Upland, California, a municipality of 63,000 people and fifteen square miles in San Bernardino County, about thirty miles east of Los Angeles. Upland, originally called North Ontario, received its current name in 1902 because it occupies the "up land," a sloping plateau where the San Gabriel Valley rises against the base of the San Gabriel Mountains. George and William Chaffey, two brothers skilled in development and irrigation, were the founders of Upland and the adjoining city of Ontario, acquiring in 1882 the tract on which the two municipalities have since been built.

The Chaffeys laid out a boulevard starting at the Southern

Euclid Avenue about 1890, looking north from downtown Ontario toward Upland and California's San Gabriel Mountains. A mule-drawn street-car prepares for a trip up the boulevard on tracks between the trees.

Pacific Railway crossing in Ontario's downtown. They ran it straight north through Upland to the foothills of the San Gabriels and named it Euclid Avenue in honor of the great Greek geometer. The Chaffeys gave the boulevard majestic dimensions; it goes on for nearly eight miles, four and half miles of which are in Upland. It has a median sixty-five feet wide. The Chaffeys planted more than 5,000 trees—chosen on the basis of their appearance and their ability to live on little water—in the center of the boulevard and along its outer edges. By 1887 people with houses in the foothills commuted up and down Euclid in open-air streetcars in the center of the boulevard, on a railbed installed between rows of pepper and palm trees. Along the outer edges of the boulevard were grevillea and eucalyptus trees, which, together with the pepper and palm trees, created a majestic procession toward the 10,000-foot mountain panorama of the San Gabriels. Initially a pair of mules pulled the streetcars up the eight-mile route. At the top of the run, the operator unhitched the mules and led them onto a platform behind the streetcar; there they rode during a gravity-powered trip back down to Ontario. Mule power was replaced by electricity before the end of the century. The electrified streetcar line was, in turn, later declared obsolete and ripped out. But the developers' initial vision of the boulevard survived. George Chaffey had insisted that Euclid Avenue should be laid out "in such a way that it will be a thing of beauty forever." It remains so today.

Upland now is a suburb, part of a continuous carpet of development extending from west of Los Angeles to east of San Bernardino. Euclid Avenue now extends from Upland and Ontario through several other towns to the south. In Upland, Euclid accommodates two lanes of moving vehicles and one lane of parking on its northbound side, the same on the southbound side. The plantings along the boulevard have changed somewhat. Palm trees did not fare well and were removed. But many of the other trees look splendid, having had a century to grow to maturity. Pepper trees form a magnificent double row up most of the median, and grevilleas remain between curb and sidewalk along much of the route. Stretching off to each side, behind the grevilleas, is a succession of front lawns and houses along most of Upland's four and a half miles of boulevard. Bungalows in the southern part of town give way to larger and increasingly impressive houses as the boulevard rises toward the mountains.

Upon first seeing the boulevard, I was struck by its beauty, which delights every newcomer to Upland. I sensed that the boulevard is more than just a municipal decoration, so I observed people using the boulevard, talked with residents, and asked Upland High School students to write essays about Euclid Avenue; from this research it became clear that the boulevard fills a series of important functions for the community. First, the boulevard is a park—a safe and attractive one, placed where it is part of the daily experience of large numbers of people. The median, its width the same sixty-five feet as in the 1880s, is broad enough that people using it feel sheltered from the vehicles going past in the street. Yet at the same time the proximity to traffic and houses encourages people to feel secure. "I feel safe when I walk my dogs or go jogging on the median," a high school girl said. "There are always cars on either side of the street, so I feel nobody would attack me because there would always be witnesses."

The boulevard accommodates leisurely enjoyment and vigorous exercise equally well. "You can walk down the median and see the trees, some hollowed out and decayed with time, and others that have withstood the ages, running on both sides for as far as the eye can see," a student wrote. Another student said that owls and other bird life and the sweet smell of berries on the trees in Autumn make it a good place to savor nature. On a balmy evening the boulevard can become romantic. One girl told of

Lined predominantly by mature trees, Euclid Avenue in Upland today is used for biking, running, and numerous other pursuits. The median is so broad and well landscaped that people feel comfortable passing leisure time there.

watching on a Friday evening as a limousine stopped at Euclid and Seventeenth Street; a young couple in formal dress got out and sat down to a candlelight dinner in the median. In the daytime the boulevard reverted to a linear park once again—a place where the high school track and cross-country teams practice and where many others run, walk, or bike. The core of the boulevard, where the mule-drawn streetcars once operated, now contains a dirt and gravel path used for walking, jogging, and horseback-riding. "One morning on my way to church," a student said, "I counted eleven runners, six walkers, and two bikers. This is the norm." A sign identifies the center as the bridle path, and motorists sometimes crane their necks to watch people riding horses up the boulevard.

Euclid is a major transportation artery, carrying 53,000 vehicles a day on its busiest section, between Foothill Boulevard—a major east-west arterial—and the San Bernardino Freeway. Buses and car pools make pickups along Euclid, stopping near benches in the median, where businesspeople read newspapers and students catch up on schoolwork while awaiting their rides.

The boulevard is a community centerpiece. Upland's most prized sculpture, August Liemback's five-ton statue *Madonna of the Trail,* commemorating the pioneer mothers who came to California in wagon caravans, has stood on Euclid at Foothill Boule-

vard (old Route 66) since 1929. Public activities ranging from
parades to protests to open-air markets are conducted or advertised on the Euclid Avenue boulevard. High school students con-
verged on the boulevard in 1991 to demonstrate against the Per-
sian Gulf War, prompting horn-honking and shouts from some of
the cars driving by. Others later tied yellow ribbons around the
boulevard's trees to show their support for soldiers. Nature and
environmental organizations meet on Euclid Avenue. There is an
abundance of spontaneous activity. The boulevard is busy many
evenings with people coming and going and talking. Pedestrians
using the sidewalks in front of the houses seem not to be bothered by the traffic in the street; the lane of parked cars and the
extra-wide planter strip along the curb make a broad buffer zone
between the sidewalks and moving vehicles.

Euclid Avenue functions effectively as a community centerpiece because it has many connections to the surrounding residential areas. The twenty-eight cross streets that tie into the four
and a half miles of boulevard in Upland allow joggers, bicyclists,
dog-walkers, picnickers, nature enthusiasts, parents with baby
carriages, students, workers—all sorts of people—to reach the
boulevard easily from the surrounding area.

For those who live in the large houses that face the boulevard
across deep front lawns, Euclid Avenue offers a deluxe address.

For those who live on the side streets, Euclid offers a sumptuous route between home and other destinations; when side-street residents have guests from out of town, they often bring them along the boulevard, assured of the favorable impression it will make. The broad median, the trees, the lawns, and the facades of large houses combine to make daily journeys through Upland pleasurable.

The boulevard is central to Upland's self-image. There are economic gradations on Euclid Avenue, and yet the grand proportions and generous planting of the boulevard create a sense of overall unity. This is not to say that the boulevard is unchanging. Streetcars have come and gone, the rows of palm trees have been replaced, and there have been other alterations. Kris Allen, who lives on Euclid, recalls that there were once "lemon groves as far as the eye could see." Most of the citrus groves have been cut down, supplanted by development. Recently residents have been arguing about whether a block of houses should be rezoned for commercial use, which would alter some of the boulevard's surroundings. Through all the changes, however, the unaltered shape and proportions of the boulevard have maintained Upland's sense of continuity. A strong physical form, such as a boulevard or a green or a square, can anchor a place in people's consciousness. No one who has been to Upland forgets Euclid Avenue. It is a key element in that suburb's identity, providing the sense of permanence that is lacking in more typical suburban thoroughfares like the transitory Rockville Pike. "I know that this particular avenue has a history that includes part of my own," an Upland student said. "When I return after being gone for a while and I see Euclid Avenue, I know I have returned home."

Boulevards, usually shorter and narrower than Upland's, were common features in communities in the late nineteenth and early twentieth centuries, especially in those with above-average aspirations. Beverly Hills, when it was begun as a real estate venture in 1906, was laid out with two boulevards. Streets of this sort are investments. They pay substantial long-term dividends. Old communities in the United States usually deteriorate as they age, as prosperous people depart for newer houses in neighborhoods where nothing has yet worn out. But boulevards are bulwarks against decline. The pleasure imparted by these streets has helped many older communities to hold their own against the forces of aging and decay.

Why, then, is such a versatile and valuable street seldom built today? Builders and developers claim that homebuyers don't want to live on a busy public thoroughfare; they want seclusion. To that, one can only say yes, there is a limit to how much traffic the homebuyer will tolerate, but perhaps it's not as stringent a limit as builders imagine. Not everyone is intent on retreating to a private street. In fact, houses on Euclid Avenue command high prices, indicating that some homebuyers place a positive value on having a grand public setting for their residence. Not everyone at the dance is a wallflower.

Second, it is claimed that residential boulevards don't work today because driveways along a well-traveled street constitute a traffic hazard. Supposedly there will be accidents because of vehicles entering or leaving the driveways. But the fact is, the Upland Police Department reports that driveway traffic has *not* caused an increase in the accident rate on Euclid Avenue. Actually, the police say, the accident rate on Euclid is low in relation to its traffic volume.

Third, it is said that frequent cross streets like those that intersect Euclid Avenue would pose a risk of accidents and also tend to slow the boulevard's through traffic. To a degree, this seems to be true. But I would avoid rushing to conclude that cross streets must therefore be eliminated or severely limited, as they are in recently developed suburbs. The overall accident rate on Euclid, after all, is low, considering the number of vehicles it carries. And the street intersections, along with residential driveways and on-street parking, have the beneficial effect of discouraging speeding and encouraging drivers to be alert. This, in turn, makes the environment much safer for bicyclists and pedestrians. The lively, pedestrian-oriented environment is able to function *because* there are frequent cross streets and other civilizing restraints on drivers' behavior.

Traffic engineers fail to appreciate boulevards and other traditional streets because the practitioners of this profession judge their work by excessively narrow objectives mainly having to do with how many vehicles they can get a road to carry. Walter Kulash says the profession is fixated on the goal of moving as many vehicles as possible, as fast as is safely possible. (Even safety, he acknowledges, is not as high a priority as is often claimed. Five thousand lives a year were willingly sacrificed in raising the speed limit on rural interstate highways from 55 to 65 miles an hour.) The crucial flaw of traffic engineering is that its work is done according to very narrow and mechanical criteria—

principally, accommodating more vehicles. Traffic engineers are not seriously interested in the aesthetic results or the social consequences of their work. Traffic engineers do not inquire, Kulash says, about the "quality of experience" of the motorists. They do not ask whether motorists feel pleased or bored, uplifted or depressed, by the roads they spend great sums of the public's money to build. It is this obliviousness to aesthetic, social, and other important qualities that helps to make modern suburbs as dull and limiting as they are. In a better-designed road network motorists would have the ability, at least some of the time, to travel on narrower, tree-lined streets graced by houses and community activity, as in Oak Park, or to travel on grand boulevards like Euclid Avenue, rather than be consigned to the kinds of roads that have been built for the past few decades. Traffic engineers as a group have not thought about what serves the full interests of motorists. They have not been told to do so. "The traffic engineers' sole charge from their employers has been to 'fix' congestion," Kulash says.

Related to this, traffic engineers have not balanced the needs of motorists against the needs of pedestrians, cyclists, and the community as a whole. The streets of old communities are appealing because they manage to serve many different interests and purposes. They encourage such activities as walking and biking. They facilitate access to mass transit. They foster community social life and neighborhood-oriented businesses. They generally produce more attractive and engaging surroundings than modern street systems do. Traffic engineers and their colleagues in development and community planning have made streets and roads into limited-purpose instruments, and for this we all pay a price.

We might begin to progress beyond the modern street hierarchy if we envisioned streets, like good conversations, as a means of making connections—as many kinds of connections as possible. We might insist on creating streets that connect pedestrians to local stores and institutions. We might demand streets that help people make contact with the other members of their community. We might require streets that nurture residents' pride and involvement in their neighborhood. We might call for streets that make it easier for people to stay in their community despite old age, an inability to drive, or other changes in condition.

We must change the instructions given to traffic engineers. We must give traffic engineers and the other technicians involved in the shaping of our communities better guidance as to what their goals should be. Their objective should be the creation of an acceptable environment. We must make it clear to them that we need streets that help connect people to the larger society, by making access to other neighborhoods plentiful.

The character of the streets has the potential to help Americans lead more satisfying lives and to create communities that uplift the spirit. This is a challenge that the makers of suburbs are honor-bound to address.

THREE

The Rise
of Marketing
and the
Decline of
Planning

We live in what may go down in history as the Age of Marketing. As the field of business that focuses on developing salable products and motivating people to buy them, marketing has penetrated nearly every corner of American life. Little has been untouched by the one-third-useful, two-thirds-manipulative tactics of marketing specialists—those ingenious businesspeople who pretend to be democratic servants of consumer needs, interested in "giving the people what they want," while in actuality they use their knowledge of human weakness to achieve what marketing values above all else: sales.

A populace whose fears and vanities have been stirred by adroit marketing will do the strangest things. Who would have believed, until it happened, that the apparel industry could persuade people to be not only willing but eager to wear manufacturers' brand labels on the outside of their clothing? There was a time when, by almost universal agreement, clothing labels were discreetly hidden from view. However, the deep human need for social approval and the equally acute fear of looking out of step have been played upon expertly by the marketers of clothing, and a metamorphosis is now complete; Americans of all levels of taste and education trot around with advertisements stitched to the fronts of their shirts, sewn on the backs of their slacks, affixed to jacket pockets, stamped into the bodies of athletic shoes, and so on. This is just one instance of marketing's successfully striking one of mankind's psychological pressure points and generating almost overnight a new custom.

Marketing imperatives influence houses and communities as forcefully as they affect the clothes that people wear. Builders and developers constantly search for techniques that will motivate people to buy houses or settle in particular subdivisions.

The builders' and developers' marketing strategies, I will attempt to show, often are obstacles to making houses and communities that satisfy residents in the long run.

Because it makes money, marketing is highly valued by businesses. Any resistance to the dictates of marketing must overcome serious obstacles. Building and development firms have placed marketing close to the top of their organizations. In the typical company, the head of sales and marketing is a member of senior management. The sales and marketing executive has the prerogative of deciding which designer to hire, setting the objectives the designer is to fulfill, and demanding changes if the designer's work deviates from the marketing concept. The architects, planners, landscape architects, and others who design houses and lay out communities are expected to behave as part of a development *team*, in which they carry the ball but only if they agree to the plays called by the coach—the sales and marketing executive. Sales and marketing personnel prevent the design professionals from getting out of line. In such a business structure, designers or others who might serve as a check on the manipulative, short-term outlook of marketing are rarely in a position to raise a challenge. Mitchell Rouda, editor of *Builder* magazine, says, "The architects are completely subservient to the marketing."

This being so, if we want to understand how modern suburbs are shaped, it is essential to know something about the ideas that marketing executives adhere to. The single most important such idea is "market segmentation," a concept that has been widely accepted in the building industry since the 1970s. Through the lens of market segmentation, developers envision the character of anything from a small subdivision to an entire town.

Market segmentation calls for dividing the market as a whole into a number of categories and then setting out to appeal, segment by segment, to whichever customer categories the firm wishes to attract. Market segmentation has altered many businesses and their products. In the magazine industry, market segmentation helped doom general-interest magazines like *Look* and the old weekly *Saturday Evening Post,* which aimed at broad, heterogeneous audiences. Instead the country is awash in special-interest periodicals, from *Coastal Cruising* to *Lefthander Magazine.*

In the building and development industry, market segmentation has encouraged developers to view prospective residents as

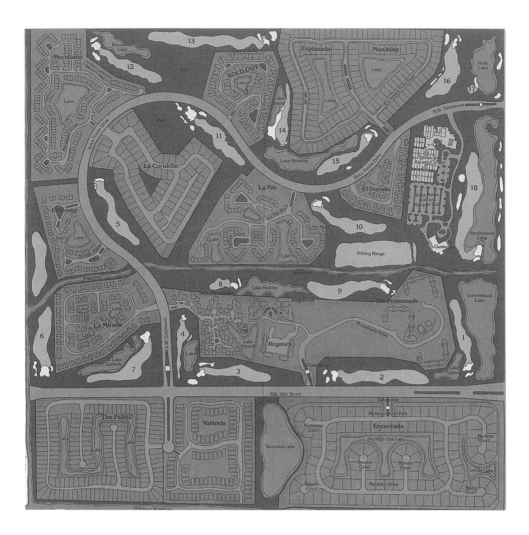

A site plan of part of Boca Pointe in Boca Raton, Florida, reveals a paucity of pedestrian or automotive connections between pod-style subdivisions. To go from one point to another within Boca Pointe usually requires driving on a major road.

a series of disparate groups who are to be kept apart from the members of other groups. The trend over the past twenty years has been to supply each segment of the paying public with an enclave segregated from the rest of the community. In small, slowly growing metropolitan areas the enclave strategy has yet to be fully embraced, but in parts of America that are quickly expanding it has become the accepted way of doing business. Nowhere is it more conspicuous than in suburban Sunbelt areas that have been swelling with affluent new arrivals.

For an example of market segmentation carried to a high level of sophistication, let's look at Boca Pointe, a 1,019-acre development in Boca Raton, Florida. The developer of Boca Pointe, situated in a part of southeastern Florida where the promise of "prestige" plays a major role in marketing campaigns, divided the site into twenty-two separate residential areas, twenty-two different enclaves, complemented by lakes, ponds, recreation complexes, and commercial areas.

The term that developers use for enclaves like Boca Pointe's is an odd-sounding one—"pods." They're called pods because the development's physical organization, looked at abstractly, is similar to the organization of a pod-producing plant. A pea plant has a stem that delivers moisture and nutrients to a series of pods, which branch off from a stem. In residential developments, the stem is the main road, off of which branch a series of building pods. Just as a pea pod has only one connection to its stem, at Boca Pointe a typical building pod has a single link to the development's main road.

By dividing the overall development into pods, marketing specialists are able to practice a high degree of market segmentation. Pods allow each residential area to be designated for a different kind of dwelling, a different kind of occupant, and a different price level. Boca Pointe has a pod of eight-story condominium buildings, a pod of townhouses, a pod of small detached houses, and so forth. Each pod specializes in one or at most two kinds of housing. Generally each pod in a development has a different builder.

Who, you might wonder, would want to live in a subdivision called a pod? It's not a term that a homeowner can warm up to. "Come visit my pad," a person might say, but not "Come visit my pod." The word sounds weird, recalling the alien beings in *Invasion of the Body Snatchers.* Marketing specialists are attentive to images and associations, so when the time comes to show a new enclave to prospective homebuyers, the marketers never, never call it a pod. They call it a village. Nearly everyone feels kindly toward villages; a village is taken to be small, intimate, human-scale. The full 1,019 acres of Boca Pointe might run the risk of seeming big and impersonal, but to live in one of its twenty-two little "villages" is to be sheltered from anonymous mass society. That is the reigning assumption. At Boca Pointe, even the shopping center hews to the village theme; it is called Wharfside Shopping Village.

All seems snug and well defined in a pod-style development like Boca Pointe. Every village has its own name—most of them melodious, exotic-sounding names like Caravelle, Mandalay,

A mail delivery point in a cul-de-sac in the "village" of Caravelle at Boca Pointe.

Valencia, and El Dorado. The builder of a village, with the approval of the developer, attempts to fashion the village into a self-contained world where every aspect of design will be harmonious. Colors, styles, house shapes, street lights, signs, pavement, planting—all these can be chosen according to a comprehensive strategy for making the village a coordinated aesthetic whole.

In the village of Caravelle, for example, all the houses—duplexes and townhouses—have orange clay barrel-tile roofs. They have driveways paved with a concrete that has been patterned to resemble brick or stone. The faux stone has an orange tone complimenting the roof color. Palm trees and other plantings provide shades of green, which look wonderfully soothing against the orange driveways and orange roofs. In Caravelle, mailboxes are not permitted to inject an unwelcome note of drabness; the mailboxes are neatly clustered together under green canvas awnings, on meticulously maintained little islands of grass and vegetation in the centers of cul-de-sacs. The mailboxes, like everything else in the design, have been made to accentuate the development's harmonious tone.

Rodney Friedman of Fisher-Friedman Architects in San Francisco calls this design approach, in which each dwelling is part

The greenness of Boca Pointe's landscape is not left to chance.

of a larger scene painting, "scenography." Even critics admit that the effect can be mesmerizing. Journalist Charlie Haas, no pushover for marketing schemes, writes that "where the period pieces are cunning and the landscaping generous, it's possible to feel a bucolic, sheltered ease, as if the whole landscape—nostalgic but inviolately new, fanciful, homey, and free of discord—were made for sunny holiday gliding." In these places everything works together, nothing seems out of sync. The enclave exudes contentment. At Boca Pointe no through streets allow one pod to come into contact with another. The developer does not want anything potentially discordant to intervene and break the golden spell.

The enclave style of development has been slower to arrive in the Northeast, the Midwest, and parts of the Mountain West, but even in these regions there are numerous moves in that direction. Marketing-oriented design and planning firms are eager to redo site plans for developments that had been laid out on paper but not yet built; often the goal is to reorganize the development to be more like pods, with houses clustered in smaller groups along cul-de-sacs instead of strung out along continuous public streets. A Colorado firm that advocates little pockets of development set apart from the more public streets uses as its sales pitch the question: "Would you rather live in an ESTATE or a SUBDIVISION?"

The lust Caravelle entrance at Boca Pointe is an indication of how far developers have come in the art of making favorable first impressions.

In the purest enclave developments there is only one entrance for each pod, and this entrance takes on tremendous importance, becoming both a symbol of the residents' social standing and a prelude to the village's interior. Builders lavish attention on entrances. Villages entrances at Boca Pointe feature fountains, waterfalls, palm trees, and terraced plantings. Above the terraced plantings is a wall on which the village name is mounted. (Some of the gold letters spelling "El Dorado" fell off their stucco wall, but fortunately for the marketing staff, the pod was sold out by the time that happened.) The use of fancy entrances is a formula promoted in building magazines and applied, with regional variations, throughout the United States. In a "Design Workshop" article, *Builder* told its readers, "A project entry will have greater visual impact and feel more inviting to prospects if it's set back from the street." Consistent with this advice, entrance walls at Boca Pointe sweep back from the road, usually in gentle curves. The article recommended using a special pavement treatment, such as scored concrete, to make buyers think they are leaving the outside world behind and crossing into a special community. On both sides of the entrance drive, ponds or other visual highlights are recommended. "After buyers pass through the entry area, give them a focus to draw them into the community," the article said. "That focus might be a recreational center, a gazebo, a pond, a fountain, a garden or simply open space; which is chosen depends on the community's character." Treatment as elaborate as this is not standard in new developments, but it is the direction in which suburban design is headed, especially in large projects for affluent people.

The entrances—and the coherence and consistency of the villages—make strong impressions on prospective homeowners. Mostly, however, they are first impressions, with all the limitations that a first impression implies. Marketing specialists often create seductive first impressions at the expense of considerations that turn out to be more important for residents as years go by. This trade-off can be seen in the pod as a whole and in the design of the individual houses or apartments.

Consider some of the housing designed by the firm that helped write the Design Workshop column—Berkus Group Architects. Based in Santa Barbara, California, with branches in Orange County, California, and Washington, D.C., Berkus Group is one of the most successful tract-house designers in the United States. Its work is emulated by many builders and architects. A Berkus project attends closely to first impressions. The walkway from the street to the front door frequently passes through a gate or a small courtyard garden or beneath the roof of an arcade; as visitors approach the front door, there's a drumroll of spatial experiences, arousing anticipation of what will come next. Inside the dwelling, the foyer may be extra high. Sunlight streams into it from above. The interiors have high, sloping ceilings, balconies, or other features possessing flair. They have generous expanses of glass, which extends the views beyond the walls and maximizes the sense of spaciousness. From the foyer, the visitor often can take in views in three different directions—upward to a staircase or to a bridge that connects the master bedroom suite, at one end of the second floor, to the rest of the second floor; downward a step or two to the family room, dining area, or other living area; and outward through glass doors or windows to the back yard. A bit of the kitchen or another room may be visible, hinting to visitors that there's more waiting to be explored.

Berkus Group and a number of other firms have done well for themselves designing tract houses of this kind. Builders erect them by the thousands in California, Arizona, other parts of the Sunbelt and to a lesser extent in other regions. They are choreographed, see-through houses, predicated on the idea that the bigger the view and the more dramatic the progression of spaces, the better the house will sell. In 1983, when I met him for the first

The recessed entrance and the partially covered walk make approaching this house's front door an event. But the more the front doors are removed from the street, the fewer opportunities there are for residents to exercise casual surveillance over the street or initiate conversations with neighbors. A California see-through house designed by Berkus Group Architects.

time, the firm's founder, Barry Berkus, said his goal is to design dwellings that are "exciting, flexible, stimulating enough, not just a filing cabinet, a cube." He portrayed such design, with its premium on views, drama, and expansiveness, as a service to the inhabitant, an improvement on the dull, closed-in tract houses and apartments that the building industry often turned out in the past and continues to turn out in some parts of the country.

By 1990, however, when Berkus made one of his many presentations for a National Association of Home Builders annual convention, even he seemed willing to acknowledge some limitations in such designs. Berkus spoke jadedly during a builders' seminar. After pointing out the visually stimulating characteristics of marketing-oriented contemporary design, he mockingly drew attention to flaws, such as the hard-to-reach, hard-to-clean surfaces in open, multilevel interiors. "Dust-catchers," he called them. Cleaning problems are probably the least of the frustrations for residents. More important is the fact that the houses often provide little visual privacy. An expansive view of the interior is made available not only to family members and friends but also to every postal worker, pizza deliverer, or petition gatherer who knocks on the front door.

Clare Cooper Marcus, Carolyn Francis, and Colette Meunier at the University of California at Berkeley examined tract houses in the Bay area and concluded that "private areas of houses are amazingly frequently violated by insensitive window location." In some of the model homes they saw, the researchers noticed that "balconies off master suites were entirely visible for blocks around." Windows into master bathrooms were placed so inappropriately that the researchers "began to wonder if the windows afforded a deliberate form of 'social flashing' of opulent bathrooms and their luxuriating owners to next-door neighbors, passersby, or, in some cases, golfers on adjacent fairways." In 1991 the *New York Times* reported that a couple in a condominium development in Tampa were arrested for lewd and lascivious conduct after they made love in a bathroom hot tub within view of an eight-year-old boy in the condo next door; the boy's father had no trouble videotaping the sex play from one of his windows to aid the prosecutors. Such are the hazards of the see-through dwelling. If visual privacy is limited, acoustic privacy is equally scarce. In many houses, noise travels without a break throughout much of the interior.

To builders these defects are no secret. Builders accept tho deficiencies because they make for effective marketing. In fact, builders joke about them. They call a dwelling that has visually impressive but hard-to-live-with features a "twenty-minute house," by which the builders mean a house designed to be so striking that it will be remembered by people who spend twenty minutes in it during a harried house-hunting expedition. What's missing from the calculations of market-driven design is sufficient concern for how people will live in the houses or the developments once they've made their purchase.

Bernard S. Schreft, a marketing consultant in Fort Lauderdale, praised one landscape architect for an ability to lay out large developments with a sequence of visual experiences, the equivalent of a musical score. There is a dramatic flourish at the entrance of the development, then a quieter period during which the opening fanfare is allowed to sink in. After this there is a second buildup, followed by another period of less-intense stimulation. As the journey proceeds toward the interior of the development, the visual experiences rhythmically continue, giving emotional resonance to the motorist's progress. Such artfully designed sequences can be a welcome relief to residents coming home after a hard day. However, a community ought to use its landscape features to do more than provide a pleasing experience for motorists. It should offer settings that people will *use* once they get out of the car. At Boca Pointe two things are noticeable about the outdoor surroundings. First, they are beautiful—much more handsome and harmonious than the usual tract developments of thirty or forty years ago. Second—and because of the favorable initial impression they make, this is recognized less quickly—they are empty. Much of the outdoor setting stands deserted even in balmy weather.

Why does so much of the suburban landscape stand empty and devoid of neighborly activity? The principal reason that I want to explore here is the developments' physical organization—the obstacles that discourage pedestrian activity. Marketing techniques favor placing community facilities where they will be on view to large numbers of visitors driving by. Boca Pointe has its Fitness and Racquet Club located at the bend in a major road, where anyone passing through the development's northeastern quarter sees it. The Tennis and Aquatic Center and the clubhouse of the Golf and Racquet Club are close to another major road. The Wharfside Shopping Village is built close to another road. All of these are virtually inaccessible to anyone who might think of walking to them from a residential area. While spending large sums on swimming, racquet sports, and golf facilities, the developer has made the most fundamental exercise of all—walking—ridiculously difficult. A sales brochure for El Dorado unwittingly draws attention to Boca Pointe's antipedestrian layout when it boasts, "El Dorado is the only community within Boca Pointe to have direct, permanent walking access to the Tennis and Aquatic Center and the Country Club."

People cannot go by foot to the shopping center, even from the adjoining residential village. The finger of a lake forms a barrier—in developers' terminology, a "buffer"—between the shopping center and the village. Lakes or other landscape features are placed where they create buffers around each pod, separating it from nearly everything in its vicinity. Marketers and designers, in their obsession with what will be seen by motorists and first-time visitors, have neglected the potential for encouraging daily neighborhood activity, which depends to a large degree on people's ability to walk to interesting or useful places. Scenographic though the layout may be, the residents have been painted into a corner.

Market segmentation, then, ends up reinforcing one of the faulty practices indulged in by traffic engineers—the creation of street and road systems that limit people's ability to get around on their own bodily power. Market segmentation favors a circuitous circulation system with few direct connections because it allows each enclave to stand apart and trumpet its separate identity. This profoundly discourages neighborhood life. Neighborhood ties flourish when people can go places on foot, encountering friends and acquaintances along the way, at a pedestrian pace. If walking is inconvenient, people simply will not walk, and the benefits of walking—among them, knowledge of the neighborhood and its residents—will be squandered. In pod-style developments, the odds are stacked against the growth of neighborliness.

The great boon of market segmentation ostensibly is that people get to live among people who are much like themselves. When the housing is of a single kind, in a narrow price range, appealing to a small slice of the market, one result is a concentration of people of the same age group, the same economic status, and other similarities. Most people find comfort in living among people who are like themselves. Since at least the nineteenth century, development has avoided a totally random distribution of people. Today that tendency is pushed to an unprecedented extreme by marketers and developers who play not only on people's positive yearnings for like-minded neighbors but also on their fears. "When you work for developers, you learn that almost everything that goes on in development is based on fear and flight," says Walter Kulash. "It's based on fear of cities, fear of the people that are in cities, and flight from them."

The consequences of this rigid segregation of different kinds of people are troubling. Tiny, separate "villages" with buffer zones on their perimeter increase the likelihood that their residents will be categorized—often in derogatory terms—by those who live outside their borders. Residents of highly segregated developments will be labeled according to whatever traits they share, or seem to share. Segregation breeds resentment. For children the experience of being labeled on the basis of where they live can be very unsettling.

More important, when people live in highly segregated residential districts, they give up experiences and satisfactions, often without knowing what they're sacrificing. People think they know a tremendous amount about the world because of television, periodicals, and other elements of modern life, but much can be learned only through direct experience, and direct experience is limited by the suburban form of development. In many suburban areas, for example, children grow up with little daily exposure to old people, a lack that may hinder their development years later. Each age of life has its own lessons to teach. Without people in their late years, it is harder for children and young adults to obtain the insights that lead to maturity.

The costs of a deliberately segregated pattern of development weigh on society as whole. Barriers between one residential area and another foster a breakdown of the larger community. It becomes harder to create towns, cities, and metropolitan areas that pull together, focusing on common interests and shared goals. Energy that could be channeled into the betterment of the society is dissipated by the growth of an "us against them" mentality. Sociologist Richard Sennett argues that the geographic separation of one group from another keeps many adults in an eternal adolescence, unable to grapple skillfully with the genuine differences among people. Segregation aggravates the fears people harbor toward those who differ from themselves. For better or worse, the United States is a diverse society, and its citizens need to acquire the skills that allow a diverse society to function well. This requires coming into contact with people from outside one's own class. It requires learning how to cooperate. We would be wise to lay out communities in ways that allow interaction with people who are not quite like ourselves. In so doing, we would make it easier to see our common humanity and cooperate in solving mutual problems.

The marketers' use of the "village" motif misrepresents what villages are really like. Genuine villages throughout most of history have not been homogeneous. They have been whole or nearly whole societies containing old, middle-aged, and young; poor, middling, and sometimes rich; people of differing talents and interests. The village of the past thrived by having individuals who were able and willing to fill many varied functions. While in a modern society with automobiles each little community no longer needs its own butcher, baker, clergyman, and so on, it is still beneficial to have people of all ages and abilities. A neighborhood of people too much alike will lack many things.

Residential areas made up solely of people in their prime working years chronically run short of volunteers for community activities. Cooperative housing complexes, which depend on volunteer activities by their residents, have learned in the past twenty years that retired people are essential, because with so many two-income families too busy to undertake community projects, retired people are the core volunteer population willing to serve on community boards and undertake neighborhood projects. If a neighborhood has no retired people, civic activity often languishes.

Communities fare best when there are no gaps in their population. Young people may be needed for mowing the lawn, running errands, and babysitting. Educated people may be needed for their contributions to culture and leadership. People with less formal education may be needed to provide services and carry on trades, from working in restaurants to cleaning houses. Women who will care for others' small children during the workday are needed almost everywhere. So are families who will run mom-and-pop stores (without which there looms the monotonous prospect of a community made up of chain stores). Societies thrive on interdependence. Modern forms of development have done a disservice by segmenting neighborhoods too narrowly.

Many people sharply sense the limitations of their current subdivision or "village." If any change occurs in their personal circumstances—whoosh, they're gone. "We figured it was time to go because most of the people who moved in about the same time

In pod-style development, a single kind of housing unit is built in large and often monotonous quantities. These townhouses are in West Chester, Pennsylvania.

we did had already moved out," a family moving out of a suburban Chicago townhouse development told me. The family's income had risen, and they felt they should not stay among townhouse dwellers any more. They should be in a neighborhood with a higher economic status, in a single-family house, now that they could afford it. The townhouse subdivision was severely limited—it had no mix of houses, little mixture of incomes, and little ambiguity about its level of prestige. It was a pigeonhole, and the family escaped it as soon as the pigeonhole no longer fit. In American suburbs, moving out is the common pattern, propelled by the narrowness of any one subdivision.

Repeated millions of times, the decision to move out robs communities of their memories and their social relationships. It leaves them shallow rooted, ill equipped to provide their residents with sustenance during hard times. Sociologists have discovered that longtime residents make a disproportionately large contribution to a community; they do much to define its character and create a sense of continuity. Market segmentation, in its push toward small, segregated categories of people and housing, gives the residents a homogeneity that may well be pleasurable—briefly—but it exacts a price in human losses. "Any human relationship takes time for seasoning, for testing, for the kind of slow, casual knitting that will not break apart under the first signs of stress or strain," John Killinger writes in *The Loneliness of Children.* Rapid mobility, Killinger observes, "does not afford the kind of time—*years and years* of time—that are necessary to become rooted in a place, to really know the neighbors, to truly belong to the community, to celebrate the great milestones of life that can be celebrated in a home church or synagogue, to feel, deeply and responsibly, that there is a bond between ourselves and the land, ourselves and the house, ourselves and the neighborhood, that nourishes and replenishes our beings."

As early as 1972 sociologist Gerald Suttles noticed that suburban areas laid out with features such as segregation from cross-traffic—a key trait of pod-style development—"seem to be among our most atomized communities and the least able to develop a corporate body of representatives and a native identity apart from the one developers have given them." In the more than twenty years since Suttles made his observations, the problems have festered.

At the root of what's wrong with the suburbs is an overreliance on business and moneymaking. Business could not have gained such a dominant influence over community development if public planning had not suffered a precipitous decline. The full story of how and why vital community planning went into eclipse is too long to be told here, but I present a much-abbreviated account of the fiasco because it may help in figuring out how the reshaping of the suburbs ought to proceed.

Every profession needs to have faith in its ability to produce the results it desires. Planning, to its great sorrow, lost that faith after the 1950s, partly because it embraced modernist principles of architecture and planning—principles that proved to be a blueprint for disaster. Urban renewal failed to produce its expected benefits in many cities. Slum clearance turned out to be a dubious practice, one that displaced large numbers of poor and black people, setting the stage for racial unrest and riots in the 1960s. Public housing, initially a bright hope, in many instances degenerated so completely that it became more notorious than the substandard buildings it had supplanted. These and other well-known failures led planners to retreat from their ambitions. Increasingly, decision making was left to market forces.

Second, planning came under attack because often it was heavily influenced by the very interests it was supposed to regulate. Many planning agencies adopted policies that differed hardly at all from what businesses and property owners wanted. For example, planners of suburban areas often zoned long stretches of highway frontage for strip commercial development, which was ugly and an impediment to travel. Such actions raised the question of why, if the planners were simply ratifying what private interests would have done, was it necessary to do planning at taxpayer expense.

Third, planners shifted their interest away from determining physical form. Some planners concentrated on the *process* of planning—making sure deliberations were handled by the proper committees, with the requisite hearings, on the right timetable, and so on. As they did so, they became less attentive to whether the physical environment itself was being shaped adequately. Planners lost much of whatever competence they once had as makers of physical form. There are still many individuals called planners, but most of them might more accurately be termed application-accepters and permit-dispensers. They are not planners in the traditional sense of the word—individuals who give physical shape to the future. Planning departments have surrendered responsibility to others, principally developers, who have become increasingly free to lay out streets, neighborhoods, and common areas as they choose.

The builders and developers always fall back on the argument that if people didn't like what was produced, they wouldn't buy it. This is a vastly oversimplified version of what's really going on. Many homebuyers buy houses or communities that they know are flawed. They buy them because of the location, the quality of the local schools, or the price, even though they might prefer houses and communities very different from what the builders and developers are offering. People also buy into flawed houses or defective communities for another important reason: They expect to make money. "Housing in this country has always been part of a process of moving up," Berkus observes. Many people take what the market produces, in the knowledge that others will most likely come along later to do the same, enabling the initial owners to step up to a more expensive house. This process encourages homebuyers to operate just like marketing specialists—conning themselves into accepting defective living environments because they will make a profit. When millions of Americans behave this way, it's easy for developers to sell "villages," "estates," and subdivisions of dubious quality. The challenge to well-conceived design has gotten tougher as people have come to see their house as their main way of accumulating money. Ethan Seltzer, of the Institute of Portland Metropolitan Studies in Portland, Oregon, says the use of houses as investments has distorted patterns of housing and community development. Seltzer suggests that the federal government should encourage some means of family saving and investment other than appreciation of residential real estate.

Despite all the problems that planning has had over the years, planning remains the most likely instrument for overcoming the defects of current suburban patterns. Marketing is not an adequate substitute for high-quality planning. On the outskirts of San Jose, I talked with a childless couple living in a new subdivision in a four-bedroom house with a three-car garage. They knew that buying the house—which was far larger than they needed—made financial sense, but they were dissatisfied nonetheless. Their dream was to move to a small town they knew in another part of the country—a nineteenth-century town with a pretty business district of two-story brick buildings along the main street, a park full of tall trees in the town center, and streets laid out like a skewed checkerboard, with sidewalks along every street. It's possible for effective public planning to nurture places like that small town into existence. Few developers can create such places on their own.

Whatever the failings of planners, we should be wary of the argument that people can find what they need if the market operates with a bare minimum of governmental direction. "The argument that people are getting what they want assumes that homebuyers are as knowledgeable about the implications of community design as professional planners are," says Daniel M. Cary. "Often they don't find the problems out until they've bought the house and lived there. Even then, they may not understand some of the subtle aspects of the problem."

Planners cannot bring about a redirection of suburban development on their own. The building and development industry has to know more and care more about the quality of community design before the situation will greatly improve. There is no magical cure that will cause the industry's failings to vanish suddenly, but there are some practical remedies that might help. One such remedy is a reform of the publications that give the building industry information. Magazines like *Builder* and *Professional Builder and Remodeler* devote tremendous energy to telling builders and developers how to achieve financial success. The theme that runs through most of the magazines' reports on design and planning is: here's how to sell houses faster, how to sell more of them, how to sell them at a bigger profit. The magazines seize on topics such as how to build bathrooms that impress prospective homebuyers, how to create compelling sales brochures, and how to design model homes that spur people to buy. In the magazines are numerous reports on builders and their latest subdivisions. *Professional Builder*'s coverage reads like puffery; *Builder*'s reporting is more probing, but it too is overly enamored with design and marketing gimmicks that boost sales in the short term at the expense of long-term buyer satisfaction.

Quite striking to anyone who reads them for an extended period is the magazines' limited interest in discovering how subdivisions and communities fare after the builder has moved on. *Builder* does avidly report the reactions of consumer "focus groups" to brand-new houses and newly opened subdivisions, but this is like asking diners for their opinion of the food before they've had an opportunity to digest it. The *experience* of living in a place is what matters in the long run, not the often shallow

The grid delivers a grand setting for a group of pedestrians: a view of Kenilworth Avenue in Oak Park, Illinois, in 1925.

first impressions. To its credit, *Builder* has checked on the performance of the "New American Home" show houses, whose construction the magazine has sponsored each year since 1984, and it has occasionally revisited a well-known community like Levittown, New York. But it is not common for the editors to visit subdivisions that have been completed for a year or five years or ten years and tell readers how these places have fared. One would think from reading the trade publications that residents' long-term satisfaction is a matter of little concern.

The magazines ought to investigate how happy people are with the places that builders and developers produce. The trade magazines would do well to ask such questions as: How have housing developments of different kinds performed over the years? Which elements of design have improved life for residents? Which elements have spawned disappointment and high turnover? Analysis of this sort might give builders and developers valuable guidance on how to revise and refine their designs. Many ideas and observations might be culled from visits to neighborhoods and suburbs that have held up well for decades—Miami's Coral Gables, Chicago's Oak Park and Evanston, Cincinnati's Mariemont, New York's Forest Hills Gardens, Baltimore's Roland Park, Kansas City's Country Club District, Camden's Yorkship Village, Los Angeles's Palos Verdes, Ladd's Addition in Portland, Oregon, and others. Exploration of communities that have weathered economic cycles and changes of fashion would be a useful corrective for an industry obsessed with the short term.

To perform this task well, the trade magazines would need the courage to criticize products of builders and developers. The magazines would have to be willing to face hostile reactions from builders and developers, who have grown unaccustomed to critical analysis from their trade publications. When *Builder*, in a departure from the norm, ran a March 1993 cover story entitled "Why I Won't Buy a New Home," containing scathing comments by people who chose to buy older houses rather than new ones, the National Association of Home Builders responded, as might be expected, with outrage. The president of the builders' association wrote a full-page commentary in *Builder*, complaining that such coverage felt like an insult because it appeared in a periodical that, although privately owned and operated by Hanley-Wood Inc., is authorized to call itself "The magazine of the National Association of Home Builders" and is sent to all dues-paying members of the association. *Builder*'s "offending" article (which was accompanied by suggestions on how builders

Gardens containing 6,000 roses embellish intersections in Ladd's Addition, a Portland, Oregon, neighborhood platted in 1891 by local businessman William S. Ladd. Volunteers help the city maintain the roses.

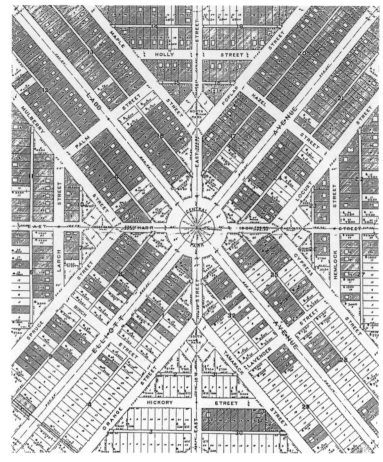

The diagonal street pattern of Ladd's Addition, shown in a 1922 promotional map, was inspired by Pierre L'Enfant's plan for Washington, D.C. It contrasts sharply with the grid layout of the surrounding neighborhoods.

can defend themselves against homebuyers' distrust of new houses) might have provoked less fury if it had been couched in calmer language. Unfortunately, this foray by *Builder* into criticism of the industry was written in the same breathless style that the magazine ordinarily uses to make new subdivisions sound like the most spectacular undertakings since the Taj Mahal. The magazines need the courage to examine issues that may cast some builders and developers in an unflattering light, but they need more than that. The magazines need a more thoughtful kind of writing; they need to rise above their instinct for glibness. Builders and developers, in my experience, tend to be bright people. They deal repeatedly with complicated situations. They are not simpletons, capable only of ingesting information about what's "hot." There is no inherent reason why their magazines have to be so oversimplified and unreflective.

For years the American Institute of Architects published an undistinguished journal. Then, in the 1970s and 1980s, under the editorship of Donald Canty, the journal, *Architecture,* enjoyed a run as a penetrating and eminently readable publication. A periodical can accomplish great things when it has ambitious leadership. Homebuilders and developers deserve a similar level of editorial ambition, for they, as much as architects and planners, are the shapers of our communities. If the magazines concern themselves not solely with financial success but also with the well-being of society, they may help to improve the quality of communities.

Any meaningful reform of the building and development industry would require businesspeople to expose themselves to different thinking. When builders and developers gather for conferences and seminars, they would do well to search for more varied sources of ideas than the ones they usually hear. Thought-provoking sources are not hard to find. There are social critics, architecture critics, think tanks, universities, foundations, and so on. There are organizations such as the Environmental Design Research Association, the American Institute of Architects, the American Society of Landscape Architects, the American Planning Association, and the Urban Land Institute, to name just a few. The Environmental Design Research Association, composed of individuals who study the design of the man-made environ-

A fountain near the center of Mariemont, Ohio, an artfully designed suburb begun in the 1920s.

An arch makes a graceful connection between a residential area in Palos Verdes, California, and Malaga Cove Plaza, a shopping center built in the 1920s.

ment and how it affects people's satisfaction and behavior, has been in existence for more than twenty years. This association as well as the architects' institute, the landscape architects' association, and the planning association all hold their conferences apart from those of developers and builders. Each group meets in isolation, their members often complaining about how little power they possess. (A sense of powerlessness comes naturally to people who shut themselves off from those in related fields.) If the people who build and develop the suburbs have the will to break out of their parochialism, useful conversations might begin. These might lead to better ways of building.

The current pattern of following one's own narrow self-interest is a sure route to social decline. In *The Rise of Selfishness in America,* James Lincoln Collier writes, "A people who will not sacrifice for the common good cannot expect to have any common good." People must routinely do things that go against their immediate self-interest if their society is to thrive and their metropolitan areas are to be healthy. This is the requirement of civilized life.

Finally, the planning profession must be repaired. Planners need to be educated in the importance of the physical settings they are shaping. They need to acquire the skills they have neglected for the past quarter-century. These skills must be linked to a compelling purpose and vision, something that planning has sorely lacked in recent years. As planners become more capable, it will be incumbent on the public and especially on business to treat planners with greater respect than has been the norm. Planners who have ideas should be prized, not punished for speaking up. A new appreciation of planners as people who *think* might begin to dispel the apprehensive atmosphere that has made planning an unappealing line of work for the bright and dynamic.

It is time to let go of the idea that marketing, without planning, is an adequate answer to society's needs. Marketing is selfishness masquerading as democratic principle. The debilitating effects of marketing need to be reversed. Americans must develop a renewed commitment to the public good, expressing it in their thinking, their behavior, and their institutions. When this happens, American communities will begin to thrive.

FOUR

Controlling the Neighborhood

Nature and community in harmony.
—Motto of the Burke Centre Conservancy, Burke, Virginia

A foolish consistency is the hobgoblin of little minds.
—Ralph Waldo Emerson

In Burke Centre, the home of 20,000 people in Fairfax County, Virginia, none of the swing sets is painted in the bright colors that children instinctively prefer. There are no brilliant oranges, no canary yellows, no fire-engine reds. All the swing sets are painted in earth tones, a muted range of colors selected by the developer in the mid-1970s and required ever since by the local homeowners' association, the Burke Centre Conservancy. Burke Centre believes in rules—for colors, materials, objects, and activities.

In Burke Centre, humankind will never have to shield its eyes from a house with striped awnings. They are not allowed. Residents will never have to worry about some renegade installing a storm door embellished with a family monogram or trimmed with machine torturings of scalloped white aluminum; elaborate storm doors are warned against in a ninety-one-page rulebook issued to all 5,860 households. Back yards will never be marred by something as plebeian as a permanently strung-up clothesline. All clotheslines must be removed when the laundry is taken in. Residents will never have to see an aboveground swimming pool. They are not permitted. A flagpole with an eagle at the top will not pass muster, nor will a chain-link fence. In this largely middle-income development, which was once described by the *Washington Post* as having a flotilla of houses in "a choice of two colors, beige and off-beige," the homeowners' association insists on an almost military degree of order. Not even the height of a pile of firewood escapes the disciplinary regimen; logs must be stacked no more than four feet above the ground.

The insistence on order runs equally strong at Blackhawk, a predominantly upper-income development twenty-five miles east of Oakland, California. At Blackhawk, in the tawny foothills of the Diablo Mountains, if a homeowner wants to put up a basketball backboard, it must be installed at the rear of the house. Blackhawk's 7,000 residents, including the exuberant sportscaster John Madden, are protected from such a baldly unarchitectonic sight. A security guard for the 4,800-acre development enjoys passing the time by telling visitors about Blackhawk's many rules, such as the ban on "for sale" signs except when placed on a mailbox or a driveway and the unconditional ban on political signs. "The residents," says the guard, "get a thick book of rules."

Such is the meticulous world of homeowners' associations, where rulebooks, boards of directors, design review committees, employees, and volunteers strive to suppress all manner of environmental and behavioral threats. What goes on at Burke Centre and Blackhawk is occurring in developments in every part of the country and at nearly every level of income.

Homeowners' associations are not new. Mandatory homeowners' associations—which all the property owners in a development are required to support through dues or assessments and compelled to obey in the design, use, and maintenance of their properties—appeared in the United States in the nineteenth century. Until about thirty years ago, they remained rare. As of 1962 there were probably no more than five hundred mandatory homeowners' associations. Since then they have grown explosively. Each year brings the formation of hundreds if not thousands of new associations. The United States now contains an estimated 130,000 mandatory homeowners' associations. More than thirty million people at least one of every eight Americans—live under the jurisdiction of a homeowners' association. Some call themselves "community associations." Others use the term "condominium association," where that applies. Still others use more stately titles like "conservancy" or "foundation." For simplicity's sake I refer to all of these as homeowners' associations.

The reasons for the surge of homeowners' associations are several. Starting in 1962, when the first American condominium was established in Salt Lake City, condominiums became a popular way for apartment dwellers to obtain the financial advantages of homeownership. People heeding the Herbert Hoover maxim that "nobody ever got sentimental over a stack of rent receipts" bought condos and became members of associations that cared for the commonly owned grounds and the common portions of buildings. Second, the desire for recreation prompted a growing number of developers to provide community swimming pools, tennis courts, and other shared amenities. To maintain these facilities, homeowners' associations were formed. Third, people who were busy, affluent, aging, or just plain lazy opted for developments where chores like lawn mowing and leaf collection would be taken care of collectively by workers hired by an association. Fourth, homeowners' associations caught on because they promised to protect and enhance property values. The associations derive their power from deed restrictions—legal covenants that set conditions on how a property may be used or maintained. Because the associations have the power to tax their members and to make and enforce rules, some political scientists classify homeowners' associations as private governments.

Whether homeowners' associations have consistently boosted property values is arguable. In some countries, the restrictions employed by homeowners' associations have been considered harmful to property values. Political scientist Evan McKenzie, author of the forthcoming *Privatopia,* a book about homeowners' associations, says that courts in Great Britain historically were reluctant to enforce property restrictions like those of homeowners' associations, out of a conviction that they would make ownership less desirable and therefore reduce real estate values. In the United States, by contrast, real estate developers have argued that restrictions uphold and elevate property values. The consistent standard of maintenance, the ability to crack down on undesirable behavior, and the organized peer pressure of an association are thought to pay off in higher real estate prices.

Douglas M. Kleine, former research director of the Community Associations Institute, an organization that promotes homeowners' associations in the United States, says there has been only one national study of the long-term effects of homeowners' associations on property values in this country. That study was prepared by the Urban Land Institute in 1964. It concluded that in homeowners' association developments established prior to 1940, properties maintained their value "strikingly in contrast to the deterioration of other housing of comparable age and location." The usual pattern is that as a neighborhood ages, its property values decline relative to the prices of newer housing; neighborhoods with mandatory homeowners' associations avoided that decline, according to the ULI study. A serious weakness of that study is that it was completed so long ago—before 99.6 percent of today's homeowners' associations were even formed.

"We used to say at CAI that a more up-to-date study should be conducted, but it never was," Kleine says. Kleine points out a second serious weakness: "That study may not have been able to measure the full cycle that neighborhoods go through, which would include reuse or adaptive reuse." He explains, "If you look at townhouses in downtown Baltimore, you see that they came back [from a period of deterioration], but through adaptation. In covenanted communities, I'm not sure there's that flexibility for the future. Can you rent out your basement? Can you run a home business? Can you use aluminum or vinyl siding?" Kleine speculates that liberties such as those may be important to a neighborhood's long-term prospects.

Whatever the merits of those arguments, millions of Americans believe homeowners' associations to be financially advantageous. And there are reasons why the number of homeowners' associations is likely to continue climbing. One is that suburbs have become large and populous, and as they have grown they have ceased to provide a close community feeling. A homeowners' association development offers, in most cases, a distinct identity on a small scale, a haven against impersonal mass society. Another reason for the continuing growth of homeowners' associations is that financially strapped local governments are often unable or unwilling to provide all the parks, recreational complexes, and other facilities that the populace wants. Residents can obtain those amenities by living in homeowners' association developments; and the residents have the satisfaction of knowing that the dues or assessments they pay to their association are being spent within their own development, not miles away on the other side of town.

Growing concern for the natural environment is another spur to homeowners' associations. Government regulations increasingly demand the preservation of marshes, swamps, and steep hillsides. Usually these natural areas must be placed under the supervision of some organization, so a homeowners' association is formed for that purpose. Some developers, especially in the West, recently have become reluctant to build developments with homeowners' associations because the associations can become forceful adversaries, suing the developer when problems are not handled to the residents' satisfaction. Nonetheless, the number of associations nationally continues to rise.

Residents are not of one mind about how an association ought to conduct itself, so as the number of associations grows, the number of conflicts mounts. Marilyn Oldham, who served on a homeowners' association review board in Columbia, Maryland, says, "There were people who moved to Columbia because they wanted the [governance] structure. They didn't want any change from the neighborhood they moved into—no paint jobs, no fences, no change. There were some who wanted more individuality. And there were some who felt it was all horse manure." These contrasting attitudes make for friction. And if attitudes toward homeowners' associations differ within Columbia—a community that from its earliest days was advertised as the ultimate in planning and organization—the likelihood of conflict in the average speculative development is higher yet. "We are a very ambiguously minded nation," says David B. Wolfe, a marketing consultant in Reston, Virginia, who helped establish more than 400 homeowners' associations in the 1970s and 1980s. "On the one hand, we want to value individuality. On the other hand, we want community and protection of property values."

"In the fifty largest metropolitan areas, community association developments account for at least 50 percent of the market share of new home sales," reports the Community Associations Institute. In Sunbelt areas like San Diego and Orange counties in California, homeowners' associations encompass the great majority of the new housing. Probably 90 percent of the new housing in the Washington, D.C., metropolitan area is in homeowners' association developments. Consequently it's common for a family to buy a house without necessarily wanting the homeowners' association that comes with it. In almost every case the homeowners' association is *preorganized* by the developer before the houses go on the market. It is the developer who draws up the bylaws and the standards of the homeowners' association. For those who move in, the homeowners' association is a fait accompli. Wolfe says the Washington area contains many homeowners who are dissatisfied with their associations.

In Burke Centre controversy recently erupted when the conservancy notified approximately twenty homeowners in the Wood Sorrel Cluster that they had violated a rule limiting houses to two exterior colors. The homeowners had installed brown Sears, Roebuck storm doors, which added an impermissible third color to the exterior. The conservancy ordered that one of the colors be repainted. "Storm doors have been a bone of contention forever," said the president of the conservancy's board of trustees. The Wood Sorrel residents argued that the rule was trivial. "How can you sit around and talk about something so inane as storm doors?" a protesting homeowner asked a trustee. The trustee replied, "You'd be surprised. You should have been here for the white-stone discussions."

At Franklin Farm, a development in Oakton, Virginia, the homeowners' association ordered a family to remove a collection of imitation pink flamingos from its grounds. The flamingos violated a strict limit on exterior decorations. In the course of enforcing its rule, the Franklin Farm Foundation discovered that the family also had a large assortment of flamingo decorations in the interior of their home. Flamingos were a family theme. Oldham recalls disputes in Columbia over a family being ordered to change the royal blue color they had painted their garage door, a man being ordered to get rid of a boarder he had taken in to cope with the financial setback of a divorce, and a family being told to raze a greenhouse that was larger and more commercial than the association allowed.

Oldham came to this conclusion: "At Columbia, people really care about their houses. They represent the financial success of the family, the unity of the family, who they are. At Columbia you couldn't put cardinals on your mailbox. You couldn't put up a sign with the family name carved in some style." The restrictions became a depressing influence. "There are a lot of creative people out there who have ideas," Oldham says, "and you defeat them." Zane Yost, a Bridgeport, Connecticut, architect who has spent his career in housing, says, "You create an alienated society in which people are intimidated and afraid." The United States has more than its share of adults who are waiting for some organization to tell them what to do. Some of them might begin to rekindle their spirit if their environment was less confining.

Homeowners' association restrictions affect many of the country's prime child-rearing neighborhoods. I know of no studies of the effects of homeowners' associations on children, but logic suggests that associations with intrusive rules diminish children's independence and self-reliance. Children learn by watching adults. When they see the adults being told what color to paint their house, which tones of basketball backboards to buy, and where not to plant a garden, children can hardly avoid concluding that the scope of individual action in contemporary America is narrow indeed. One wonders whether a young Abraham Lincoln could have grown up successfully in a homeowners' association development. The society in which Lincoln came of age was one that gave individuals ample latitude to make their own decisions. The liberty to succeed or fail by one's own lights always has value. If children see adults following their own disparate enthusiasms, they might conclude that sooner or later they too will be able to do the same. In a community where freedom is respected, there will be individuals who do unusual things in building, planting, decorating, and in conducting other aspects of their lives. Examples of independent behavior teach children to respect their own capacities.

Homeowners' association restrictions have a mixture of effects on the neighborhood as a whole and neighborhood activity. They enable the neighborhood to act against nuisances and threats. As municipal governments become concerned with bigger issues, the homeowners' association fills a gap, attending to matters that escape municipal attention. Neighborhoods can obtain a satisfying sense of control over their affairs. But there are serious hazards. Oldham says that in the section of Columbia where she lived, the homeowners' association tried to achieve consensus on neighborhood changes and usually succeeded in doing so. "But there were always some who disagreed," she says. When a dispute flared up, the coercive power available to the association sometimes enlarged the conflict. What might, in an unorganized neighborhood, have remained a disagreement between two unhappy neighbors escalated into a fight in which nearly everyone in the vicinity took sides. "On the greenhouse issue the whole street got in a big fight," Oldham says. "Neighbors stopped speaking. To some people, that's pretty offensive. The people who had the greenhouse eventually moved."

Many of the more serious nuisances addressed by homeowners' associations, such as junked cars, noise, pollution, and home businesses that generate heavy traffic, are issues that fall within the scope of a municipal zoning ordinance. It may be harder to get the attention of a municipality, but municipal action, if and when it comes, will probably not arouse as much neighborhood division as action by a homeowners' association. Those who serve on homeowners' associations already know something about the bitterness that the association can arouse. A 1987 study in California found that during a one-year period 44 percent of the homeowners' association boards in that state had been "harassed" or threatened with lawsuits. "Private governments" can be heartily disliked—even more intensely than public governments.

Why do homeowners' associations adopt rules telling people how many colors they may paint their house, which kind of

fences to install, how high to stack their firewood, where they may and may not plant vegetables, and so on? The answer is no mystery: People feel a need for consistency and visual harmony. They wish for things to fit together. They yearn for coherence. The desire for harmony runs deep in human beings, and it forms the fundamental basis of design regulations.

Harmony is a virtue. Yet it is a complex virtue, and not one that should be sought to the exclusion of all other qualities. The full dimensions of physical harmony, including both its satisfactions and its limitations, need to be understood if homeowners' associations are to arrive at a sensible policy on aesthetic matters. A good place to study physical harmony is in a community renowned for its appeal. Let's look closely, then, at how harmony operates in one place that attracts residents and admirers from near and far. That place is Nantucket, Massachusetts, a 300-year-old island town off Cape Cod.

When the great white car ferries from Hyannisport dock in Nantucket harbor and disgorge their polo-shirted passengers onto the cobblestone streets, harmony is one of the qualities the vacationers discern through the tint of their sunglasses. The for-

A front door in Nantucket, facing the public way. The meticulously clipped hedge hides this house's windows from the sidewalk.

mer whaling center is a handsome sight. It is handsome because the buildings along Nantucket's aged streets fit together well. The buildings share many traits. Nantucket houses have simple, almost austere shapes, which were dictated by the stern attitude of the Quakers, who dominated island life in the 1700s, and dictated, too, by the harsh winters, whose driving rain and steady thirteen-mile-an-hour winds put a premium on uncomplicated, water-tight architectural forms. The houses generally agree on choices of materials and colors. More often than not the walls are wrapped in natural-toned cedar shingles, accented by wooden trim that has been painted white. The facade of the typical Nantucket house is simple—a single, relatively flat wall from foundation to eaves, with decidedly restrained decoration around the doorway. More than two-thirds of the houses surviving from before the Civil War are two stories or higher. The proportions of the facades make a consistent pattern; for every two to three feet of height there are three to four feet of width—a ratio that is visually restful. Windows are consistently vertical in their proportions. The similarity from one house to another fosters a sense of unity.

The placement of the houses' main entrances close to the street, on sparsely adorned facades, gives them an appealing directness, which fits the historical image of early New Englanders as individuals who faced their fellow townspeople plainly and straightforwardly, whether in the democratic give-and-take of the town hall or in the conduct of their daily lives.

The rows of houses, most of them set back only a short distance from sidewalks made of concrete, stone, or brick, create comfortable and well-defined perimeters for the public environment. White-painted fences, one after another, pleasantly separate the public domain from the owners' yards and make the atmosphere cozy. "In between houses and along empty lots, fences were built linking house to house," writes J. Christopher Lang. "Big houses on larger lots were graced by fences across their fronts. The combined effect on many streets was the creation of a continuous physical edge along the street, punctuated by doorstoops and entrance walks."

So far, this is an argument for consistency. The proposition, however, is not yet complete. While consistency does attract admirers to the narrow streets of Nantucket, consistency is not what *keeps* people interested for long. To motivate pedestrians to continue exploring their surroundings after the initial burst of discovery has faded, a place must offer variety. Buildings in Nantucket possess more than consistency; they possess a wealth of subtle variations. Some houses are three windows wide; some are four windows wide. Some have windows pressed tight against the cornerboard at one end of the facade, making the house look quaintly off-balance. Other houses are composed more symmetrically. Most houses have their roof ridge parallel with the street, but here and there a house is positioned gable-end to the street. Dark-green louvered shutters embellish some houses and not others. Some houses have shed-roofed additions to one side or the other. Unembellished center chimneys rise from many of the pre–Civil War houses, but there are other houses with an end chimney, a pair of chimneys, or a white-painted widow's walk on the roof. Wooden steps lead up to most of the front doors, but a smaller number of houses have steps of stone or concrete.

The fences along the sidewalks are not uniform. Some are simple white picket fences with pointed tops. Others have a horizontal rail over their tops, a carryover from ship carpentry, which was one of Nantucket's principal occupations. Wood baluster fences, with round vertical balusters beneath a molded or round top rail, accompany the more elegant houses that began to be built after 1800. There are other kinds of fences too—most of wood, a few of wrought iron, especially in front of the town's small number of brick houses.

The grounds provide additional variety. Around the 1870s, residents began planting hedges, which have softened the once-stark appearance of the town. Some of the hedges have grown up and created a living green wall between the sidewalks and the front yards. Side yards have been tended according to individual taste. The degree of care given to planting differs from one property to another. The wealth of distinctions is not lost on those walking by. Consciously or unconsciously, passersby are encouraged to take an interest in the surroundings because of the variety.

The lesson of Nantucket is twofold. First, there is enough consistency to draw the community into a harmonious whole. Second, there is a wealth of variation within the basic unity. The virtue of consistency is well understood by today's developers, who establish homeowners' associations with rules that insist upon a high degree of uniformity. What tends to be neglected is the second half of the equation: the need for variety to make a place interesting to explore day after day.

Human beings are designed to walk. To make their walking pleasurable they require a continual succession of new sights or experiences. Every few paces there should be something more to notice. It is the succession of views, sounds, smells, and experiences that causes pedestrians to take renewed interest in their surroundings. Variations of some kind should occur frequently—probably every several feet. Variations should be allowed to arise not only as *distance* is traversed but also as *time* passes, as a place ages. The unfolding that comes with the passage of time accentuates interest for those walking through a place.

The objection most commonly raised against allowing variety is that people will introduce *bad* variations, not *good* ones. A resident of Burke Centre defended the development's rules by insisting, "If you could trust that people would use good judgment, you wouldn't need controls. But they don't." This pessimistic view is by no means rare. At Providence Point, a retirement community in Issaquah, Washington, I was being given a tour of the development when suddenly I noticed, fifty feet ahead, bright orange draperies in the windows of one of the condominium units that had recently sold for $200,000. On an overcast afternoon the resplendent orange color caught my eye, and I lightheartedly pointed out the draperies to the marketing director, who was driving me around. With not a moment's hesitation the marketing director said, "They can't do that! I'll make them take those out!" Clearly, no one is exempt from the distrust of individual decisionmaking, not even retired people who have invested much of their life's savings in a new home.

This fastidiousness is unfortunate. Instances of "bad" taste are rarely as ruinous as Providence Point's punctilious marketing director seems to think. Unless a development's design is extraordinarily delicate, an occasional lapse in taste will not make the place a shambles. On the contrary, a deviation from the prevailing standard may add a humanizing touch to the community. In John Kennedy Toole's novel *A Confederacy of Dunces* the main character, Ignatius Reilly, makes a show of being repelled by other people's bad taste in dress or behavior; the reader notices, however, that despite Reilly's professions of disgust, he is in fact fascinated and delighted by what he identifies as "offenses against taste." The sights that fall short of his lofty standards entertain him and feed his self-esteem, which hungers for the bolstering effect of comparisons. "Bad taste," in limited doses, is often good for people. At the very least, it provides a rich source of humor, one of the most gladdening qualities available to human beings.

When my wife and I go for walks after dinner, we often talk about what we see on our perambulations. There are things we find fault with—the funereal black trim on a house a couple of blocks away, a set of windows that are too large for the dormer in which they've been installed, the strange, struggling plantings in a neighbor's front yard, the boat that was propped up in someone's driveway for a year and a half. Aesthetically, all these sights seem of dubious value. Yet they do not justify imposing a battery of rules and regulations on the neighborhood. The varied choices that people make in building, painting, decorating, planting, and undertaking other activities provide a neighborhood with points of potential interest. The contrasts between the houses and grounds my wife and I like and those we don't like have sparked more conversations than I can count.

If bad decisions run rampant, of course, visual harmony will be eroded and perhaps sacrificed altogether. This is a genuine loss. But if neighbors have such "bad" or conflicting taste, one wonders whether a tight series of rules and regulations will save the situation; the rules will then have an alien quality, subduing the natural impulses of the neighborhood and draining its spontaneity. Excessive rules may not so much improve a neighborhood as straitjacket it. Harmony is valuable, but even more valuable is the liberating feeling of freedom.

Lest I leave the impression that when people are free they promptly lapse into poor taste, I should point out that freedom clears the way for agreeable and sometimes beautiful creations. One family near us took a dull gray house and repainted it in a buoyant combination of light colors, transforming its dour visage into something refreshingly cheerful. Another family restored the cedar-shingle exterior of their house and painted the window sash maroon, which, in combination with cream-colored window casings and tan-colored walls, gave it a gratifying vigor. Sometimes a building or landscape project goes on for a long time. Watching its progress gives the neighbors a feeling of involvement in community life. The continual arrival of new individual expressions gives people reason to explore the neighborhood. This is quite different from conditions in a highly regulated development like Burke Centre. When people are not at liberty to paint their houses as they like or make other decisions, what rewards await the pedestrian? If down the block is more of what one has already seen, why bother to go look? The mind is repulsed by too much repetition.

Developers often think that if they can give a development the appropriate physical form at the start and set up a homeowners' association to ward off changes, the results will be beyond reproach. For example, less than a mile from the old Main Street of Nantucket is a new subdivision called "Nashaquisset, a Village of Nantucket." Nashaquisset has won a slew of awards from the home-building industry because of the quality of its layout, landscaping, and house designs. "Every exterior detail was approved for accuracy by the uncompromising Nantucket Historic District Commission," *Builder* magazine enthused. Natural cedar shingles, white-painted trim, vertically proportioned windows, old-style street lights, granite curbs, brick sidewalks, picket fences, small gardens, houses placed close to the street—Nashaquisset has many of the characteristics that have made the old town of Nantucket appealing. But something is not quite right. An administrator of the Historic District Commission privately admitted that she is disturbed with the results. "It's like canned

Nashaquisset, a new development intended to capture the character of old Nantucket.

Nantucket," she said. "The developers chose all the plants and established the gardens. All the residents have to do is put things in their closets. Nashaquisset feels overplanned. It feels fake. It's always bothered me. It's just too imposed, that's what it is. I think Nashaquisset is awful."

Nashaquisset fails an important test of pedestrian interest: It has too few individual touches. It lacks idiosyncrasies. Because virtually everything has been planned and carried out by the developer, down to the planting of gardens, which are now maintained by a homeowners' association, the setting feels constrained. It lacks the personal passions and predilections that give the old town of Nantucket much of its authenticity. The "village" of Nashaquisset feels disturbingly like a theme park.

My hunch is that in the long run Nashaquisset will turn out all right. Personal expressions inevitably will appear, and the houses and grounds will acquire individual histories. The seeming artificiality of the development—now so troubling to people who have thought about Nashaquisset's integrity—will dissipate as Nashaquisset becomes an established part of the landscape. As Nashaquisset ages and its occupants leave their marks on the various properties, the community will benefit from the unifying influence of its white picket fences, its cozy streets and lanes, and its consistent choices in proportions, styling, and materials. The elements that make Nashaquisset's design coherent will almost certainly help to sustain the community's long-term appeal.

Still, Nashaquisset stands as a warning against the notion that a place can achieve perfection at the start. The old places that most provoke admiration are the result of a long period of evolution. "Things like Nantucket don't happen overnight," the Historic District Commission administrator said. "Nantucket looked like a wasteland, very stark. It's taken 150 years to develop all that character and flavor." Insisting that a community settle upon its final form immediately, without change and experimentation, is as foolish as expecting individuals to achieve maturity without the trials of childhood, adolescence, and early adulthood.

Time and a large degree of freedom can work marvels. Levittown, New York, is an example. Commentators lambasted the regimented appearance of Levittown when its 17,000 mass-produced houses rose from the flat potato fields of Long Island in the late 1940s and early 1950s. But with the passage of four decades and more, Levittown has made tremendous progress. Families have repainted and redecorated the houses' exteriors, added wings and dormers, planted trees and flowers, and made innumerable other enhancements. The story-and-a-half frame dwellings that the critics initially found so monotonous have become surprisingly varied. Freedom accommodates improvements.

Given time, the subdivisions being built today could evolve into interesting places too. For that to happen, distinctiveness must flourish. In *Care of the Soul,* psychotherapist Thomas Moore writes, "One of the strongest needs of the soul is for community. . . . Soul yearns for attachment, for variety in personality, for intimacy and particularity. So it is these qualities in community that the soul seeks out, and not likemindedness and uniformity."

Distinctiveness is important not only within a community but also between one community and another. There can be no single blueprint for community design or governance. Some communities will have homeowners' associations. Others will not. Communities that are satisfying will take different physical forms, depending upon the desires of their residents, among other things. So it is difficult to make general recommendations for places that, ideally, are greatly varied. But let me make a stab at it.

The pitfalls of homeowners' associations might diminish if the designers laid out communities differently than most of them do now. One way to begin is by organizing communities around strong, well-defined public spaces. Small parks, greens, commons, or other public areas—interspersed through the neighborhoods—can establish a sense of community identity, a quality that homeowners' associations rightly value. The streets should be distinctive, ranging perhaps from gracious boulevards to intimate lanes. It would be good to lay the streets out in strong, legible patterns, with rows of trees planted along them, and perhaps with hedges or low fences along the sidewalks. Landscape elements can help make the streets and public places memorable. The idea is to let the public spaces—the parks, greens, streets, street trees, sidewalks, and vegetation—carry the main burden of creating community harmony and consistency. If the public spaces achieve a strong coherence, people will be free to infuse their houses and grounds with many variations without causing the neighborhood to appear chaotic or unsightly—the feared condition that underlies typical homeowners' association regulations.

Gillet Avenue in Waukegan, Illinois, as it appeared in 1962 and seven years later after its elm trees had been killed by Dutch elm disease. The two photos illustrate the ability of street trees to create a beautifully cohesive setting. With trees, the variations among individual houses are agreeable. Without trees, the varying house styles and materials start to clash.

Municipal regulations usually stipulate how far back the houses must be from the streets. In large-lot suburban areas, sometimes they stand so far back that the streets become dull and lifeless. It might be better to insist the houses come closer to the streets and have their facades form a fairly steady line. Houses in a more or less even line along the street accentuate the feeling of unity and strengthen the public areas. If developers or home-owners' associations think it is necessary to subject the houses to aesthetic rules, the rules might concentrate on proportions, shapes, and materials, leaving many details free to vary from one property to another. When houses agree in their basic elements, it is usually possible for residents to personalize them in numerous ways without destroying the coherence of the neighborhood. In this way, a balance might be achieved between harmony and variety, between community cohesiveness and individual liberty.

Developers and designers would be wise to identify the elements of design that most commonly lead to troublesome rule enforcement. A different choice of design elements at the start might make much regulation and enforcement superfluous. Let me cite two examples of rules that could be eliminated by changes in the initial design of the community. In Irvine, California, homeowners' associations have rules saying how long a household may leave its garage door open. The reason is that garages attached to the houses dominate the streets, and the streets look shabby when the doors are left open. At Virginia Run, a 1,000-house development near Manassas, Virginia, there are strict rules about trash containers. All the trash containers must be dark blue. They must, according to the Virginia Run *Book of Regulations,* be taken into the house or garage the same day the trash is collected. To enforce this, Missy Knicely, a community manager, drives the streets each week looking for trash containers that have not been put away promptly. She then sends notices to violators, many of whom are offended at receiving the warnings or fines.

Yale's Patrick Pinnell says a different site design could make such garage-door and trash-container rules unnecessary. If Irvine had been built with the garages facing alleys rather than facing the more formal streets, it would not matter how long the garage doors were open. If Virginia Run had been built with alleys, where the containers could sit without making the front streets look unkempt, it would not matter how long they stood there or

*Front and rear
views of a block in
Ontario, California.
Because the alley
accommodates the
garages and gar-
bage collection, the
street in front of the
houses retains a
parklike expanse of
trees and lawns.*

what color they were. Beverly Hills, California, which no one has
ever accused of looking unsightly, has alleys, and they work just
fine, allowing the streets in front of the houses to remain beautiful even on garbage day. If communities are planned so that drab
objects and irritating activities are accommodated in inconspicuous locations, this would take some of the friction out of daily
life. Intelligent design that reduces or erases potential sources of
neighborhood conflict can eliminate some of the nit-picking regulation to which homeowners' associations fall prey.

Improvements in homeowners' association governance could
also reduce the unnecessary intrusiveness of the associations.
David Wolfe, after many years of helping to organize homeowners' associations, became convinced that associations often dis-
ply troubling traits. In the past several years he has been thinking

about how to reform homeowners' associations. When Wolfe was hired to help organize the homeowners' association of Kentlands, a 352-acre development in Gaithersburg, Maryland, he insisted that the association and its committees be given names that might foster improved behavior. He named the association the "Kentlands Citizens Assembly" to encourage people to regard it as a grass-roots democracy. Instead of an architectural review committee, he suggested establishing a "Kentlands Historical Trust." Instead of a legalistic statement of the association's powers, he saw that Kentlands had a "community charter."

Along with the different names, Wolfe altered some of the ways in which Kentlands' homeowners' association functions. Kentlands allows voting by all residents aged eighteen and older, in contrast to the typical homeowners' association, which gives the voting rights to property owners and disenfranchises renters. Rather than concentrating all power in a board of directors, the Kentlands Citizens Assembly attempts a division of powers more like that of a public government. The president is directly elected by the citizenry. Legislative, judicial, and executive powers are separated from each other to the extent that state statutes for homeowners' associations allow. The goal is to make Kentlands a place where self-government is vigorous and broad-based.

The Kentlands Citizens Assembly tries to achieve a balance between community responsibilities and individual rights. It declares that its purpose is "to safeguard the integrity of community traditions in a manner that is responsive to the welfare of the community *and its individual citizens.*" The charter says that Kentlands aims to "provide opportunities for individual, personal growth to better enable each person to more fully fulfill his or her human potential." It attempts to "foster a strong sense of inter-connectedness" among citizens, in the knowledge that "for a community to be able to give its utmost to its individual constituents, its individual constituents must give their practical utmost to the community." The charter recognizes that "so long as a person's expression of his individuality does not encroach upon the comfort and rights of others and does not compromise the integrity of his or her community, he or she is fully entitled to express his or her individuality in any fashion."

Homeowners' association specialists such as Atlanta attorney Wayne Hyatt are pursuing other changes. Hyatt and others try to write covenants so that they set forth general goals for the association rather than detailed rules. This enables residents to draw up the rules after they've moved in rather than having the rules decided in advance by the developer. Residents also gain the ability to eliminate or alter rules more easily, in response to changing conditions or different attitudes within the community. Andres Duany, one of the planners of Kentlands, says homeowners' associations need such flexibility so that they can respond to altered needs as years go by.

The approaches advocated by Wolfe, Hyatt, and others hold the potential for improved decision making in homeowners' associations. But let's return to the main concern of this chapter, which is the physical design of communities. Why is so much attention in modern developments directed at matters as trivial as the colors of swing sets, the ornateness of storm doors, and the presence of clotheslines? Quite possibly it is because these developments lack more important issues and lack more satisfying forms of community involvement. The communities are simply too narrow; they contain too small a spectrum of places and activities.

A partial solution might be to lay out communities so that they contain a more generous range of settings and activities. If a suburban development includes stores, restaurants, and work-

Community orchards occupy part of the land at Village Homes in Davis, California. Income from fruitgrowing supports community activities.

places, people might relax their worries about the color of a mailbox or the presence of a political sign in the front yard. Shops and other nonresidential elements can give people important sources of enjoyment and a more balanced perspective. More of the residents might enter into what the poet Robert Bly calls "joyful participation in the tensions of the world."

It might also be helpful if homeowners' associations had significant work to do. At Village Homes in Davis, California, the residents' association cares about more than how the development looks. At Village Homes much of the common land is an "edible landscape," planted with grapevines and orchards. Residents act as stewards of the land, deciding how to care for the agricultural area and what to do with the produce. Some of the Village Homes children earn money by working in the twelve acres of vineyards and plum, peach, apricot, and cherry orchards. Sales from the harvests generate income for the association, which helps pay for community activities. Village Homes avoids the trap of making appearance the community's main concern. At Village Homes people are concerned with community activity and responsibility toward nature.

Finally, homeowners' associations might become less obsessed with trivial matters of appearance if suburban developments were less isolated from the larger world. Fewer obstacles and more connections, such as through streets, might spur residents to recognize that they are part of a broader community—one that is probably more interesting and less threatening than they had imagined. Suburban developments would benefit from being linked more extensively to their surroundings. The suburbs need to become less fragmented, more whole. One way to do that is to build suburbs to be more like towns.

Florida's "redneck Riviera" is quite an unlikely place for launching a new way of designing suburbs. The stretch of Florida panhandle between Panama City and Pensacola is a getaway spot for Alabamians, Georgians, and northern Floridians. In the daytime they lie on beaches of blindingly white sand or thrash around in the shallow Gulf of Mexico. In the evening, after dinner at one of the restaurants where deep fryers are bubbling, they patronize shops selling airbrushed T-shirts or pause to play miniature golf at Zoo-Land, whose mascot is an upright, red-eyed, nine-foot concrete crocodile that quick inspection reveals to be missing a chunk of its belly at automobile-fender height. Then they get into their cars and pickups and head back to their lodgings for the night. This description hardly applies to everyone, but it does indicate the tone of this northern Florida vacationland.

Lodgings in this section of the Gulf employ almost every formula that commercial ingenuity has devised. Lining the black-top of the coast highway are blocky motels up to six stories high, rustic log cabins, weathered cedar-shake apartments, gray clapboard row houses, staggered stucco-and-tile condominiums, townhouses harkening back to Tudor England, and more. Scattered along the way are diminutive refreshment stands and "Jr. Food Stores."

And then there is Seaside. A billboard on Route 98 hails it with a verb-free slogan: "The New Town. The Old Ways." Seaside makes an arresting contrast to nearly everything else on the two-lane coast road. Its gleaming little skyline comes into view like a fantasy of yesteryear. From the shoreline to about a quarter-mile inland rise the silver-colored slopes of several hundred metal roofs—pristine versions of the rust-streaked tin roofs found on houses throughout the rural South. The shiny crimped-metal roofs keep the rain out of old-fashioned-looking wooden houses, which have all been built since 1981. From the tops of many of the roofs, towers shoot up in quirky, picturesque shapes. The towers climb as high as their owners wish to build them. The only limitation is that they must be narrow, their floor area restricted to a little over 200 square feet, so as not to block their neighbors' views.

Once travelers enter the eighty acres of Seaside, they discover a network of narrow streets surfaced with reddish concrete pavers—the contemporary, pale-looking equivalent of the red brick streets that rumble beneath motorists' tires in many old communities. Most of Seaside's streets are paved just eighteen feet wide, limiting the room for movement. Restricting passage further, vehicles park on the streets or the shoulders. Motorists have little choice but to slow down. Individuals on foot and on fat-tired bicycles give every impression of feeling on equal terms with cars, vans, and pickups.

The streets have been designed with affectionate detail. Enclosing their sides are white picket fences in dozens of different designs. Property owners individually select or invent the style of their own fence, which must differ from all others on their block. About sixteen feet behind the fences stand front porches. The distance was set so that people sitting on the porches can

Plan of Seaside, Florida. In the tradition of old towns, Seaside has a mixture of stores, public buildings, and houses of many sizes, all linked together by a network of comfortable streets.

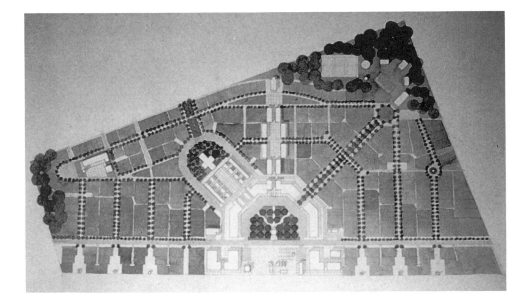

Seaside, on the Gulf of Mexico, seen from the air. On the dunes above the shore are a series of beach pavilions, each designed by a different architect. Each pavilion connects one of Seaside's streets to the beach.

hold conversations with those going past without having to raise their voices.

By Seaside regulation, the porch typically extends along at least half of the house's facade, and it must be no less than eight feet deep—big enough so that people can use it comfortably. The houses are clad in clapboard, shingles, or board-and-batten siding—no vinyl, no aluminum. Their windows are mostly tall and narrow, in keeping with the old-fashioned character of picket fences and spacious wooden porches. Festive colors such as pink, yellow, and aqua predominate.

A network of sandy footpaths, bordered by more rows of picket fences, runs through the middle of many of the blocks. The footpaths were envisioned as a safe, convenient alternative to walking in the streets, but once the streets were paved, the footpaths lost most of their pedestrian use. This is probably just as well. It seems more respectful to walk by a procession of front porches than to slip down the mid-block footpaths, close to windows that expose the houses' interiors. One person dubbed the footpaths the "voyeur system."

Nearly all the streets run in straight lines, which were anath-

A street scene at Seaside.
The post office, one of Seaside's first buildings, designed by developer Robert S. Davis.

ema to the vast majority of American designers when Seaside was being planned in the early 1980s. Conventional opinion held straight streets to be the epitome of dullness. But Seaside's streets are not dull—they are visual knockouts, in part because no street goes on for long without providing something more to look at, often something with charm. Each street leading to the Gulf points toward one of a series of captivating beach pavilions, each pavilion the creation of a different designer. Streets meet in interesting ways. Where Tupelo Street and Grove Avenue come together, a gazebo stands in the middle of the intersection. Streets sometimes jog left or right when they pass through an intersection. In almost every case, there is something to gaze at close ahead. Only the main road through Seaside—the coast highway— runs straight for as far as the eye can see.

In the evening, when summer's heat begins to dissipate, the streets are the scene of leisurely promenades. But they are used in the daytime as well, and for more than aimless strolls. People walk to the post office, a tiny, white classical building that Seaside's developer, Robert S. Davis, designed himself and built before there were more than a few dozen inhabitants to support it. People walk to the wooden Sip and Dip refreshment stand, where the employees behind the counter squeeze fresh lemons for each lemonade. They walk to Bud & Alley's, a seafood restaurant named in honor of Davis's miniature dachshund, Budweiser, and his cat. They walk to a gourmet grocery store operated by a couple who relocated from Bessemer, Alabama, where they had owned a food store for thirty-eight years. They walk to a gift store, a conference center, a circular community pool, and other centers of activity. As with densely developed old summer colonies like Chautauqua in western New York, which was one of Davis's models, people *drive* to this place to have the pleasure of walking.

Seaside, the "new town" with the "old ways," captured many people's imaginations. Although only a small resort, Seaside departed so exultantly from development-as-usual that it emerged as the most celebrated new place of the 1980s. Robert Davis and

The views down Seaside streets focus on houses, like this one, or on gazebos, beach pavilions, or other points of visual interest. No street stretches infinitely to the horizon.

his architects, Andres Duany and Elizabeth Plater-Zyberk of Miami, believe the eighty-acre development illustrates ways in which not only resorts but communities of many kinds, including suburbs, can be greatly improved. Seaside has come to be hailed as the beginning of "neotraditionalism," the use of design traditions from old places to shape new communities. The neotraditionalists—it's simpler and equally accurate to call them traditionalists, the term I use—are intent on employing the wisdom and experience of old places to create new settlements of all sizes.

Sandy footpaths through the middle of the blocks are an alternative to walking on the streets.

Davis, born in Birmingham, Alabama, in 1943, is an articulate, soft-spoken man imbued with idealism, which has expressed itself in varied ways over the years. As an undergraduate at Antioch College in Ohio, he thought the path to improving society lay on the political left and joined the Socialist Workers' party. After graduation he recruited black and poverty-stricken students for that progressive-minded school. Later he worked for a couple of Miami developers active in the Federal Housing Authority's Section 236 program, which he summed up as "subsidizing the very rich to provide housing for the poor."

In 1979 Davis inherited the Florida oceanfront land, which his grandfather, the founder of a Birmingham department store, had purchased before World War II. Davis wanted to develop the tract in a more humanly appealing manner than the typical waterfront development. He thought he might be able to accomplish that if he carefully studied old towns. So, with his wife, Daryl, he got into his red 1975 Pontiac Bonneville convertible—a sturdy land cruiser that eventually racked up more than 150,000 miles—and went off to examine old communities, among them Grayton Beach, Apalachicola, and Key West, Florida; Charleston, South Carolina; and Savannah, Georgia. He intended to identify elements that have made those places physically appealing and socially rewarding.

Traveling along in the Bonneville at times were Andres Duany and Elizabeth Plater-Zyberk, a bright, tireless husband-and-wife team of architects educated at Princeton and Yale. Both architects come from families with cataclysmic histories. Plater-Zyberk's parents, once members of the professional elite in Poland, were refugees from that country's Communist dictatorship after World War II. Duany's father was a developer in Cuba who took his family into exile after the Castro revolution. Those calamities seem, if anything, to have fortified the two architects' resolve to lead a kind of cultural resistance against destructive and foolish practices. Unlike totally assimilated Americans who take their culture and their communities for granted—which leads to complacency—Duany and Plater-Zyberk recognized that magnificent transformations or terrible destruction are always possible and that it is up to responsible individuals to choose the outcome. Voracious readers who had spent time in Europe, they revered the cultural and architectural accomplishments of Western civilization; at the same time, they saw much of that physical and cultural heritage being trampled in the United States by the forces of modern planning, modern architecture, and modern development.

The original market area of Seaside, with shops and eating and drinking places close to the beach.

Plater-Zyberk, born in 1950, is a native of Paoli, Pennsylvania, a rail-commuter suburb at the end of Philadelphia's Main Line. Her father, a not very well-paid architect for the Philadelphia Savings Fund Society, and her mother, a French teacher and garden designer, had settled there after emigrating from Poland following the horrific experiences of 1939 to 1945—the conquest by

Nazi Germany and then the Soviet Union, culminating in the Communist takeover. Thin and red-haired, Plater-Zyberk was a diligent student who traveled more than two hours a day by train and bus between her home and the Country Day School of the Sacred Heart at Overbrook, near Philadelphia. "We skimped and saved, and we all had scholarships," recalls Plater-Zyberk, who grew up with a brother and two sisters. Skilled as a designer and adept at theory, sometimes called Lizzie Planning-Zoning during her postgraduate years at Yale, she excelled in the academic world and in time became influential in university teaching about design and planning and instrumental in the rebuilding of South Florida after Hurricane Andrew. Though she regularly gave meticulously organized lectures and presentations, outside of professional and academic circles she tended to let Duany do most of the public speaking.

Duany, born in 1949, was reared for his first ten years in Santiago, Cuba, where his father was a developer. After his family fled the revolution of 1959, he was brought up on Long Island, spending his vacations in Barcelona, Spain. Of medium height, cocksure and handsome with short black hair swept back, Duany was blessed with a charismatic personality. Like Plater-Zyberk, he zealously studied the history of towns, cities, and architecture. But unlike Plater-Zyberk, who was instinctively diplomatic and averse to exaggeration, Duany reveled in verbal combativeness, thrusting his chin forward as he made scathing attacks on his enemies—in most cases, developers, planners, and architects who did not think along his lines, or who hardly thought at all.

Countless architects before Duany had criticized suburbs, but no one had done it so engagingly. For his travels away from Miami, Duany packed carousels of 35-millimeter slides, the weapons with which he identified suburban communities' defects— houses whose facades were dominated by bleak garage doors, shopping centers that were impossible to get to without a car, circuitous street layouts and services so far away that they "make the child-rearing age an age of driving." Duany traveled incessantly. In his illustrated talks, which he honed to razor's-edge wit, Duany ridiculed conventional development practices and set forth a contrasting vision of community life—employing earnestness, evangelism, common sense, and withering mockery, as the pacing of the lecture demanded. ("Sarcasm," he once confided, "is a great tool.") Unlike that earlier scourge of the suburbs, the great architectural critic Lewis Mumford, who issued pronouncements from on high, Duany knew how to be funny, usually at the expense of designers and developers. Showing a picture of a silly-looking townhouse complex designed with each unit's facade projecting or receding from its neighbors, he would say, "This facade is supposed to tell you that your unit has individuality; what it really tells you is how many other people got exactly the same thing." The targets of his barbs sometimes took offense, but nearly everybody laughed at the absurdities of suburban development and ended up reflecting on how things could be done better. Anton Nelessen, a planning consultant from Princeton, New Jersey, and teacher at Rutgers University who has shared the podium with Duany, says, "He's got it down to a nightclub act." Unlike a nightclub act, however, the duration of a Duany performance had no limit. It was not uncommon for Duany to stay at conferences of two hundred or three hundred people, arguing his point of view, until the last person who wanted to talk with him had every question answered.

By the late 1970s, when Duany and Plater-Zyberk began working with Davis, the fields of architecture and development had grown flabbily self-indulgent. Architects had cultivated a long-standing obsession with *originality,* as if every designer were this year's Le Corbusier. Architects tried to have their buildings stand out from their surroundings. Developers sought to set each of their projects apart from the neighbors. Unifying elements that would have made places coherent were pitifully few. Duany and Plater-Zyberk saw a need for restoring visual cohesiveness to the sorely fragmented environment. They would accomplish this by reviving older design traditions, even while trying to recognize today's economic and psychological realities.

The reform of community design was, especially for Duany, a glorious cause. He passionately advocated "dignity" in community design—a standard of judgment rarely heard in the United States in the past forty years. His highest praise for a street was to call it civilized. In sharp distinction to the typical developer, who viewed the suburb as a "market" composed of "consum-ers," Duany saw the suburb as part of a "civilization," made up of "citizens" who need to make wise choices if their society is to remain vital.

Duany and Plater-Zyberk argued that streets should be envisioned as public rooms—places that are pleasurable to occupy and that invite human interchange. To make a street feel like a public room rather than simply a leftover space between buildings, the street must have steady walls, Duany said. He disdained "wiggly" townhouse developments in which each unit's facade projected or receded from the facade of the adjoining unit. He rebuked the curving streets of many modern suburbs for meandering without discipline, like strands of cooked spaghetti. Buildings need uniform setbacks from the street, Duany believes. Just as a room is defined by even walls, a street feels right when the buildings facing it form a steady wall.

The street should be kept as narrow as is practical, Duany argued. When overly wide, it ceases to feel like an outdoor room. Duany and Plater-Zyberk recognized, however, that American communities could not be designed as tightly as the European streets they admired. "American space is larger, more expansive," Duany said. Americans expect bigger distances between themselves and their neighbors. Therefore Duany and Plater-Zyberk came to rely heavily on trees and fences to subdivide the outdoor areas. Trees are planted in steady rows along the streets. If a street curves, it usually does so with a consistent, disciplined shape, such as a crescent. Fences paralleling the streets make the streets cozier. Such tools are not new. They have existed for centuries. They can be seen in countless old towns and old neighborhoods. "We don't have to invent a thing," declared Duany. "It's all been done."

Before laying out Seaside, Duany and Plater-Zyberk designed Charleston Place, a suburban subdivision in Boca Raton, Florida. There they placed townhouses side by side in straight rows, close to the streets. To open the townhouses to ample sunlight and breezes and to confer a pleasant rhythm on the street, they placed a second-story terrace alongside each dwelling's upper floor. The alternation of terraces and gabled second stories overlooking the street created a graceful cadence while the line of houses remained steady.

The design of Charleston Place was loosely based on long, narrow old detached houses in Charleston, South Carolina, that have porches on one side, overlooking lovely secluded gardens. "Sideyard houses," Duany and Plater-Zyberk called them. In the Boca Raton subdivision each house similarly has a garden on one side, hidden from the street. The garden extends to the property's rear, where its privacy is protected by a five-foot-high stuccoed wall. On the other side of the wall is a mid-block pedestrian passageway, which goes from one street to the next. These narrow public walkways—intimately proportioned, paved with red

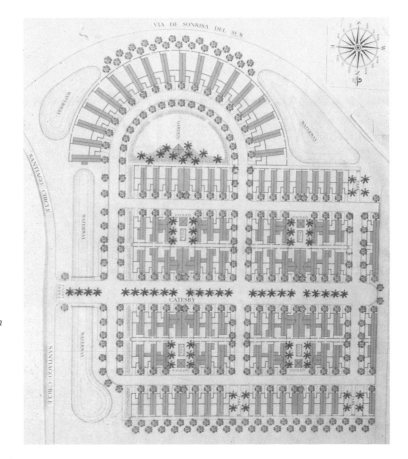

Plan of Charleston Place in Boca Raton, Florida, with its short, straight streets, mid-block walkways, and great crescent.

brick, enclosed by stuccoed walls, and embellished by roses that gently arc overhead—are some of the most romantic places in the subdivision.

When I visited Charleston Place about two years after its completion, residents were outdoors on nearly every block during the evening. They were out in pairs and in groups, walking or talking—while the conventional subdivisions nearby were devoid of activity. On one block at Charleston Place a man wheeled a barbecue grill to his small lawn and did his outdoor cooking there, where he could watch the parade of people. The development looked handsome, as Duany and Plater-Zyberk had intended; more important, it succeeded in becoming a place where people are drawn into conversation with their neighbors. Charleston Place suggests that when the streets are "public rooms," they stand a good chance of generating community activity.

Rose-covered brick walkways run behind the walled rear yards of Charleston Place houses, connecting one street to another. Facing page: *Townhouses at Charleston Place—adaptations of narrow Charleston, South Carolina, houses with porches overlooking side gardens—have second-floor terraces above the street. Each house also has a garden court secluded from the street.*

Charleston Place, for all its virtues, was only a housing subdivision. Seaside was more comprehensive; it came closer to being a town, but a very small one, containing a limited range of enterprises. After Seaside Duany and Plater-Zyberk received much more planning work, some of it on projects that were larger and more complex. They designed a 5,000-acre suburban development called Blount Springs, north of Birmingham. They laid out a 9,400-acre development called Avalon Park, in Orlando, Florida. They laid out Windsor, a 400-acre resort village in Vero Beach, Florida, and Tannin, a 60-acre resort on Alabama's Gulf coast. They designed a 1,475-acre extension of the Wellington development west of West Palm Beach, Florida. They laid out several developments in Virginia and Maryland, including Haymount, a 1,582-acre undertaking near Fredericksburg, Virginia; Belmont, a 273-acre project in Virginia's Loudoun County; and—by far their best-known suburban project—Kentlands, a 352-acre development on the Kent farm in Gaithersburg, Maryland, northwest of Washington, D.C. They won commissions as far distant as West Rockport, Maine, and Chico, California. More than seventy places in several states have been designed by Duany and Plater-Zyberk's small, well-traveled firm, which identifies itself as "architects and town planners."

Among privately commissioned designers, the term "town

planner" had been out of fashion for decades, but as the 1980s ended and the 1990s began, the term seemed worthy of revival. Interest in fashioning new developments so that they would capture qualities of traditional towns was growing. The American small town, though it is now home to only a small portion of the nation's population, retains widespread popular appeal. When the Gallup Organization asked Americans in 1989 what kind of place they would like to live in, 34 percent chose a small town, as compared with 24 percent who chose a suburb, 22 percent a farm, and 19 percent a city. Anton Nelessen found similar results when he showed New Jersey residents scenes in small communities, rural areas, suburbs, and cities. Most New Jersey residents live in suburbs of New York or Philadelphia, but they told Nelessen they preferred a hamlet or village, followed by a large-lot rural location, then a suburb, and, at the bottom of the list, a city. The majority of Americans may find it necessary to work in metropolitan areas and live in suburbs, but many of them say they would prefer to be in a traditional small town. Some of this may be idle dreaming. But clearly the small town has appeal, and it's worthwhile for designers to find out which elements of small towns can successfully be infused into new suburbs.

Duany and Plater-Zyberk have not been alone in their advocacy of traditional community design. In most instances they produced their initial design at the project site during a week-long charette—an intensive series of design sessions during which information and ideas were gathered from public officials, consultants, neighbors, and ordinary citizens. Teams of planners and designers continually revised their sketches and computer models during the charettes, whose workdays often stretched long into the evening. In nearly every charette Duany and Plater-Zyberk had the enthusiastic participation of a few architects, landscape architects, or urban designers from the region.

A number of other planners and designers around the country have gravitated toward traditional community design. They do not so much form a unified movement as they agree that there are virtues to traditional design, which each person adapts to today's conditions in his or her own way. The New York architect Robert A. M. Stern, for whom Duany had once worked, has designed projects reminiscent of traditional neighborhoods, towns, or resorts. Nelessen, in New Jersey, has used the old villages and small towns of the Northeast as models for developing new small communities. William Rawn, briefly famous as the Boston architect in Tracy Kidder's best-selling book *House,* has designed residential projects employing principles from historic New England settlements. Alex Krieger, a Cambridge architect on the faculty of Harvard's Graduate School of Design, has promoted the relevance of traditional designs for today's communities. Fred Koetter, the dean of Yale's School of Architecture, has focused attention on traditional models of urbanism, as have such Yale faculty members as Patrick Pinnell, Alan Plattus, and Peter de Bretteville. In Westchester County, New York, architect John Montague Massengale has promoted traditional town planning. Large international design and planning firms like Sasaki Associates, of Watertown, Massachusetts, and RTKL, of Baltimore, have tested the waters of tradition. RTKL planned a development called Harbor Town, on Mud Island in the Mississippi River just a bridge trip away from downtown Memphis. In Loudoun County, Virginia, northwest of Washington, Sasaki designed two as-yet-unbuilt traditional developments.

Scattered around the country are other architects and urban designers who have shown an interest in tradition, among them Robert Orr and Melanie Taylor in New Haven; Jonathan Barnett in New York and Washington; Alexander Cooper, Steven Peterson, and Barbara Littenberg in New York; James Wentling in Philadelphia; Williams & Dynerman in Washington; Peter Brown's firm EDI in Houston, Texas, and Alexandria, Virginia; Stefanos Polyzoides and Elizabeth Moule in Los Angeles; Looney Ricks Kiss Architects in Memphis; Portuondo Perotti Architects in Miami; and Dover Correa Kohl Cockshutte Valle in Coral Gables, Florida. Some designers have been emboldened by Duany and Plater-Zyberk's success to look for opportunities to try traditional approaches for the first time. Others had been involved in some traditional elements of planning and design for a long time. For example, Robert Teska, head of a planning consulting firm in Evanston, Illinois, had advocated a grid system of streets for many years and has laid out several traditional communities in the Midwest. Architect Daniel Solomon in San Francisco had helped rewrite building regulations to preserve the small-scale and pedestrian orientation of San Francisco in the 1970s and has since devoted much of his attention to improving existing suburbs and giving emerging suburbs a more interesting and attractive public environment. In 1993 many of these designers and planners formed an organization, Congress for the New Urbanism, to advance their ideas.

Another San Francisco architect who became prominently associated with some elements of traditional community design is Peter Calthorpe. Calthorpe comes from the side of the profession that was intent in the 1970s on developing solar energy, reducing waste, and improving society. He started out with modernist inclinations and has consistently avoided calling himself a traditionalist or neotraditionalist—terms that in any event would not fly nearly as well in California as on the eastern seaboard, where history is held in higher regard. Calthorpe worked under state architect Sim Van der Ryn at a time when the administration of Governor Jerry Brown was eager to make state office buildings models of energy conservation. Born in England in 1949, Calthorpe spent his high school years in Palo Alto. A tall, lean man with brown hair, intense, quick to discuss ideas, Calthorpe was one of the first individuals during the Vietnam War to be given conscientious objector status on a basis other than religious affiliation.

For a long while Calthorpe led the lonely fight to concentrate the Bay area's growth into developments of greater density organized along mass transit lines. The centers, near the transit stops, he dubbed pedestrian pockets, since they would be compact enough for people to traverse them on foot. In the past few years he has switched to the term "transit-oriented development" and has formulated the idea that outside each dense pedestrian pocket there would be a "secondary area" of lower density where, for instance, neighborhoods of detached houses could be built. Whereas Duany and Plater-Zyberk's work seems to have grown out of a passionate love for classic European and American streets, squares, buildings, and towns, and whereas the Miami architects live themselves in the kind of place they are trying to re-create—the beautiful early twentieth-century suburb Coral Gables—Calthorpe is much less inclined to wax eloquent about the architectural qualities of particular places. He is more the abstract, "big picture" thinker, a man with a social agenda who wants to change the way an entire region is organized. For several years he did not live in either a classic suburb or an urban precinct; he made his home in a houseboat in Sausalito. He now lives in a Berkeley neighborhood chosen largely for the benefit of his young son Asa, who can walk from home to school and other destinations that would have been hard to reach from a houseboat community.

Though trained as an architect, Calthorpe seems more fascinated with large-scale planning than with the details of design. As developers and governments in areas such as Sacramento and the Pacific Northwest have begun paying serious attention to Calthorpe's ideas, he has had to flesh out his "transit-oriented development" concepts in greater specificity, and many of the elements he has adopted resemble those favored by Duany, Plater-Zyberk, and other traditionalists—street trees, sidewalks, front porches, town greens. In a sense, Calthorpe is moving from a general vision of regional growth to the particularities of laying out projects in individual places, while Duany and Plater-Zyberk are expanding their thinking in the opposite direction—attempting to build their ideas about streets, squares, neighborhoods, and towns into a model of overall metropolitan development. To some extent, then, the paths of Calthorpe and of Duany and Plater-Zyberk are converging.

Because Calthorpe calls for compact town centers that many people can walk to, he is often lumped with traditionalists. In truth, he defies easy classification. He would never say, as Duany did (with a touch of hyperbole) that "we don't have to invent a thing—it's all been done." To Calthorpe it is incontrovertible that the economy and the society of the 1990s require solutions different from those that worked in the 1920s. Yet he does find genuine virtues in the compact towns that Americans used to build. "Development was centered on *towns* before World War II," Calthorpe says. "When America was housed in those traditional communities, America was a much more radical place." Calthorpe associates the era of traditional, close-knit communities with political ferment that he approves of, like the era of Franklin Roosevelt. One might retort that when small towns were strong, the country sometimes produced very conservative leaders such as Warren Harding and Calvin Coolidge. The fact is, planners and designers who draw from tradition span the political spectrum, from Calthorpe on the left to Duany, Plater-Zyberk, and Robert Stern on the conservative end, each valuing different elements of traditional towns. In any event, Calthorpe's central point—that the close-knit towns of the past provided the potential for collective action and for connections among people of different economic and social classes—largely rings true. Now that the United States is typified more by suburban sprawl than by compact communities containing diverse social classes that have daily dealings with one another, Calthorpe believes that the country suffers from too many divisions. "Culturally and socially today we are split into groups that oppose one another," he says. "People feel isolated and alienated." Duany and Plater-Zyberk say essentially the same thing. Community and public well-being are in jeopardy.

A single word sums up the traditionalist approach to planning: *connection.* Most traditionalists attempt to make several kinds of connections. First, they try to connect the streets into a network so that people can readily reach other sections of their neighborhood or town. Second, they try to connect residents to shops and services by encouraging retail and institutional development within walking distance of where people live. Third, they try to connect individuals to one another by insisting that walkways be sociable—usually running alongside narrow streets, rows of trees, picket fences, and front porches, balconies, terraces, or other inviting exterior elements of houses. Fourth, they try to bridge the divide of age, household size, and economic status by mixing together houses and apartments of assorted sizes and prices. Fifth, they try to connect the new developments to mass transit. Sixth, they try to connect individuals to civic ideals and public responsibilities.

The shape and character of the streets play a key role in the traditionalist approach. It's common for traditionalists to speak about the virtues of a *grid* of streets. A better word would be *network*. What matters is not that the streets cross at right angles but that they connect frequently and extensively to one another. On flat midwestern land Teska generally recommends a grid of major streets, although he allows that the minor streets in between the arterials might follow a different configuration than a checkerboard. RTKL's Harbor Town development combines radial boulevards, crescents, straight streets, traffic circles, and squares into a sophisticated and complex pattern.

Duany and Plater-Zyberk frequently design street networks that are quirky and complicated. They do much of their planning on site rather than in their Miami office (an elegantly spare former airplane engine factory in a largely working-class neighborhood), and this gives them opportunities to walk the land repeatedly and organize the streets to suit any irregularities they discover. One might conclude, looking at their designs, that

There are many ways of laying out highly connected street networks. A is a grid with "T" intersections that discourage regional traffic from using minor streets. B is a curvilinear grid. C is a random arrangement like that of old New England towns whose roads conformed to irregular topography, in the absence of a master plan. D is a radial street plan loosely based on the Yorkship Village neighborhood (now called Fairview) built in 1918 in Camden, New Jersey.

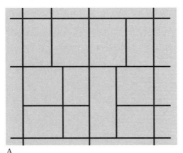

A

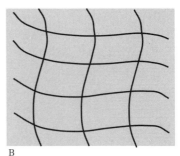

B

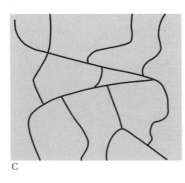

C

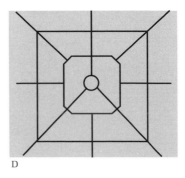

D

Original plan of Harbor Town on the Mississippi River, later revised. Small parks, squares, ponds, and natural areas are interspersed through a distinctive street network. A commercial center is to be built in the southern part of the development, near a bridge to Memphis.

Duany and Plater-Zyberk welcome every slope, every swamp, every outcropping. "Though still recognizable, the blocks are bent, squeezed, stretched, chopped, or inflected expediently to suit terrain, orientation, or what have you in the way of local circumstance," writes Patrick Pinnell, who participated in the Kentlands charette. "This makes for places that are easily legible and navigable on the ground," Pinnell says, "but very hard to hold as *overall* patterns in the memory." The legibility of traditional street networks contrasts with the confusing curves, loops, and cul-de-sacs of conventionally designed suburbs. Traditionalists' streets have memorable points that help visitors avoid getting lost—and that make the communities enticing to explore again and again.

Traditionalists' streets are partly successful, partly not, at pulling people out of their homes and into the public sphere. It would be unrealistic to expect the residents of Kentlands or Harbor Town or other traditionalist suburban developments to spend most of their free time sitting on their front porches, swapping stories with the neighbors; good American consumers that they are, they have TV sets, VCRs, and the rest of the electronic panoply that has turned the houses of the 1990s into indoor en-

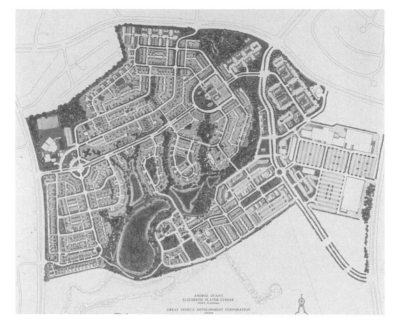

Plan of Kentlands in Gaithersburg, Maryland. Natural features form some of the neighborhood edges. Outdoor and recreation areas are within walking distance of homes.

tertainment retreats. Most of the adults in new traditional developments live mobile, metropolitan lives—traveling across the region for employment, goods, culture, and services. The constraints of the small towns of seventy years ago have been exploded. Nonetheless, new traditionalist communities seem more gregarious than conventional suburbs. The front porches, the houses' closeness to the street, and other sociable aspects of the design make for a friendly atmosphere. Some residents take their cues from the physical setting and spend more time in public than they otherwise would. A pedestrian certainly has more opportunities to see and talk with people in a new traditional community than in a conventional subdivision.

Neighborhood size receives careful consideration. The goal of many traditionalists is to design neighborhoods on a quarter-mile radius, so that in five minutes a person can walk from the neighborhood's edge to its center. This is an old idea, used in the 1929 Regional Plan for New York and elsewhere. If amenities such as a convenience store, a child care center, a meeting hall, and a bus stop are placed in the neighborhood's center, five minutes of walking at an average pace will take a person from home to basic everyday services. Duany and Plater-Zyberk usually try to cluster such facilities next to a small park at the core of the neighborhood. As an alternative, these services might be placed at the neighborhood's edge, particularly if the edge is a major street. Gathering places are crucial to a rich neighborhood life—probably just as crucial as pleasant streets. Duany and Plater-Zyberk believe that whenever possible, each neighborhood should have a meeting hall where a neighborhood or homeowners' association, garden clubs, and other local groups can get together. During the day the meeting hall might serve as a child care center and a place where people get their mail and drop off clothes for cleaning. With all these comings and goings, it could

Houses close to the street, some of them with porches and picket fences, make it easy for Kentlands neighbors to meet.

A bus stop in Charleston, South Carolina, sheltered from rain and sun.

evolve into a center for informal socializing. Gathering places have the potential to provide enjoyment, foster local ties, and offset the loneliness and stress associated with today's impersonal contemporary consumer culture.

One of the places where traditionalists expect people's paths to cross is at the neighborhood store—essentially a convenience store. It's possible that prospective residents will have qualms about a convenience store being built close to homes, thinking it will be a blight on the neighborhood. Actually, such stores look attractive and function satisfactorily when developers, neighborhoods, or homeowners' associations insist on it. For example, in Mariemont, Ohio, a traditional suburb begun in the 1920s, red brick Jacobean-style neighborhood shops with apartments above them are handsome and well kept; they make the neighborhood more appealing, not less. Properly operated, a neighborhood store is a boon to people nearby.

If enough demand materializes, buses or other forms of mass transit are expected to serve some neighborhood centers. Plater-Zyberk recalls that when she was growing up in suburban Philadelphia in the 1950s and 1960s, adults and children routinely traveled to jobs, schools, cultural events, and meetings with

*A business area
known as the old
town center in
Mariemont, Ohio,
contains a restau-
rant and retailers
surrounded by a
predominantly
residential
neighborhood.*

friends by train and bus. "Tiny kids," she says, "would commute
on the train." Conventional wisdom now holds that middle-class
suburbanites overwhelmingly prefer to travel by personal vehicle and dislike commuting by bus. One reason for resistance to
buses is that waiting for the bus is a miserable experience. Duany
argues that a neighborhood store should be required to provide a
comfortable place where people waiting for the bus can sit in-
doors, reading or enjoying food and beverages. A drab experience
could be transformed. To further improve the situation, buses
might signal their anticipated arrival time electronically to a display that would announce it automatically inside the neighborhood store. This is already done in Europe and Japan, and it
makes for a less anxious wait. There are many ways in which
daily life could be improved at the neighborhood level.

The feasibility of developing retailing in a neighborhood center is a subject of much debate. Unless some form of subsidy is
provided initially, it is not clear whether stores will open and
prosper in the center of a neighborhood, away from crosstown
traffic. Bob Gorman, the head of planning, landscape architecture, and urban design at RTKL, says, "If the amenities are more
recreation-oriented, they could be in the center. If they're more

A shopping center in Mashpee, Massachusetts, as it looked in the early 1960s.

retail-oriented, they probably need to be on an artery to get business from traffic passing by." In Charleston Place, each section of the development contains a neighborhood swimming pool for the people of the surrounding blocks. But retailing lies outside the development. Calthorpe does not believe stores can thrive in the center of a neighborhood; he argues it is more logical to place most services not in each residential neighborhood but in a town center, which can draw customers from several neighborhoods.

Calthorpe planned Laguna West, a 1,000-acre development eleven miles south of downtown Sacramento. There he concentrated shopping, child care, and other services in the town center, which he has laid out with small, regular blocks. As it fills up, the town center should become a lively place, patronized by a substantial population—those who live in the surrounding neighborhoods, those who live or work in town center itself, and those who are employed in Laguna West's offices and industrial facilities nearby. Calthorpe believes in the importance of a walkable environment, but he defines it more loosely, using a ten-minute rather than a five-minute walk as the basis of his planning.

There seems little doubt that the town center at Laguna West will be comfortable for pedestrians. Calthorpe expects that the outlying area's streets will be walkable, too, lined by sociable front porches and rows of saplings that will eventually shade the sidewalks. But the streets in the neighborhoods outside the town center are far from ideal. Many of the blocks in the residential neighborhoods are long, and many contain cul-de-sacs, which typically discourage walking. It remains to be seen whether pedestrian activity in the residential neighborhoods of Laguna

West will be much greater than in ordinary subdivisions. Generally, short blocks and frequent intersections are an important part of the recipe for encouraging walking, biking, and neighborhood activity. Nelessen says that to make communities walkable, blocks should be no more than 400 feet long. "My preference," Nelessen says, "is for blocks 300 feet long. A length of 200 feet is ideal." He observes, "Typically suburban developers make the blocks as long as possible. They don't want the cross streets, which reduce the number of lots they can create." Nelessen is convinced that frequent cross streets not only give people more choices of how to get around but also make a place more engaging by increasing the number of corner houses. "Corner houses," he says, "are usually more interesting than houses in mid-block."

A portion of the altered and expanded shopping center, now called Mashpee Commons, after the addition of traditional-style business buildings, sidewalks, and streets.

The rediscovery of the town has brought some surprising transformations. One such transformation has taken place in Mashpee, Massachusetts, on Cape Cod. In 1962 the Fields Point Partnership built a small one-story shopping center near a traffic circle in Mashpee. It was for many years a prosaic, pseudo-mansard-roofed shopping center surrounded by blacktop park-

The theater entrance at Mashpee Commons fronts on a public plaza.

ing lots. After Arnold B. Chace, Jr., became president of Fields Point in 1979, the company decided to remake the center. "We both hate shopping centers," says Douglas S. Storrs, Fields Point's vice president of planning and development. "We don't think shopping centers are enjoyable places to shop. We like places that meet the full needs of residents and visitors." To transform the shopping center into a traditional small downtown, the company constructed two-story buildings on portions of the parking lots, installed sidewalks, and formed narrow streets. Public plazas were created where they would encourage conviviality. Fields Point added a six-screen movie complex. Instead of having people enter and exit the theater by way of a parking lot, the company insisted that theatergoers should be funneled through a public plaza facing the center of the business district. The theater's designers, Melanie Taylor and Robert Orr, wrapped storefronts around part of the theater exterior to make it more conducive to pedestrian life.

"People will walk a thousand feet in a downtown if they're seeing interesting things, walking past the fronts of buildings," Storrs says. "If it's beyond a 300-foot distance in a parking lot, they feel they're being forced to walk too far." The redone shopping complex, called Mashpee Commons, has parking, but much of it is broken up into smaller lots. Vehicles also park on the streets; the stationary vehicles at the curb provide a buffer between the pedestrians on the sidewalks and the moving automobiles in the streets. Fields Point sought and obtained a post office, which brings in a steady flow of people from morning to night. The town center needs further development—the parking lots still stand out—but the start that has been made is promising. On streets directly connected to the downtown, Fields Point is planning to build houses, which will make the community more complete.

Planners of new traditional communities try to find prominent sites for civic, religious, and cultural institutions. Placing a church at a turn in the road or the head of a T intersection, for example, makes for a more memorable impression. It also serves to remind people that life involves values higher than money-making, shopping, and domesticity. At Mashpee Commons a new town green was created, with a bandstand in its center and a town library and a Catholic church and rectory on two of its sides. In Kentlands, a church commands a circle just off the main road into the development.

When I first discovered the church at Kentlands, it was not yet completed, and a sign next to the building said tersely: "Future Site of the Church." Whose church was it? It seemed peculiar that a church building, even an unfinished one, did not have a sign identifying its denomination. Upon inquiring, I found the new orange-brick structure with a white steeple did in fact have an affiliation—the Church of Jesus Christ of Latter-Day Saints, or Mormon church. The land it stood on had been donated by the initial developer of Kentlands, Joseph Alfandre, who is a Mormon. The absence of a full identification made me wonder whether the vagueness of the sign—"the Church"—was meant to avert potentially negative reactions from non-Mormon home-buyers coming to look at model homes. A religion that until recently limited blacks to the lowest rungs of the church hierarchy and that continues to restrict the rights of women may not do much to boost sales of spec houses in suburban Washington. While the idea of using churches as landmarks seems a good one, the case at Kentlands suggests that there are hazards in putting one denomination on a pedestal.

Conspicuous sites best fit institutions that serve the entire community—public institutions such as libraries, schools, and town halls. The most numerous of these institutions—the schools—certainly deserve a newfound prominence. Schools in the late nineteenth and early twentieth centuries strove for stateliness

Entrance to the Rachel Carson School at Kentlands.

and grandeur. That sort of civic symbolism unfortunately went into decline after the Second World War as school districts settled for dully functional building exteriors and lackluster locations. Countless high schools and middle schools slunk out of the center of town, gaining sites that were several times larger—the better to accommodate parking, athletic fields, and fleets of school buses—but that were pitifully humdrum. Looking at the typical suburban school, one wants to exhort it: "Buck up! Show some pride! Remember that you're crucial to the community!"

At Kentlands the local school district agreed to build the Rachel Carson Elementary School on a prime site that Alfandre donated, a rise of land overlooking Darnestown Road—a main road on Kentlands' perimeter—and Tschiffely Square Road, a principal entrance into the development. However, the school district insisted on using one of the district's stock building designs, and the new two-story red brick school ended up with its face looking away from the intersection, oblivious to the potential for civic expression. Those who drive past on Darnestown Road see the building's backside—a featureless expanse of orange brick punctuated by four big louvered vents. What sort of symbolism is it when a building turns its back on passersby and blows air at them?

To salvage what he could of the school's dignity, Alfandre, at his own expense, had Duany and Plater-Zyberk add a classical white-columned portico to the building's entrance on the opposite side of the building, invisible from Darnestown Road but prominently on view inside Kentlands. Better a last-minute embellishment than a school devoid of symbolic expression. Traditionalists argue that society needs proud statements of civic responsibility and public achievement. Institutions that serve public well-being deserve to command community notice, and they have the obligation to behave properly.

Most traditionalists admire the ability of old towns to bring together people of differing ages, backgrounds, and economic levels, allowing them to get to know and appreciate one another. Daniel Cary is a fan of old towns and a man who hopes that new traditional communities can re-create some of their social connections. Cary grew up in Ripley, New York, a small town surrounded by grape vineyards on the south shore of Lake Erie. As a youth, he worked in the nearby resort town of Chautauqua, a tightly built, culturally ambitious little place that became one of Robert Davis's models for Seaside.

"My father, Martin Cary, built cabinets in a barn in the back yard," says Cary. "He also made birdhouses. We had a sign out front saying 'Martin House,' which people could interpret in more than one way. My grandmother, Flora Cary, lived in Fredonia, another small town in Chautauqua County. She supported herself by sewing dresses and baking sweet rolls for people and renting rooms in her house to women students at Fredonia State College. When she became older, my parents added an apartment onto our house, and she lived there. She continued to sew and bake. That was a very viable business that sustained her for twenty-some years when she was 'retired' on Social Security."

"In a traditional town, where things are close enough together, there is a network of people," Cary says. The closeness, the network of people, and the ability to use residential properties flexibly allowed individuals like Martin Cary and Flora Cary to maintain flourishing cottage industries in their homes. The closeness meant that everyone in the community knew people from other walks of life, and knew them well. "I knew doctors and their children, the janitor's children, the mortician's son," Cary says. "I knew farmers and carpenters and wealthy people and professionals." Firsthand experience with many kinds of people, Cary contends, makes individuals more sympathetic to the needs of others. "It's different than in a monoculture where you only have

$100,000 houses, where the kids never have any exposure to, let's say, a farmer," Cary says. "When it comes time to vote, will they be as sensitive to the needs of the farmer?"

"Real towns need poor people and rich people," Cary observes. "Rich people kick in money for things like a library or a cultural center. If there are no poor people, the rich people have to clean their own houses." Cary believes the interplay of different kinds of people inculcates a sense of responsibility, especially when people are exposed to how other people make a living. "It's important to citizenship," he says.

Elizabeth Plater-Zyberk remembers her hometown of Paoli, Pennsylvania, as a place where social divisions were stronger than in Cary's country town of Ripley, New York. "We grew up close to the train station and the downtown in Paoli," Plater-Zyberk says. "It was a low-income area. The neighborhood was Italian and Irish working class. A wooded ravine separated it from a black neighborhood. In our town the neighborhoods were classified by income and color."

"But," Plater-Zyberk says, "there was a meeting in the town and in the schools. It was a ten- to fifteen-minute walk into town. We would go food-shopping, walking, and it would take all morning because we talked to people. Along the way you met neighbors."

Paoli and Ripley indicate that traditional towns were not made from a single mold. Consistent with that fact, new traditional communities employ differing strategies to bring people with different characteristics together. One strategy, akin to what Plater-Zyberk experienced in socially stratified Paoli in the 1950s, is to build neighborhoods that are relatively homogeneous but to make sure that there are places where people from the divergent neighborhoods can come together—such as in a downtown. The other strategy is to mix assorted sizes and kinds of housing close together. Different kinds of housing may coexist on the same block, or housing may vary from one block to the next. "As we work around the country, we find there are a surprising number of people who are open to mixing incomes and colors," Plater-Zyberk says. Compared with forty years ago, "I think there's a lot more of that kind of openness," she says.

Many of Duany and Plater-Zyberk's town plans encourage a mixture of ages, incomes, and household sizes by allowing each single-family house to have a garage apartment or cottage at the rear of its lot. The inhabitants of these small units are likely to be in a different income bracket or a different stage of life than the people living in the main houses. The mixture stands to benefit people of many ages. Young adults, for instance, may be able to find small apartments for themselves in family-oriented neighborhoods, as opposed to living in big rental-housing complexes. Cary recalls that as a university student, he lived in a South Miami garage that he and the owner—one of his professors—converted into an apartment. Cary lived rent-free in exchange for doing chores for the professor's family (including six children), which occupied the house in front of the garage apartment. "I cleaned the pool, mowed the lawn, ran kids to school, and did a little babysitting," Cary says. Besides the financial advantage, this arrangement offered a more civilized life than that of a typical student holed up in a dormitory room or an apartment complex. "These people kind of adopted me," Cary says. "I ate with them three meals a day. For the time I was in school, I had a *family.*"

In new communities like Kentlands and Laguna West, garage apartments or cottages are often called granny flats or in-law units, indicating that some of the individuals living in them are expected to be the grandmothers of the children in the single-family houses. Grandmothers may be available for babysitting and other household assistance, but without the friction of sharing their children's living quarters twenty-four hours a day.

Grandparents are not the only ones able to occupy apartments of this kind. They can just as easily be used by sons and daughters old enough to live on their own, or grown children who want to move back home after a divorce, a job layoff, or other upheaval. In the past twenty years grown children in the United States have been living in their parents' homes for an increasing number of years because of marital breakups, high housing costs, and other difficulties. Granny flats allow them to live at home without being so much underfoot.

Usually granny flats or cottages may be rented to nonrelatives as well. Calthorpe has designed subdivisions with townhouses that have garage apartments behind them. The rental income from the garage apartments is expected to help families to make the mortgage payments on the townhouses. This extends home-ownership to people otherwise unable to buy a home of their own.

At Kentlands, one of the first dozen garage apartments was rented to a teacher at the Rachel Carson School. As additional

The corner house of this Kentlands block has a granny flat above the garage. The flats let households respond to changing needs.

garage apartments are built, more young, single teachers may choose to live within walking distance of work—eliminating the cost of commuting. Some of the school's faculty could become more of a presence among the children and their parents.

Whoever lives in the granny flats remains under the eyes of the homeowners in the main dwelling, so conditions in the rental housing are not apt to get out of hand. Risk to the neighborhood from undesirable tenant behavior—an objection often raised against rental housing—should be minimal. For families, such housing offers the advantage of flexibility; families can respond naturally to their changing needs and to ups and downs in their finances. One Kentlands homeowner lives in her garage apartment and rents her house out, collecting $100 more per month than her mortgage payment.

Many of Duany and Plater-Zyberk's developments are planned so that even if no one builds garage apartments or cottages, it is still possible to have houses of varied sizes and prices on a single block. An example is one of the streets facing the central hill-top green in Kentlands, which mixes together two-story and three-story dwellings. Most of the dwellings are townhouses; others are detached houses. A small three-bedroom townhouse in the middle of the block sells for about half the price of a five-bedroom detached house on the corner. This does not mean the poor will live cheek by jowl with the rich, but it does enable the block to accommodate people with different sizes of families, different budgets, different ages—a broader mix than is usually found in brand-new suburban developments.

Detached houses and townhouses near the central green of Kentlands have been built in a variety of sizes with a wide range of prices.

Another form of housing favored in new traditional developments is apartments above stores and offices. Like granny flats, such apartments allow people to live in a community that otherwise would be beyond their financial means; the monthly rent charged for an apartment over a store is typically not as daunting as the price of other kinds of housing. Because some shopping is close by and because public transportation, when it operates in the suburbs, is likely to focus on mixed-use areas, some tenants of upper-story apartments may be able to do without a car, thus reducing their cost of living. Apartments of this sort can be a godsend during periods when an individual's income is low.

Traditionalist designers generally (though not always) favor laying out communities so that they have a considerable range of housing. Some of the new developments borrow ideas from old planned communities like Mariemont, a four-square-mile Cincinnati suburb that was begun in 1923 and promoted at the time as a "national exemplar" of town planning. Mariemont was the work of John Nolen, a Cambridge, Massachusetts, planner who in the early decades of the century laid out towns, neighborhoods, parks, and urban projects throughout the United States. Seven decades after its founding, Mariemont, population 3,300, remains a very desirable place to live. In the town's most affordable area, the northwest quadrant, many young couples rent apartments. Families with children, a considerable number of them one-parent households, live in some of the northwest section's row houses, conveniently close to an elementary school and a child care center. As families become acquainted with the town and their finances improve, some of them buy small detached houses or two-family houses in the northwest. Those with more money gravitate toward other parts of town, the most luxurious area being the southern portion of Mariemont, overlooking the Little Miami River, where larger detached houses predominate. The mixture of housing allows people to relocate as their needs change and yet remain in the same small community where they know the schools, stores, services, and many of the neighbors. When residents reach their sixties or seventies, some of them move to apartment buildings near the town center, within a short walk of a bank, library, movie theater, stores, and restaurants. Sara Lutz, a real estate broker with an office in the town center, each day watches a procession of elderly individuals walking across the circle to the Village Kitchen restaurant in the late afternoon. She observes, "It's like a retirement community for a lot of people."

Many new traditionalist developments aim to offer a choice of flats, townhouses, small detached houses, large detached houses, and so on—all on an interconnected network of streets so that people can readily walk from one area to another. Some blocks may be considerably wealthier and more elaborate than others, but they compose a community more integrated and interdependent than the usual postwar suburb. Henry Turley, developer of Harbor Town, says, "We want our neighborhoods to be home to a mixed group of people: old and young; rich and not so rich; working and retired; even black and white—whoever might want to live there—a group representative of the city as a whole. We think that it's important that diverse people live together. Democracy assumes—no, demands—that we know, understand, and respect our fellow citizens. How can we appreciate them if we never see them?" Designers have learned from Mariemont and other old communities that people prefer to see housing similar to their own across the street. So the general rule in traditionalist developments is that *like faces like.* Row houses face row houses. Detached houses face detached houses. People seem willing to accept a different kind of housing behind them, so shifts in the type of housing mostly occur from one street to another or from one block to the next.

What proportion of the population in new traditionalist developments will be families of modest means or racial minorities remains to be seen. The relatively high cost of today's developable suburban land, the resistance of many local governments to lower-income people, and the dictates of the market mean that suburban development is geared mainly toward the wealthier classes. This is a major obstacle to hopes of making new traditionalist developments as diverse as the population of old towns. Will the doctor's children meet the janitor's children, the way they did in a small town like Ripley, New York? For that to happen, more will be needed than the skill of a good designer or the aspiration of an unusual developer. In most suburban areas, economic mixing on a large scale would require a state or regional government policy, one that insists on the development of affordable family housing in new communities. This, along with other government responsibilities, is discussed in chapter 8.

There remains a sense in which new traditionalist developments are not as fully connected as the communities that Americans built fifty or a hundred years ago. Although traditionalists make it easy to get from one point to another within the neighborhood, the number of connections between adjacent neighborhoods is sometimes limited. This is partly the result of *greenbelts*—open, natural areas preserved at the edges of neighborhoods. Duany and Plater-Zyberk call for greenbelts next to many of the neighborhoods they design. In a hilly development, the greenbelt may be a tree-covered slope set aside as parkland. In a low-lying area the greenbelt may be a marsh. In Florida, where the high water table has to be accommodated, greenbelts often are man-made lakes or canals.

In one form or another, greenbelts have long been used to save distinctive landscapes and supply metropolitan residents with natural areas that otherwise would be eradicated by continuous development. Greenbelts provide community breathing spaces— places to enjoy nature and find relief from an increasingly urbanized environment. Where greenbelts follow a region's natural systems, they help protect ecology and give people opportunities to become better acquainted with plant and animal life.

Greenbelts define neighborhoods by giving them clear boundaries, and to some extent they shield the neighborhoods against intrusions by outsiders. Although streets may cut through greenbelts at some points, it's common for sizable stretches of greenbelt to be uninterrupted; thus the greenbelt prevents some metropolitan traffic from finding its way onto the neighborhood's minor streets. Many designers and planners believe identifiable boundaries between neighborhoods are sorely needed. "We're so desperate today for a sense of neighborhood," says Alan Ward, a principal at Sasaki Associates. "If you have a physical expression of it, it reinforces the feeling of neighborhood." A linear green area, in Ward's view, "is a powerful structuring device."

Ward sees some greenbelts—especially parks—as connectors, bringing together people from adjoining neighborhoods. But they may also be dividers, defining the edge of the neighborhood so distinctly that they say to residents: "The area on this side of the natural area is our neighborhood; the area that lies beyond is someone else's." Such sharp demarcations are a mixed blessing. They raise an issue that confronts every generation of metropolitan dwellers: To what extent should people be encouraged to think of themselves as residents of a particular neighborhood, and to what extent should they see themselves as citizens of the entire urban region? In each stage of urban history people have had to search for a suitable balance between the claims of neighborhood, on the one hand, and the claims of the greater urban region, on the other.

The closest Duany and Plater-Zyberk have come to formulating a rule about how extensively to link neighborhoods together is their guideline that "there should be at least three connections in any direction." This is more connections than in many recent suburban subdivisions. It is far fewer than most old communities possess. The old approach was to connect neighborhoods and towns to one another as liberally as the landscape allowed. If we were to do this today, we would probably sacrifice some neighborhood identity. People would have a harder time identifying where their neighborhood begins and ends. But there might be advantages that would make this approach worthwhile.

The typical suburb built in the nineteenth or early twentieth century was laid out predominantly on an interconnected web of streets, without greenbelts to act as boundaries or buffers. The web of streets may have had some kinks and irregularities, but on the whole it was a continuous network, one that maximized access to the world beyond one's block. If a resident developed friendships with people in an adjacent neighborhood, reaching them was simple because there were plenty of streets tying the two neighborhoods together. If a family liked the bakery or the dry cleaner in the next community more than those in its own, it was easy to get there. People have always found an enormous number of reasons for traveling beyond their own neighborhood. In Oak Park, Illinois, which we looked at in Chapter 2, people find it easy to walk from neighborhood to neighborhood and even to other municipalities. An Oak Park resident can follow any of a large number of streets into Chicago on the north and east, the suburban towns of River Forest and Forest Park on the west, and the suburban towns of Berwyn and Cicero on the south.

The continuous network has the virtue of not reining in a person's loyalties. It is easy for people to become acquainted with areas beyond their own neighborhood, and as they become more knowledgeable, they are likely to become more empathetic toward those places and their inhabitants. In Oak Park, one writer observed, "Sense of neighborhood is vague, far overshadowed by the sense of belonging to Oak Park." A broad-minded individual has the opportunity to identify with an ever more extensive territory as his or her forays into distant places grow. The continuous web of streets may be the best physical structure ever devised for breaking down provincialism. The network of streets encourages people to cast the net wide when thinking about who and what are part of their community.

Occasionally a suburb becomes nervous about its exposure to other communities. Chicago has been deteriorating for decades, and as the western part of the city has decayed, Oak Park has closed some of the streets along the Chicago border, trying to shield itself from encroaching urban blight. This may be the expedient thing to do in some circumstances, but it does not refute the fact that there are many benefits in letting one neighborhood flow into another, free of barriers. Oak Park continues to have an open grid on most of its borders, as has been the case for more than a century. In most places and in most times, obstructions are unwise because they reduce people's knowledge of surrounding areas and undermine the sense of being part of a metropolitan community. Exposure to life beyond one's own neighborhood increases the likelihood that people will take an interest in the problems of the urban region and help act to solve them.

It is not clear, either, that neighborhoods need greenbelts to protect themselves from the intrusion of metropolitan traffic. In old suburbs and urban neighborhoods, most of the through traffic avoids minor residential streets. The common pattern in most American urban areas was to lay out a grid or web of streets; at frequent intervals there was a street carrying crosstown traffic. Often every sixth, seventh, or eighth street filled this function. On many of these crosstown streets, stores thrived because they attracted a double quotient of customers—those traveling a

This street in Seattle has been narrowed to slow traffic and protect the peacefulness of a residential neighborhood. The narrowing provides a handy place for a basketball hoop.

few miles by vehicle and those living within walking distance. Apartments naturally developed along some of the crosstown streets. Buses or other forms of mass transit served these routes efficiently. In Oak Park the requirements of crosstown traffic and the desire for quiet side streets have found a fairly effective balance. The minor residential streets are more irregular than the crosstown streets. Minor streets jog left or right at certain intersections, discouraging drivers who might be tempted to use them as shortcuts. Some minor streets come to T intersections. Other streets are closed off at one end to motor vehicles. Still others are one-way. These techniques limit the speed and volume of traffic on minor streets. The minor streets remain safe and pleasant places for families with children.

Because the crosstown streets are only about six to eight streets apart, few of them become so broad or so jammed with heavy traffic that they cut one neighborhood off from one another. More commonly the crosstown streets have exactly the opposite effect: they bring together people from neighborhoods on each side. This community structure is an often advantageous alternative to greenbelts. Crosstown streets—especially if they are boulevards or contain businesses—function well as boundaries between one neighborhood and another. These boundaries, being permeable, are not impediments to movement between neighborhoods, nor do they interfere with the formation of the broad community spirit that our metropolitan areas need today. Major streets, when used as neighborhood edges, can deliver benefits that traffic-blocking greenbelts often lack.

One of the many planted circles in Seattle neighborhood intersections. The circles permit through traffic but lower its speed.

In Seattle, a hilly city laid out almost entirely on a grid, there are several crosstown streets per mile. On these streets—which generally have two lanes of moving traffic and two lanes of vehicles parked at the curbs—neighborhood business centers grew up before World War II. Recently they have been showing renewed vitality. "Those are the business districts that have picked up in the last ten to fifteen years," says Richard K. Untermann. "Proba bly thirty neighborhood centers have come back." The neighborhood centers on these crosstown streets have restaurants, banks, pharmacies, small grocery stores, offices, bus service, and sometimes more. On Seattle's Capitol Hill, for instance, Nineteenth Avenue East contains a thriving business district, including a cafe that has become a popular gathering place for residents of the surrounding neighborhoods. A fine-grained pattern repeats itself across large portions of Seattle—lively crosstown streets and their gathering places alternating with more tranquil residential areas.

The side streets in Seattle were laid out on a more rigid grid than those in Oak Park. To compensate for that, Seattle has been adding "traffic-calming devices," also known locally as chicanes, to protect the residential side streets from excessive through traffic. In certain locations streets have been narrowed so that only one lane of traffic can proceed at a time. Circular gardens have been planted in the centers of many intersections, forcing drivers to slow down. "What's important is the *speed* of the cars that come through a neighborhood," says Anton Ne-lessen. Neighborhood residents maintain the gardens, each of

Chippewa Square, interrupting the grid of streets in Savannah and giving a neighborhood a small park.

which is planted differently. Instruments such as these civilize the grid without sacrificing its advantages.

When a continuous grid spreads across a large area, it is sometimes accused of making the urban or suburban region monotonous. But this need not be the case. Communities have plenty of ways to make their streets distinctive and prevent themselves from being inundated by a sea of sameness. Where the Wooster Pike (U.S. 50) enters Mariemont, the road broadens into a beautiful tree-lined boulevard. A few blocks later the boulevard brings traffic through a Tudor-style business district in the center of town. Traffic is diverted from its straight line by a square in the town center. Mariemont, though it has no greenbelts on most of its borders, nonetheless makes a memorable impression, standing out from the rest of suburban Cincinnati.

Communities with fewer resources than Mariemont might create special features on major streets at their borders to set themselves off from neighboring municipalities. These features might take the form of a burst of planting, a length of boulevard, a sculpture, a historical tableau, a change in the pavement, or any of a long list of possibilities. Where techniques such as these have been employed in old communities, they break the metropolitan areas into distinctive and enjoyable parts. In Westchester County, New York, where U.S. 1 leaves the town of Harrison and enters the town of Rye, suddenly there are stands of trees nearly a hundred feet high on both sides of the road. In the old section of Savannah, Georgia, planned by James Oglethorpe in the 1730s, the rigid grid is gloriously broken up by a series of shaded squares that function as neighborhood parks. There is a wealth of ways to bestow character upon a continuous grid.

Sometimes areas distinguish themselves from one another without consciously trying to do so. One neighborhood may stand out because its buildings were constructed a decade later than those in the adjoining neighborhood, or because its buildings were fashioned from different materials or built on a larger scale or made with a greater or lesser degree of luxury. Working-class neighborhoods look different from executive neighborhoods and consequently create character even in a simple grid network of streets. Where there are hills and valleys or other topographic changes, distinctiveness abounds.

Finally, it is worth emphasizing that the distinctiveness of a town or neighborhood does not consist solely of physical characteristics. What also matters is the social and institutional connections from which residents derive their sense of community. In many communities, elementary-school attendance areas or parish boundaries create a sense of neighborhood. If there is a feeling of mutual attachment among the people, it is not absolutely necessary that each neighborhood *look* different. Much of the point of reviving the ideal of the town has, after all, been to provide people with the satisfaction of knowing their neighbors and caring about one another. This concern for social, intellectual, and spiritual connection runs strong in the work of many traditionalists—almost as strong as the emphasis on what things look like and how and where they are built. If the sense of connection grows and flourishes, the traditionalists will have achieved a large measure of success.

We think that there is an imbalance growing between our commitment to sumptuous private buildings—our homes—and spare public and community facilities—our parks, town squares, and such. And we believe that this parallels an imbalance between our private lives and our civic or public lives that is not good for our country.—Henry Turley, developer of Harbor Town, Memphis, Tennessee.

To create vigorous suburban neighborhoods, houses must be designed in ways that encourage people to spend time in public. In most of the suburbs built during the past few decades, however, the development of outgoing, community-oriented houses has become a lost art. Increasingly American houses have emphasized the private life and private possessions of each household, at the expense of daily involvement in the community.

The comforts and amenities in new houses' interiors have grown enormously since the Second World War. Today's new houses contain twice as many bathrooms as houses built just after the war. Kitchens have expanded and taken on a higher level of finish. Family rooms, unknown before the late 1940s, have become commonplace. The percentage of new houses with central air conditioning has jumped from zero to eighty-three. The array of technology intended to make life easier grows constantly. Marcus, Francis, and Meunier examined single-family model homes in the San Francisco Bay area for five years in the 1980s and were amazed by how much equipment the houses contained. "A virtual showroom of energy-consuming appliances adorns each of the model homes," observed the Berkeley researchers. In the kitchen they found not only the long-established appliances—refrigerators, stoves, and dishwashers—but newer features such as indoor barbecue grills, microwave ovens, trash compactors, and instant hot-water dispensers. Some bathrooms featured whirlpool tubs. Many houses had intercoms for calling from one room to another, even though the open-plan interiors allowed voices to carry throughout the house with no electronic help. Burglar alarms promised to prevent the growing accumulation of household goods from being pilfered. Many living areas possessed lofts or extra-high ceilings. Frequently there was a huge master "retreat," of which Marcus and her colleagues said: "This cluster of rooms, often entered through double doors, provides a seemingly luxurious setting for eating, sleeping, relaxing and bathing quite separate from the rest of the house." Along with becoming more lavishly outfitted, interiors have also become substantially larger. In the late 1940s the typical new single-family house contained approximately 1,300 square feet. By 1992 it had grown to 1,920 square feet, an increase of nearly 50 percent.

During the past several decades, outdoor life has shifted away from the fronts of the houses. Before the Second World War, even fairly humble houses had front porches where people spent part of their free time. Upper-middle-class houses frequently had side porches. Since the war, family leisure has gravitated to back yards, which are now routinely equipped with decks or patios. In other words, private areas behind the houses have been upgraded, while public areas facing the streets and sidewalks have surrendered much of their social importance.

Houses and neighborhoods have also been affected by the ever-increasing number of vehicles in each household and changing ideas about where to store them. Before the war, the garage—usually big enough for just one automobile—was almost always a free-standing structure in the back yard. After the war the garage moved forward and was attached to the side of the house. Where lots were small, garages frequently became protuberances on the houses' facades. From 1969 to 1990 the number of cars, trucks, and other vehicles for household use in the United States shot up 105 percent, to 165 million. Household vehicles grew more than two and a half times as fast as the number of households and four times as fast as the nation's population. In 1990, for the first time in American history, the number of household vehicles exceeded the number of individuals licensed to drive them. Garages hurried to keep pace with vehicle production. The National Association of Home Builders reports that by 1990, fully 72 percent of new detached houses had at least a two-car garage, and 14 percent had a *three-car* garage. In California, at last count, 35 percent of new detached houses had three-car garages. Other parts of the country are following California's lead. Minnesota, North Dakota, and Nebraska are among the states where at least a quarter of new detached houses have three-car garages. It is difficult for a house not to be greatly affected by such a substantial enclosure.

A three-car garage requires approximately 700 square feet of floor space—nearly as much space as the entire finished interior of the first Levittown houses built in 1947.

In California and some other western states, where lots for detached houses have been pared down to minimal dimensions, garages have overwhelmed the houses and the streets. Philadelphia architect James W. Wentling, who works for homebuilders in several states, says that some western builders construct a two-story house with 2,500 square feet of living space *plus* an attached three-car garage on a lot containing just 3,000 square feet (the equivalent of forty by seventy-five feet). Wentling describes the results as pathetic: "Streets are nothing more than wall-to-wall garage doors, often with no signs of habitable life visible from the sidewalk. It is frequently difficult to find the entrance to the home."

Moreno Valley, southeast of Riverside in California, is one suburb where garages set the tone for their neighborhoods. A typical Moreno Valley house occupies a narrow lot and has a two-car garage projecting from its front. The most conspicuous exterior feature of such a house is the garage door—commonly sixteen feet wide and windowless. Rows of closed garage doors cast a forlorn expression upon the streets for most of each day. When

schoolchildren and parents begin to arrive home in the afternoon, the situation changes, but not much for the better. The big,
windowless doors slide overhead, and—voila!—the garages' contents become visible to all. In late afternoon in Moreno Valley, by
my observation, more than one of every ten garage doors is likely
to stand open. Anyone who goes down the street gets a view of
garage shelves stocked with auto supplies, washer-dryers against
the garages' back walls, bicycles hanging from the ceilings, lawn-
mowers, refrigerators, boxes full of household goods, and other
effluvia of the consumer age. It's as if a succession of enormous,
messy closets had been opened to public inspection.

People occupy some of Moreno Valley's garages. Men operate
table saws or work on cars. Children play on driveways. Occasionally a hardy soul sits on a lawn chair at the mouth of a garage,
there being no front porch available. But more often than not the
visible adult population is sparse. Life in public, life with any
semblance of dignity, has been made uninviting by the garage-
dominated houses. Often the house's front door and living-room
window are grimly half-hidden in the garage's shadow. Almost
everyone except children and people engaged in chores has instinctively abandoned this drab environment.

There is, to be sure, a degree of convenience in designs that
integrate the garage into the house. On a foul day a resident arriving home with a load of groceries from the supermarket can drive
right into the attached garage and be only a few steps from the
kitchen, sheltered from the weather. "Driving to the kitchen has
become something more than a standard," Daniel Solomon and

*A house in Moreno
Valley, California,
dominated by its
three-car garage.*

Susan Haviland have remarked acerbically. "It is like an inalienable right, something the absence of which is unimaginable." Convenience of this sort, however, is a poor standard for community design. Single-minded pursuit of convenience does more harm than good. As the Reverend Jesse Jackson once said in a different context, "the laws of convenience lead to collapse, the laws of sacrifice lead to greatness."

What has foolishly been forfeited in the emphasis on "convenient" house design, comfortable interiors, and leisure-oriented back yards is a vigorous neighborhood life. People know their neighbors less well, or hardly know them at all. Most suburbanites spend little time in the kinds of public or semipublic settings where conversations with neighbors spontaneously occurred in the past. Places that used to foster community life have been drained of vitality.

Some social commentators profess not to be bothered by the decline of neighborhood life. One modern train of thought contends that people today get the information and entertainment they need from television and other forms of indoor diversion, from modern communication, and from traveling by car to destinations spread across the metropolitan area. According to this argument, people no longer depend on the neighborhood for information and social contact. This assumes—erroneously—that modern technology is largely benign in its effects and that it is an adequate substitute for having social contacts available within walking distance of home. While some people may fare well without neighborhood activity, for many people the lack of neighborhood vitality is deeply troublesome, in part because the modern technology that people have become dependent on leaves many needs unsatisfied. Cultural critic Neil Postman argues in *Technopoly* that television and other modern technologies have aggravated serious social ills in the United States. Modern technology has flooded the household with more stimuli, more information, than people can digest. Much of what people are exposed to, Postman says, is useless, contradictory, or harmful, "a source of confusion rather than coherence." According to Postman, "When the supply of information is no longer controllable, a general breakdown in psychic tranquillity and social purpose occurs."

That is why life in public places continues to be enormously valuable. Traditionally the neighborhood was an important social network that stabilized people, helping them to evaluate the world and find a path to satisfaction. The neighborhood was an anchor for the individual, providing emotional, spiritual, and intellectual support. When a neighborhood has an animated public life, residents benefit. They obtain greater opportunities to find companionship, develop friendships, and form ideas. They are led toward balanced lives. Their ability to cooperate in solving community problems and carrying out community improvements multiplies.

To improve the depressed state of today's neighborhood life substantially, houses must be designed in a different spirit. But more than design must change. There also must be a less obsessively private and materialistic attitude if neighborhood life is to flourish. Neighborhood life now suffers not only from the antisocial character of the houses and the unattractiveness of the public realm but also from the hurried pace at which people live. Many people will not have much time to spend on neighborhood and public life as long as they remain under intense pressure to generate income. So one element in restoring neighborhood vitality consists of persuading people that they do not need so many alluring but ultimately burdensome possessions. The American "dream house" promoted for the past couple of decades is so costly—so stuffed with "conveniences," comforts, and expensive goods—that its occupants place themselves on a financial treadmill. The more money they spend on the house, appliances, electronics, automobiles, and other things, the less time they have for being part of the community. People become mired in a hectic and in many respects impersonal way of life.

Throughout history, wise individuals have pointed out the hazards of excessive materialism. "That man is richest whose pleasures are the cheapest," wrote Henry David Thoreau. The poet Horace wrote,

> But as wealth into our coffers flows in still increasing store,
> so, too, still our care increases and the hunger still for more

One of the most insightful books of recent times is E. F. Schumacher's *Small Is Beautiful,* published in 1973. In it, Schumacher, a British economist, writes: "The cultivation of needs is the antithesis of wisdom. It is also the antithesis of freedom and peace. Every increase of needs tends to increase one's dependence on outside forces over which one cannot have control, and therefore increases existential fear."

The prevailing American attitude toward material possessions has been that "more is better." But such an attitude is a sure route to frustration during a period of income stagnation. Since the early 1970s, roughly 80 percent of the nation's households have failed to gain ground financially. Median household income in 1990, adjusted for inflation, was $29,943, or $1,000 less than it was in 1973, according to the Census Bureau. For all but the top fifth of the population, making more than $80,000 a year, income has stagnated.

There comes a time when people must consider what it is they value. Unconstrained materialism came under widespread challenge in the 1960s and early 1970s. Some believe that the sharp questioning during that era may have planted the seeds for a more balanced way of living. David B. Wolfe, who has focused on stages of personal and societal development, says that as the postwar baby boomers advance into middle age, they will be motivated to question anew their beliefs and their country's behavior. Wolfe predicts that because of the baby boom's large size and influence, there will be a rekindling of idealism and a renewed desire to put the nation on a path toward wisdom. Many people have recognized for a long time that excessive consumption—of vehicles, petroleum, and other resources—harms the air, land, and water. In the future, it may become more widely understood that excessive consumption also damages the lives of individuals, households, and communities.

Governments could help clear a path for people to choose a less expensive and harried way of life. Many local building and zoning codes force new houses to be larger than necessary and to occupy more land than they need. Many municipalities in the East and the Midwest, Wentling notes, require half-acre to two-acre lots, which drive up housing costs. When large lots prevail, young children cannot find enough playmates within walking distance; they have to be driven to their friends. Teenagers in large-lot communities depend on having cars to reach everyday activities, as do adults. A house on a big lot weighs on people in many ways. State or regional governments should press recalcitrant local governments to reduce exorbitant house and lot-size requirements. The federal government might help by limiting how much mortgage interest can be deducted from federal income taxes. There is no excuse for encouraging people to build lavishly at government subsidy.

If people spend less money on houses and private possessions, three things may happen. First, some of the savings may be avail-

After a certain point, as residential lots grow larger and the houses retreat from the street, the sense of neighborhood diminishes. This is in a new subdivision in Lincoln, Nebraska.

able for spending on improvements to the public environment. Money that now goes into making the interior as large and plush as possible might be used instead to plant trees along the streets, to create small neighborhood parks, to build alleys behind the houses, to build smaller neighborhood schools, and to make other improvements in the public sphere. Second, some people may find more time for community life; some families may not need to hold two full-time jobs or work such long hours. Third, if people look at their transportation needs more critically, they might decide they can live with fewer cars and smaller garages.

To make the neighborhood function better, streets and sidewalks must become more congenial places. Houses must not have big garages dominating the street. "No architect is skillful enough to make human life project itself on the facade of a house when sixty percent of it is given over to garage doors," say Andres Duany and Elizabeth Plater-Zyberk. There are many ways to make garages less obtrusive. Traditionalist designers often lay out communities to have garages at the rear, along alleys. By this simple stroke the houses are freed to have attractive, communicative fronts. The areas in front of the houses, uninterrupted by driveways, can then be landscaped much more generously. The setting can become more gardenlike, which might encourage people to spend time out front, where they will be apt to encounter neighbors and passersby.

When the garage disappears from the front of the house, it becomes much easier to make the house's facade attractive. Wentling suggests a number of techniques that make facades and streets inviting. One of them is to place the house's main entrance in a prominent location in the facade—a commonsense idea that has been ignored by many designers in recent decades. He suggests having glass in the front door or to one or both sides of the door—perhaps by installing side lights. "This simple gesture acknowledges that people like to see who they will be greeting (or not greeting) at the door," Wentling says. It also allows natural light into the home. In front of the door, a stoop, court, or porch might be provided—spacious enough to accommodate a small group of visitors. The stoop and steps may be brick or stone instead of concrete. Rich veneers may be used on walls around the entrance. "The entry is the place to use quality building materials," Wentling says. Over the front entrance, some protection from the weather is welcome.

A usable front porch—which Wentling describes as at least six to eight feet deep and ten to twelve feet wide—encourages residents to occupy the area in front of the house, where there are opportunities for contact with neighbors. A porch invariably softens the house's facade and supplies a more graceful transition between exterior and interior. Some built-in seating might also be installed in the vicinity of the front door. All of these measures give the streets a measure of dignity and personality. They invite people to linger.

Wentling also recommends giving the house an informal or utilitarian entrance, providing direct access from the outdoors to the kitchen and the informal part of the house. In older houses, this informal door was located on the side or back of the house; it was the door where good friends called. In contemporary house design, the informal entrance became the door from the house to the attached garage—which is not suitable as an entrance for visitors. Ideally, says Wentling, the informal door should be located on the side of the house, easily accessible to visitors—not on the back or in the garage. Where there is enough room, one solution he recommends "is to attach the garage to the house with a breezeway." The breezeway is inviting to visitors. It has the potential to become a screened outdoor sitting area or an enclosed room, depending on the household's preference. And it provides a direct, covered path from the garage to the house. A garage attached to the house via a breezeway does not detract from the house's appearance. On the contrary, it usually creates a pleasing composition.

The locations chosen for garages exert a major effect on the street and on community life. If garages are built along alleys at the rear of the lots, people can do messy chores like changing the car's motor oil without making the whole neighborhood seem unkempt. People need places where they can conduct unpolished activities. In a well-designed community, the street and the alley complement each other like feminine and masculine, yin and yang. The alleys also provide a good place for utilities, such as electrical boxes, which otherwise tend to clutter the streets and front yards. The land and paving required for alleys may increase the cost of development, but the cost may be offset somewhat by a reduction in the need for multiple private driveways.

Where alleys are not feasible, an alternative is to place the garages near the backs of the lots, with driveways running by the sides of the houses to the streets. Garages kept near the rear of

These four layouts suggested by Peter Calthorpe prevent garages from overpowering the streets.

A house in Blount Springs, Alabama, with a front porch elevated above the street. Two garage doors are inconspicuously placed on the side of the house.

the property allow the houses to look more attractive. One of the reasons old neighborhoods often look good is that their garages are far in the background. Some freestanding garages, especially those with second stories for storage, apartments, home offices, or other uses, are handsome. The garage, which tends to debase the house when directly attached to it, frequently becomes appealing when it is an independent structure. The chief disadvantage of placing the garage at the back of the lot is that the long driveway is expensive and land-consuming. In some cases, two adjoining houses may share a driveway to reduce the cost.

Another alternative, consuming less of the back yard, is to attach the garage to a back corner of the house. The garage might extend ten to twenty feet into the back yard beyond the house's rear wall. For the past ten years I've lived in an old house that had a garage added to a rear corner in the 1950s, and I've discovered that it magnifies enjoyment of the area behind the house. One wall of our garage borders a back patio; it gives the patio a privacy that would otherwise be lacking. My wife or I and our visitors can go out-of-doors without being on display to the people next door; people need sanctuaries from their neighbors just as much as they need places where they can rub shoulders with them. Our garage, built of concrete block, has had vines trained to grow on the walls bordering the patio; the foliage makes it look pleasant year-round.

Yet another alternative is to build the garage attached to the

Each house in this row at Harbor Town has a carport on the side with enough room to park two vehicles one behind the other. Each lot measures about thirty-seven by 100 feet. The house entrances and carports were styled by Looney Ricks Kiss Architects to resemble porches.

side of the house but recessed from the house's facade. At Harbor Town, near downtown Memphis, houses are not allowed to have garages flush with the facade. Many of the garages are on alleys; some of the others are attached to the sides of the houses but recessed several feet so that they are inconspicuous. Often some other part of the house, such as a porch, embellishes the front of the house and further draws attention away from the garage door.

When a three-car garage is a necessity, it can be made to look like a two-car garage by arranging two of the stalls one behind the other, in what is known as tandem parking. If one stall is for a car that isn't driven much or is for a workshop or storage, there is no need for each of three stalls to have its own garage door.

In any event, designers should do their utmost to avoid having the garage advance beyond the facade of the house. A garage does not merit being the house's center of attention, nor should it be the dominant influence on the street.

Residential streets that look good and encourage human activity usually have a healthy balance of harmony and variety in their architecture. No single approach to the question of consistency and variation is appropriate in every situation. We can look to historic communities to see the range of possibilities. In Bos-

Harmonious streetscapes with plenty of variety are foreseen in Duany and Plater-Zyberk sketches of Haymount, east of Fredericksburg, Virginia.

ton's Back Bay the buildings have great uniformity in scale, style, and relationship to the street. They are the same height, they are made of the same materials, and they adhere to the same "build-to" line (the distance of the building facade from the street). In Leesburg, Virginia, the handsome county seat of Loudoun County, harmony is strong, but there is less uniformity. Small and large houses sit side by side on small and large lots, with short and long front yards. In Leesburg the buildings' scale and their relationship to the street vary; it is architectural style and materials that give the town visual harmony.

These examples suggest that two different factors are at work in creating physical coherence. One is the design, materials, size, style, and scale of individual buildings. Many developers of upper-priced subdivisions now require individual buildings to adhere to a single esthetic. It's common for developers to require that houses employ specific colors, materials, sizes, and scale that will harmonize together. Those aspects can be categorized as *architectural control.*

The other factor is *urban design control.* Urban design—the three-dimensional relationship of the buildings, the open spaces, and the streets—has received much less attention from developers. Yet urban design is not something unimportant. Adroit urban design gives a neighborhood or community much of its spiritual appeal and its real estate value. Skillful urban design is a principal reason why the Back Bay has for more than a century remained one of the premier sections of Boston. The streets and outdoor spaces feel right; they are deftly shaped, consistently organized in relation to the buildings. Traditionalists, more than most Americans, recognize the importance of urban design and the contribution it makes to human happiness.

Elizabeth Plater-Zyberk suggests that if a community is to achieve a pleasant environment, it must pursue either architectural control or urban design control or both. In the absence of meaningful architectural or urban design control, a place is often not enjoyable; this is true of most highway commercial strips, for instance. Places where control is exerted over both architecture and urban design are among our most valuable real estate. Forest Hills Gardens in Queens, New York; Shaker Heights, Ohio; and Santa Barbara, California, are three demonstrations of this. In Duany and Plater-Zyberk developments there is more often than not both an architectural code that has to be followed—governing the proportions, styles, materials, and other aspects of the buildings—and an urban design code, which regulates the placement of streets, sidewalks, building facades, porches, and other elements in the public realm. While the development is under construction, the developer exercises the controls. After the community is occupied, a homeowners' association assumes those powers.

To make a great place, Plater-Zyberk believes, it is necessary to have some degree of intentional interrelationship between the architecture and the urban design. Great places these days do not come into being unless there is purposeful coordination. Without some sort of concern for compatibility, a community ends up being a mishmash. So many choices of materials, shapes, styles, and other elements are available in the modern American economy that coherence comes about only as a result of conscious effort to make things fit well together.

Many traditionalist developments require colors that are considered compatible with one another. Some artificial materials, such as aluminum siding, may be prohibited. In Seaside the proportions of window openings must be predominantly vertical, like the long, narrow shapes of windows in nineteenth-century houses. Many traditionalist developments emulate historical styles of their regions. Houses in Virginia are intended to resemble those built by Virginians in the eighteenth or nineteenth century.

At Harbor Town, developer Henry Turley limited the use of brick exteriors, partly to prevent builders from erecting the same brick-veneered houses they routinely erect in Memphis's suburban subdivisions. "We were looking for something that recalls the imagery of the late nineteenth-century and early twentieth-century frame homes in the Memphis region," says Memphis architect J. Carson Looney, who reviews architects' and builders' plans for Harbor Town. Exteriors at Harbor Town are largely wood. Foundations, whether concrete slab or conventional, must rise at least thirty inches above the ground, giving the house a different aspect than modern houses, which have concrete slab foundations with their first floor only four to eight inches above the ground. Windows must be predominantly vertical, and they must be tall enough to complement the high ceilings inside. Usable porches are strongly encouraged.

These Harbor Town houses are about eighteen by sixty feet and fit onto lots approximately forty feet wide. Each has a porch on the side, facing the street.

Looney discovered that an effective way to get builders to understand and adhere to Harbor Town's architectural guidelines was to assemble "image boards" displaying photographs and drawings of a wide assortment of houses that would satisfy the developer's expectations. The images—taken from books and magazines showing houses around the United States and interspersed with photos of exemplary houses in the Memphis area—have given builders a clear sense of the character being sought. At the same time, they have demonstrated how much variety is

At Laguna West near Sacramento, trees have been planted in the streets to provide greenery and shade in a hot climate.

possible within the developer's vision of the community. Perhaps because of this, Harbor Town has achieved great diversity, with houses ranging from literal recreations of historic architecture to contemporary adaptations of motifs from the past. For the most part they fit into a coherent and attractive streetscape.

As I indicated in Chapter 4, my own inclination is to try to achieve harmony mainly through urban design and to allow the individual homeowner plenty of latitude about other issues, such as what color to paint the houses. Individuals, it seems to me, need and deserve outlets for creativity and autonomy. The problem is that it takes years for some elements of urban design, such as street trees, to develop fully. In the early stages of a subdivision, when the trees are mere twigs, there is a tendency not to recognize how much will eventually be accomplished through skillful urban design. Instead, developers and homeowners' associations impose stultifying uniformity on the houses and grounds because the visual impact of the houses has not yet been softened by an established landscape. Many people—marketing specialists especially—do not have the patience to wait for the trees to grow.

There is no denying that houses' proportions, materials, construction quality, color, and style do make a difference to the quality of the public experience on the streets and sidewalks. If the houses' facades are the "walls" of the outdoor "public room," it is hard to argue against taking steps to ensure that these walls are attractive. At Laguna West, Peter Calthorpe agreed to let builders use their stock suburban house designs in the outlying neighborhoods with just a few modifications, such as adding porches to their fronts and making their garages less conspicuous. That seems to have been a mistake; some observers have complained that visually the houses are a letdown. Calthorpe has tried to supply shade and greenery by insisting that trees be planted in the small front yards and by installing little concrete planters in the perimeters of the streets. It's expected that saplings growing in the planters will mature into rows of street trees like those in old Sacramento neighborhoods, where dense arboreal canopies help to make the ninety-degree-plus summer days bearable and actually reduce the ambient temperature by several degrees. But the truth is, the planters—small rectangles stranded amid the asphalt and concrete of the streets, with precious little soil surface to support thirsty trees—are inelegant. And so are many of the houses. Both the architecture and the urban design of the initial portions of Laguna West seem to have been done without the passion that makes America's best neighborhoods pleasurable. In a prototype community as widely heralded as Laguna West, such shortcomings are dangerous. Bad architecture can blind people to what's good about the planning.

At Kentlands there is also a gap, but a less yawning one, between the lofty hopes of the planners and the realities of everyday construction. Builders at Kentlands have failed to make some of the houses look as authentically historical and regional as the tantalizing sketches initially produced by the Duany and Plater-Zyberk staff. Fake muntins in the windows and other modern short-cuts detract somewhat from the atmosphere—especially if one had been led to believe the development would look like a newly minted eighteenth-century Annapolis. Yet if Kentlands does not possess all the charm of a 200-year-old town, it does look much better than the typical Washington area subdivision.

The ideal situation would be to have every house designed individually, as at Seaside, where the great majority of dwellings are well crafted and interesting to look at in addition to being reasonably harmonious. Economics makes this impossible in most suburbs. In the realm of "production homebuilding" (as tract homebuilding is called within the construction industry), aesthetic compromises on architecture and craftsmanship are common. Some compromises stem from a need to rein in construction costs so that buyers can afford the housing. But much of the cheapening of the houses' architectural and construction quality stems from a more dubious motive—a desire to spend the inhabitants' money on wet bars in the family rooms, lavish bathrooms in the master suites, TV sets in every corner, and other interior embellishments that humanity for centuries managed to live quite satisfactorily without. The peculiar trade-off between architectural quality and craftsmanship, on the one hand, and the bloating of interiors, on the other, is most striking in high-priced production houses. The construction, proportions, and detailing of an expensive house are often no better than those of houses that sell for much less; the expensive houses just have

Peter Calthorpe's design for an affordable house on a narrow lot includes an "in-law unit" over the garage along a rear alley. Rental income from the small apartment may make it possible for a family to buy the front house.

165

A U-*shaped pre–World War II apartment building in New Haven has proportions that blend into a block made up mostly of one- and two-family houses.*

more square footage, extra appliances, bigger bathtubs, and other upgrading of this sort. Clearly, in some suburban developments it is financially possible to produce much better-looking houses—dwellings that will contribute to the attractiveness of the public environment. But there is no simple or single answer to how to achieve this. A great deal depends on the skill and determination of developers, architects, and builders who know their locality and its history.

Interesting, lively neighborhoods are more likely when there is an intimate mixture of *types* of housing—detached houses, duplexes, row houses, apartments, and possibly others. Currently it is difficult to obtain the leavening influence of variety in some parts of the country. Calthorpe says that in California and other western states, developers insist on limiting each large tract to single kind of housing. "In the West no homebuilder works with less than 150 housing units at a time," he says. Consequently all that the resident of a detached house will find nearby is more detached houses. All that an apartment dweller will experience in the vicinity is dozens more apartments. Such uniformity makes a neighborhood visually less interesting and socially less stimulating. Developments designed this way may be simpler to finance, build, and sell, but they are deficient places for living. Calthorpe has pragmatically accepted the developers' routine practice, laying out some neighborhoods composed solely of detached houses. He has tried to offset their deficiencies by linking the streets of single-family houses to a nearby mixed-use town center, to which the residents can walk, bike, or drive. The center possesses higher-density housing, offices, stores, services, mass transit, and local institutions.

Traditionalists in other parts of the country have succeeded in getting developers to sprinkle a mixture of dwellings throughout their communities. Harbor Town contains apartments, row houses, duplexes, and detached houses. Kentlands, too, contains a range of housing. Buildings of different sizes, containing varied households, help to make a more interdependent neighborhood—one that is more apt to develop a vigorous public life.

Apartments can be compatible with detached houses, Duany and Plater-Zyberk believe, if the shape and scale of the apartment buildings resemble those of individual houses. An example of the successful blending of apartment buildings and detached houses prior to the Second World War is the very common 2- or 2½-story apartment building with a U-shaped ground plan. The two legs of the U face the street, as does the open center of the U, which is a gracious landscaped approach to the building's main door. The width of each leg of the U is often the width of a nearby detached house. The height of the apartment building is the same

A street in Buffalo where houses with first- and second-floor front porches keep the streets under the residents' watchful eyes.

as a house's. Other details are also patterned after single-family construction. On the street, as a consequence, the apartment building fits in well with detached houses.

The U-shaped apartment building is one of many older types of housing that composed eminently walkable and pleasant neighborhoods. Another example from the American past is the two-family, 2½-story house, which was built in great numbers in the early decades of the twentieth century in the Northeast and Great Lakes regions. Cities such as New Haven, Buffalo, and Cleveland and their suburbs are full of these two-family houses, which are often intermixed with detached houses and an occasional apartment building. The family that owns the house occupies the first floor and rents the second floor to a tenant. When I was a young newspaper reporter, my wife and I lived in Buffalo in the second floor of what is known in that city as a two-flat. We discovered that two-flats mixed in with single-family houses and an occasional four- to six-unit apartment building form highly agreeable neighborhoods. The lots the two-flats occupy are about thirty-five feet wide, producing a population density sufficient to support stores and restaurants within walking distance. The

A one-family house at Harbor Town with first- and second-floor front porches. A garage is at the rear, attached to the house through a small screened porch. The house fits on a 42-by-110-foot lot.

houses' outdoor areas are allocated unequally, yet in a manner that works out satisfactorily. Typically the owner gets the use of the small back yard and the first-floor front porch. The tenant gets a second-floor front porch with a bird's-eye view of the block. The result is that in good weather plenty of porches are occupied. Opportunities for mischief on the block practically disappear during waking hours because whatever happens in the street, on the sidewalks, or around the fronts of the houses is likely to be observed.

The benefits of the second-floor porch were impressed upon me one hot Labor Day weekend when friends from Pennsylvania came to visit and spent much of the holiday on our second-floor porch. In the evening, as we sat drinking ale, a car came down narrow St. James Place, its engine making a metallic sound— *ching-ching-ching*—which drew our attention. Looking down, my friend Charlie Madigan and I saw the car creeping along in front of us, perhaps three miles an hour. It scraped the sides of one parked car. Then it scraped a second car. At that point we realized that the driver was drunk and shouldn't be at the wheel of an automobile. Charlie ran down the stairs, caught up with the

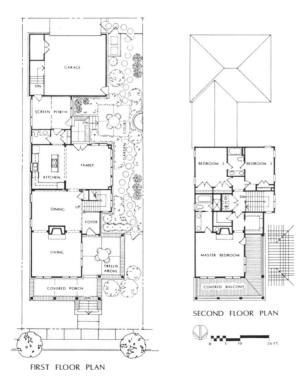

FIRST FLOOR PLAN

SECOND FLOOR PLAN

car, and persuaded the driver to pull over to the curb. An avid conversationalist, Charlie soon learned the driver's name, talked to him about being Irish, and in a couple of minutes convinced him to entrust him with the car keys. That evening the driver never reached the corner—heavily traveled Elmwood Avenue, where he might have gotten into a serious collision. The episode left me with an increased awareness that sociably designed houses, oriented toward the street, can help people in ways that no one is able to foresee. Sometimes they might make the difference between life and death.

The two-flat with its pair of porches embodied, I now realize, a whole series of beneficial attributes. It made the streets safer and more civilized. It allowed people to see their neighbors and watch out for their well-being. It gave renters the opportunity to live in settled, family-oriented neighborhoods. It fostered a personal bond between landlords and tenants, as landlords acquainted their tenants with neighborhood stores, restaurants, and activities. Because of the income from the rental units, it brought homeownership within the reach of more families. It enhanced the lives of individuals, families, and the community.

On the block of two-flats on thirty-five-foot lots, there weren't enough garages or driveways for all the cars. The homeowners had the use of the driveways along the sides of the houses, leading to garages near the backs of the lots. If tenants owned cars, they parked them in the street—which kept the speed down and made the street safe enough for children to play hockey in it during the winter. Between the time school let out for the day and when dinner began, St. James Place always seemed to have a hockey game in progress. If people want satisfying lives and thriving neighborhoods, they learn to trade some private conveniences, such as plentiful off-street parking, for public benefits. They strive to balance competing benefits rather than pursue private comforts and private possessions into what turns out to be a dead end.

House designs of this sort are not obsolete. Harbor Town has a new two-family house similar to a Buffalo two-flat. The Harbor Town house has an owner on the ground floor and a tenant above, with first- and second-floor front porches. A few modifications have been made to the design popular in the northern United States in the 1910s and 1920s. The lot in Harbor Town is fifty-five rather than thirty-five feet wide. The rear of the house, facing an alley, has a large attached garage containing two parking stalls for the owner and two for the tenant. To give the tenant a somewhat private outdoor area, there is a deck on top of the garage—an alternative to the more public front porch. Harbor Town also has single-family houses with first- and second-floor front porches.

Houses of the past have lessons from which today's suburbs can profit. In recent decades Americans have been focusing too much on the house itself and too little on the neighborhood, too much on interior luxury and too little on public amenity. By reconsidering the design of our houses, we might begin again to create walkable, stimulating, more affordable neighborhoods where sociable pleasures are always within reach. The country can learn much from the neighborly kinds of housing we used to build. They made—and continue to make—good places for living.

In August 1992 the retail giant Sears, Roebuck began emptying nearly all its offices in the world's tallest building, the 110-story Sears Tower in downtown Chicago. On seventeen consecutive weekends, a schedule chosen so as not to disrupt the company's daily business operations, movers loaded the records of the Sears Merchandise Group into a convoy of trucks and transported them thirty miles to the northwest. Their destination: 120 acres of a new business park called Prairie Stone, where Sears had constructed five flat-roofed buildings of light blue reflective glass, linked by a central atrium and augmented by two parking garages, three parking lots, a child care center, and large expanses of open land. By Thanksgiving the relocation was complete. The five buildings, none more than six stories high, yet enclosing an enormous 1,973,000 square feet of office space, reverberated with the sounds of Sears employees. Five thousand office jobs had bid farewell to Chicago's Loop and settled in a suburb called Hoffman Estates.

Officials of Hoffman Estates were jubilant. In just four months the village's employment base jumped by two-thirds, and the municipality stood to gain property taxes amounting eventually to more than $2.9 million a year. It was the most far-reaching step yet in the transformation of a nineteen-square-mile village which as late as 1959 had been an unincorporated area that busied itself mainly with raising corn and soybeans.

Hoffman Estates had begun to develop in the mid-1950s, when builders, led by Sam and Jack Hoffman's Father and Son Construction Company, started converting the corn and soybean fields into subdivisions of ranch and split-level houses. By the 1970s Hoffman Estates had become a middle-class bedroom community—white-collar and affluent, though not nearly as posh as its ostentatious name would suggest. Toward the end of the 1970s Hoffman Estates began to get not only new housing developments but employers. At first most of the enterprises that arrived were small. But in the late 1980s and the early 1990s the balance shifted. Siemens, a huge German conglomerate, built a research center and a medical equipment assembly plant employing 950 people. Ameritech Services, a telephone industry company serving five midwestern states, built offices for 2,500 of its employees. And Sears occupied its new complex near the Northwest Tollway. By 1993 Hoffman Estates, with a population of 48,000, boasted more than 12,000 jobs.

Hoffman Estates' evolution into a business center is not unusual. Throughout Chicago's western and northern suburbs, business is arriving and expanding rapidly. Oak Brook, sixteen miles west of the Loop, now contains more than 45,000 jobs, including the headquarters of the McDonald's restaurant chain. Naperville, ten miles beyond Oak Brook, has more than 40,000 jobs. Northbrook, sixteen miles north of the Loop, has over 43,000 jobs. Schaumburg, the next suburb in from Hoffman Estates, has nearly 55,000 jobs. Other suburbs also possess significant shares of the region's employment.

All of this reflects a historic shift in where people work, a shift that has been under way throughout the United States since the 1960s, gathering force with each decade. In 1972 more than half the employment in metropolitan Chicago, not counting government work, was concentrated in the city of Chicago. By 1990 more than three of every five nongovernment jobs were *outside* the city. Employment in Chicago's central business district, with its skyscrapers and its nineteen commuter rail and rapid transit lines, inched up by 6 percent during those eighteen years, to a new high of 533,000. But in the rest of the city the story was different. In the outlying portions of the city, 175,000 jobs disappeared; by 1990 one in five Chicago jobs beyond the Loop was gone. The unmistakable trend was a rapid decline of employment in the city and a rapid expansion of employment in the suburbs. By 1990 the suburban portions of Cook County, including Hoffman Estates, possessed more than a million nongovernment jobs, an increase of 50 percent. Farther out, explosive job growth occurred in the five surrounding counties, known as the "collar counties." From 1972 to 1990, jobs in those rapidly suburbanizing counties more than doubled, to 812,000. Perhaps most telling, from 1985 to 1990 the collar counties accounted for 54 percent of the metropolitan area's job growth.

The trend in the Chicago area parallels what is happening nationally. "Two-thirds of all job growth in the United States is going on in the suburbs," says Alan E. Pisarski, a national authority on transportation and commuting. "Basically the whole country is shifting in the suburban direction." The move of employment is exerting a major influence on the character of suburbs.

Most historians view employment as the latest of three waves of development to occur in the suburbs. The first wave of suburban development, which started in the nineteenth century and gathered momentum after World War II, was residential. People moved to homes beyond the city's borders, while in most cases the families' breadwinners continued to work in the city.

In the second wave, retailing and services migrated to the suburbs. In many metropolitan areas the retail exodus was heavy. Detroit, for instance, has been left without any downtown department stores. Downtown Dallas has a single holdout, Neiman-Marcus. In the Chicago area the shift of retailing to the suburbs has been less massive. North Michigan Avenue, longtime center of the carriage trade in downtown Chicago, has seen its sales volume greatly increase since the opening in 1976 of the city's first "vertical mall," Water Tower Place, where a hotel, several floors of professional offices, and many more floors of condominium apartments are situated on top of seven levels of fashionable stores. State Street, traditionally the region's premier shopping destination, has not fared as well. Retailing on State Street has contracted into fewer blocks. Since 1960 five full-line department stores have left State Street—Wieboldt's, the Boston Store, Montgomery Ward, Goldblatt's, and Sears, which now has no store in downtown Chicago. The Carson Pirie Scott department store continues to operate on State, and the Marshall Field Company maintains its flagship store at the northern end of the street. Many other stores, including some newcomers such as Filene's Basement, still draw hundreds of thousands of shoppers to State Street from neighborhoods throughout the southern and western sections of the city.

The bulk of the Chicago area's retail growth, nonetheless, has been on fresh sites in the suburbs. Oakbrook Center, a mall built in Oak Brook in the 1960s, has continuously expanded, to the point that it now has six department store anchors, including Neiman-Marcus, Lord & Taylor, and Saks Fifth Avenue. Woodfield Mall, which ranked as the country's largest shopping mall when it opened in Schaumburg in 1971, has continued to grow since then (even while losing its number-one status nationally). Gurnee Mills, a gigantic outlet mall in Gurnee, thirty-five miles north of State Street, opened in the fall of 1990 with ten anchors and 200 smaller stores arranged along an S-shaped concourse that goes on for a full mile.

Besides malls, other types of retail establishments, from warehouselike home improvement centers to small stores in strip shopping centers, have multiplied outside the city. Golf Road in Schaumburg abounds with home improvement centers and discount stores behind ample parking lots. Roosevelt Road through Lombard and Glen Ellyn has turned into a merchandising corridor. Even in the historically less monied southwestern suburbs, busy shopping strips sprouted in the 1980s on thoroughfares like LaGrange Road and 159th Street in Orland Park. In a few suburban locations, like Seventh-fifth Street and Lemont Road in Downers Grove, large retail centers now occupy all four corners of an intersection.

The dispersal of employment and shopping imposes heavy burdens on some of the populace. Sears, which has been more attentive than most suburban employers to employees' transportation needs, is served at Prairie Stone by forty-eight van pools and ninety bus trips a day. Nonetheless, the daily journeys can be extremely time consuming. From the South Side of Chicago, where many of Sears's lower-paid employees live, the one-way commute by automobile to the new quarters in Hoffman Estates is an hour and a half to two hours on overcrowded expressways. Rush-hour traffic on the Northwest Tollway, which delivers workers to the Sears complex, often slows to five to fifteen miles an hour through Schaumburg. Employees from the South Side have found little relief in options such as subscription buses, which are trapped in tollway traffic jams the same as everyone else.

Commutes in the Chicago region illustrate the difficulties that beset many of the nation's largest metropolitan areas. According to the Texas Transportation Institute, the number of urban areas suffering from serious traffic congestion grew from ten in 1982 to eighteen in 1988. The greater the population growth or job growth in a metropolitan area, the worse the traffic congestion became. The average speed on freeways in the Los Angeles area has fallen precipitously in recent years, and paralysis is being predicted on many important commuter routes. Anthony Downs of the Brookings Institution writes in his book *Stuck in Traffic:*

Parking for 12,000 vehicles at Mall of America in Bloomington, Minnesota. Elsewhere on the mall's property are facilities that bring the parking capacity to 24,000 vehicles.

"In a few metropolitan areas, peak-hour congestion is so bad that reducing it is widely perceived as the central issue facing local governments."

The migration of employment to the suburbs has not been devoid of benefits, of course. Some suburbanites have seen their commuting time shortened as jobs have moved closer to their homes. When decreases in commuting time for some workers and increases for others are averaged together, commuting time turns out not to have changed much in many regions of the country. Since 1980 the average commute in the Chicago area has remained steady at about thirty-eight minutes, according to census figures. But the reasons behind the apparent steadiness in average commuting time are not cheering. These are a few of factors: First, people spent more money buying and maintaining automobiles. Money that could have been devoted to education, culture, housing, recreation, and savings has been spent instead on motor vehicles. Second, workers increasingly have traveled in the most energy-profligate way possible: each in a separate vehicle. A growing number have dropped out of car pools and other ride-sharing arrangements. Third, people have continued to abandon bus and train systems. Mass transit systems capture an ever-declining proportion of the trips in the Chicago area and in most metropolitan regions. The trend away from mass transit undermines the future of public transportation systems. Every year the Chicago Transit Authority is forced to cut service and

raises fares to make ends meet; suburbanization is reducing both its ridership and its (largely sales-tax based) revenue.

No matter what the current length of time devoted to commuting, the long-term outlook is cause for concern. Pisarski, author of *Commuting in America,* says, "As trends continue, travel times should get worse."

Heavy traffic is no longer restricted to a couple of hours in the morning and a couple of hours in the evening. In large metropolitan areas, the highways are becoming filled for several hours a day. Noontime is becoming a third rush hour in employment-rich suburban areas as workers use their cars to go to lunch or run errands. Weekends also are feeling the crush of traffic. "More and more, drivers encounter the worst traffic congestion not during commuters' rush hours but on Saturdays, the day for errands and shopping," the *New York Times* reported in 1989. In New Jersey, which has some of the most heavily traveled roads in the nation, the *Times* said, "Traffic congestion on Saturdays is expected to exceed that of the evening rush in the next few years." If these trends continue, the relaxed atmosphere that initially made the suburbs appealing will increasingly give way to a hectic and irritating daily life.

From the standpoint of public transportation and the billions of dollars the country has already invested in its urban infrastructure, it makes sense to encourage much of the nation's employment to concentrate in cities. The distances that people have to travel are generally shorter in cities. In cities it is easier to bring housing, retailing, and employment close together, producing efficiency gains and other benefits. When cities contain plentiful employment, the opportunities for healing America's racial and class divisions and for other social benefits grow. It is not feasible, however, to undo all of the vast outward migration of the past thirty years. Even if we wanted to, we could not put all the jobs and merchants back in the cities. Most of the employment, retailing, and traffic that has accumulated in the suburbs is there to stay. Consequently, it is imperative to design suburbs in ways that make transportation difficulties less onerous and that foster a more enjoyable and convenient way of life. To do so, there will have to be a more coordinated approach to transportation, employment, shopping, and services. More of the suburbs' employment, shopping, and services will need to be concentrated in places that are compact and walkable. Suburban job centers will need to become more like traditional downtowns. To understand what this might mean for the character of suburban development, it's useful to look at two downtownlike centers that have been started in the past several years.

One of these is the Miami Lakes Town Center in Miami Lakes, Florida. The core of the Miami Lakes Town Center is Main Street, a narrow thoroughfare designed to make walking an efficient and pleasant way of getting around. The distance from the buildings facing one side of Miami Lakes' Main Street to those on the other is only sixty feet. In the center of the street is a line of trees, and along the fronts of the buildings are arcades protecting people from sun and rain. Retailing occupies the ground floor along Main Street, with offices and apartments above. "We wanted small stores," said Lester Collins, the landscape architect who laid out Miami Lakes. "And we were interested in the guy who wanted to bake bread and live upstairs."

The guiding principle at Miami Lakes is that the ninety-acre town center must strive for a variety of activities and enterprises that reinforce one another. A hotel, a conference center, an athletic club, and a ten-screen movie theater are in the town center, along with office buildings and stores. Since the start of construction in the mid-1980s, businesses have found advantages to having their offices in the town center. Employees can shop at lunchtime without need of a car. Out-of-town clients and guests can stay at the hotel and walk to businesses where they have appointments—a refreshing alternative to staying at a hotel miles

The Miami Lakes Town Center in Florida combines ground-floor retailing, upper-floor apartments, and nearby offices to create a center for a 1960s New Town.

away and driving. So well do office employers like the center that they are willing to pay 10 to 15 percent higher rents than they would pay in conventional office parks elsewhere in Miami Lakes.

Downtown-style centers like Miami Lakes are known in planners' parlance as mixed-use areas. At Miami Lakes, where most of the buildings are two to four stories, housing is part of the mix. The forty-six apartments in the first two finished blocks of Main Street have helped to make retailing, restaurants, and entertainment in the town center successful, according to Carol Graham Wyllie, an executive with the Graham Companies, developer of Miami Lakes. "It gives it a different feel," she says. "You can be going to shop or to a movie and you see people eating by candlelight on their balconies. You hear jazz music coming out of the apartments."

A downtown-style center on a larger scale is the Reston Town Center in Reston, Virginia. The spine of Reston's town center, like that of Miami Lakes, is a narrow street—in this case Market Street, a tree-lined way with buildings three to fourteen stories high facing broad sidewalks. A stroll down the first two completed blocks of Market Street takes a person past the Hyatt Regency Reston Hotel, the entrances of two eleven-story office buildings, a plaza that doubles as an outdoor cafe, an eleven-screen movie theater, a collection of stores and restaurants, and a pavilion that in the winter features outdoor ice skating and in the warm months accommodates concerts, weddings, bar mitzvahs, and business gatherings. As years go by, the eighty-five acres in the town center's core are to fill out with a cultural exhibition center, parks, additional offices and stores, and probably more than 2,000 housing units, many of them apartments, townhouses, and condominium towers.

Once the housing is built, some residents of the Reston Town Center may walk to work—something almost impossible to do in conventional postwar suburbs. Even before the housing is constructed, the Reston Town Center is giving people important freedoms, sources of enjoyment, and opportunities to exercise responsibility. One of those freedoms involves mobility and household spending. People who work in the Reston Town Center can choose from among various means of getting to work. They can drive their own car if they wish, but they can also go without a car—saving a considerable sum of money and doing their part to reduce the strain on the world's resources. They are less trapped in the high-consumption way of life that suburbs

Reston Town Center in Virginia, with tall office buildings, a hotel, stores, shopping, entertainment, and recreation, is a pedestrian-oriented development in an otherwise automobile-oriented New Town.

routinely impose on Americans. They can begin, if they choose, to fulfill the environmental responsibility of "living lightly on the planet."

When a person has the good fortune to work in surroundings like the Reston Town Center—or other downtown-style centers—the idea of sharing a ride to work becomes much more feasible. At lunchtime in the Reston Town Center it is possible to walk from the office to a restaurant, a bar, a health club, a book store, an art gallery, a bike shop, or a clothing store. In any traditional downtown the lunch hour is a busy and fruitful time of day. People escape their bosses, desks, and computer terminals and obtain a salutary change of pace—out in the downtown district, where there are things to do and people to observe. There is a pickup of activity as the legs move and the lungs breathe more deeply. Instead of sitting in automobiles, prone to irritability while struggling for space on the roads, people in an old down-town or a new one get around largely on foot, which puts them in a better frame of mind to appreciate their surroundings and their fellow human beings. The pedestrian takes enjoyment from join-ing in the stream of people on the sidewalks.

In a town center with a dense and varied character, people reach destinations quickly and accomplish many of the day's errands without the bother of driving and parking. When it be-comes plain that they can easily get around during the workday without a private vehicle, some of them decide to use a bus for their commute. A dense and compact center encourages individ-uals to make that decision; the more workers rely on buses, the more extensive the bus service becomes. The flourishing of car-pooling, buses, and in some cases rail transportation in turn makes conditions better for those who do commute by car. Every-one benefits.

An effective center relies on a network of interconnected streets. Streets with plentiful links to one another provide opti-mal circulation both for pedestrians and for motorists. The core of the Reston Town Center, for example, is laid out with a grid of streets. Without such a network, a suburb asks for trouble. Most suburbs built in the past few decades do not have such networks. They have had what Dennis McClendon of *Planning* magazine calls a "dendritic" system, which forces most traffic to flow onto a few arterials and expressways—which then become clogged because there are too many vehicles trying to use too few roads. The area around Woodfield Mall in Schaumburg, Illinois, is an example. Too many people are trying to reach the mall or the many offices near the mall, on a very limited number of roads. "The number of trips in the greater Woodfield area is probably a quarter of the number of trips in the Chicago Loop," says McClendon, "but the congestion is seen as much greater because traffic has to go over very few paths. The traffic that downtown Chicago accommodates without a whimper chokes Schaumburg."

In this regard the Reston Town Center is not ideal. Though its core consists of a grid of streets, the grid is connected at only a few points to the areas lying beyond. This is a result of the modern system of planning and traffic engineering, which segregates each area from its neighbors and channels most of the traffic onto a limited number of arterial roads. This system, which has been relied upon in Reston since the 1960s, will make it harder for people to reach some destinations—such as apartment buildings across the broad Reston Parkway from the town center—on foot. It also threatens in the long run to aggravate traffic congestion on the major roads. It would be better to have a more extensively connected street network, distributing traffic on a large number of minor streets rather than relying so heavily on arterials. One need only look at two other Washington suburban areas—Tyson's Corner and Old Town Alexandria—to see that a network of many interconnected streets is superior to the modern system of a few very busy wide roads. The offices and shopping centers in Tyson's Corner are separated from one another by the few wide, high-volume arterials, which serve motorists poorly and mock the rare pedestrian. A few miles away, the narrow streets and small blocks of eighteenth-century Old Town Alexandria's gridiron handle heavy commuter traffic successfully while providing a pleasing, human-scale environment for pedestrians. The Reston Town Center's design is better than that of the typical suburban business center. It could be improved, however, with a continuous street network that ties into the surrounding area.

Parking for cars exerts a critical influence on conventional suburbs and especially on their workplaces and shopping areas. "Everything in the suburbs is geared to making the car comfortable," Andres Duany observes with equal measures of sarcasm and accuracy. A suburban store's parking lot often covers twice as much land as the store itself. A four-story suburban office development may cover four times as much land with parking lots as with buildings. The big parking areas make it unpleasant to walk from building to building. As long as parking occupies

The conventional suburban retailing formula: big parking lots out front, buildings in the background.

most of the suburban commercial landscape, it will be difficult to produce developments in which people will be inclined to walk.

Urban design consultant Jonathan Barnett says one remedy is to develop town centers that mix together a variety of enterprises with different peak hours so that they can share the parking areas. An office building needs parking mainly on Monday through Friday between nine in the morning and five in the afternoon, Barnett notes. Movie theaters need parking mostly on weekends and after the offices empty out on weekdays. Many stores need most of their parking in late afternoons and in the evenings and on weekends. Restaurants may generate their biggest parking demands in the evenings. A hotel's peak parking period arrives after the end of the workday. When each of these businesses is developed individually, it has to build large parking lots or garages that remain only partly occupied for much of each twenty-four hours. Money, land, and resources go to waste. But when offices, stores, restaurants, hotels, movie theaters, and other uses locate close to one another and agree to share parking, the total parking area needed is reduced. Parking is shared in both the Miami Lakes and the Reston town centers. The centers function with fewer parking spaces than would otherwise be required.

Placement of the parking matters greatly. Even relatively small gaps between buildings can kill people's willingness to walk farther and cause retail establishments to lose business. Successful downtown-style shopping areas are careful not to let parking lots disrupt the continuity of the shopfronts. In Miami Lakes and Reston, parking is positioned behind the buildings of the principal street; there are no parking lots interrupting Main Street or Market Street. As the town centers develop, plans call for some of the surface parking lots to give way to parking garages (which take up less land) and to additional stores and office buildings. "If you want to make a town center look like a town center," Barnett says, "you've got to make a lot of rules about where the parking goes." Only when parking and policies on accommodating vehicles are handled better than they've been for the past few decades will we get suburban places that are comfortable for people, not just for their cars.

The difficulty is compounded by the fact that many of today's stores and offices come in sizes that do not easily fit into compact, walkable surroundings. One of the trends in retailing has been toward construction of big discount stores, giant specialty stores (sometimes called power stores), and supermarkets that make the grocery stores of thirty years ago seem almost puny. Enormous one-story buildings that are essentially big boxes, with even bigger parking lots, defy designers to create pedestrian-scale communities. The Reston and Miami Lakes town centers simply do without such stores—Big Boxes, as they're called by one designer. It could be argued that the Big Boxes should be relegated to some other place, such as the roadside strip (their usual habitat) or a warehouse zone, as Anton Nelessen suggests. In certain instances, however, it may be possible to make large, single-story retail buildings mesh successfully with neighboring small-scale shops and streets.

Duany and Plater-Zyberk dealt with two Big Boxes when they developed designs for Avalon Park, a large planned community east of Orlando, Florida. Duany and Plater-Zyberk's designs call for a supermarket and a drug store, each of them covering 50,000 square feet, to be located in an Avalon Park town center. Their design proposal would allow each of the large one-story buildings to have only a small proportion of its parking in the front. Most of the parking would be in parking lots behind the stores, in the interior of the blocks. The interior parking lots would be surrounded on most sides by traditional, small-scale buildings at least two stories high. These buildings, with offices and apartments in their upper floors, would give the parking lot attractive, spatially defined edges, making the parking lots more pleasant. Rows of trees in the parking lots would further improve the parking lots' character. The traditional, pedestrian-scale buildings would link up to the sides of the supermarket and drug store. If this plan is realized, Avalon Park's commercial center would be walkable despite the presence of a pair of Big Boxes. The supermarket and drug store would, of course, occupy locations that are easy for motorists to see from major roads—a seemingly nonnegotiable requirement of retail chains.

Duany and Plater-Zyberk devised a similar answer to the question of how to fit a regional shopping mall into a walkable town center. They agreed to place the mall within sight of a major intersection, as conventional practice dictates. Between the mall and the road would be acres of parking, which mall developers insist upon. However, Duany and Plater-Zyberk laid out the proposed complex so that it could evolve over the years into a more dense and walkable development. Parking garages and additional buildings are envisioned as eventually replacing surface parking lots; when that happens, the driving areas would take on

At Avalon Park in Florida, Duany and Plater-Zyberk envision a large supermarket and a large drugstore (the bulky flat-roofed structures) being joined by traditional buildings of more than one story, which would wrap around parking areas planted with rows of trees.

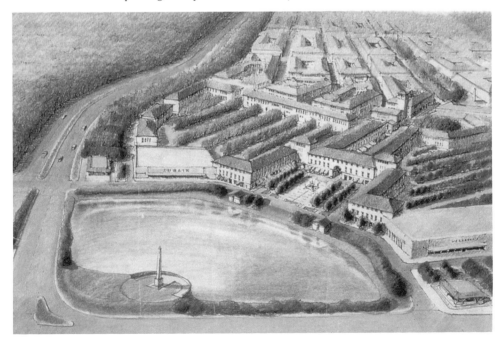

the character of traditional streets. On a side of the mall away from large parking areas and major roads, Duany and Plater-Zyberk would create a more traditional pedestrian-oriented town center. Offices, stores, apartments, and civic structures, all occupying buildings more than one story high, would face sidewalks and narrow streets. The mall entrance itself or one of its department stores might open directly onto the town streets or town squares. These streets would connect the mall to the surrounding community. To state it another way, the traditional streets and buildings would make the mall part of a multipurpose town center. It would not be an island unto itself.

In this Avalon Park proposal by Duany and Plater-Zyberk, a suburban shopping mall would merge into a pedestrian-oriented town center. Most parking would face a major road.

Only the naive would expect national developers and chain retailers to embrace such changes without first sending up howls of protest. In most big businesses there is a fixed way of organizing a building. "If you ask retailers for pedestrian access from the rear, you screw up their templates," says Peter Calthorpe. "They say, 'This is our loading area. We've got semis coming through here. It's dangerous to have pedestrians or access to the neighborhood behind the store.'" Some of these objections can be overcome through skillful designs, and a period of adjustment and

experimentation may be needed. But it would be a mistake to assume that most businesses cannot operate in buildings arranged in a more pedestrian-oriented manner. Plater-Zyberk tells of the resistance a national mall developer once raised to the idea of laying out the mall so that an anchor store would face a town square instead of facing a big road and a parking lot. The mall developer was sure that such a major change of orientation would be unacceptable to the department stores that the developer wanted to attract. The developer resisted and resisted. And then it turned out that to the developer's surprise, Saks Fifth Avenue indicated it would actually *prefer* to have its store face the town square. The mall, which was to have been built at Kentlands, ultimately was cancelled because of other factors. The jousting over its design indicates, nonetheless, that there may be more opportunity for altering suburban design than conventional developers are willing to admit.

Difficult community design problems are presented by much of the light industrial and office employment that has been arriving in the suburbs. Manufacturing, data processing, and other business operations have gravitated in recent years toward single-story buildings, often on the region's periphery. At least in the short run, one-story buildings are likely to continue proliferating because they are cheap to construct and the land they occupy is inexpensive. What's cheap for an industry's owners, however, is often expensive and inconvenient for the workers. These low, outlying buildings tend to be isolated from mass transit, with the result that workers (many of them women who are paid low to middling wages) must spend much of their limited income on automobiles.

Calthorpe argues that buildings of this sort should be gathered more closely together, in well-chosen locations, so that mass transit can reach them. Workplaces could be built within walking distance of child care, other services, retailing, and housing. Calthorpe calls his approach transit-oriented design. He urges that a series of pockets of development be built along mass transit lines, preferably commuter rail, making it easy to travel from one such center to another with no waste of resources. Some skeptics wonder whether the companies that have been seeking cheap outlying sites for their facilities will be amenable to settling in compact districts, where the land, theoretically, would be more expensive. Calthorpe believes land cost is not a serious deterrent. Land in a newly developing town center, he says, is relatively

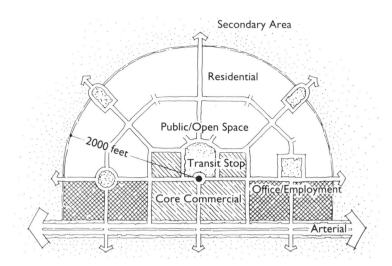

Peter Calthorpe's plan for transit-oriented development places retailing, services, office employment, community facilities, and some dense housing near a mass transit stop. From the transit stop it would be about a ten-minute walk to a secondary area of residential neighborhoods.

inexpensive. Furthermore, Calthorpe says, "most companies are not miserly and just looking for cheap land. Companies are looking for subregions where the housing stock matches the salaries they pay." If a community contains housing that the companies' employees can afford, that is a major attraction for employers, Calthorpe says.

The closest Calthorpe has come to bringing transit-oriented design to fruition is Laguna West, under construction on a thousand acres of former grazing land in the Sacramento area. The developer of Laguna West, Phil Angelides, is encouraging light industry to locate within a short distance of the 120-acre mixed-use town center. Apple Computer Corporation, which has been disturbed by the exorbitant housing costs of the San Francisco Bay area, where the company got its start, has so far built three 150,000-square-foot plants at Laguna West. Other companies are expected to follow suit. Grouping the light industry along the main road through Laguna West, not far from the town center, should help workers to reach transportation, eating places, shopping, child care, and other services. Many of the plant sites are within walking distance of the town center. At this writing the town center has a Town Square Park, a "village green" containing recreation and child care facilities, and a "town hall," which contains offices of community associations, a theater, class-rooms, and a part-time public library. Additional plans for the town center call for stores to be built facing the sidewalks of narrow Laguna Main Street and for construction of offices, 300 townhouses, and approximately 1,500 apartments. Beyond the town center are lower-density "secondary areas"—residential areas where approximately 1,800 detached houses are being built. Streets radiating outward from the town center will make it fairly easy for residents of those single-family areas to reach the services and amenities in the center.

A circular street in front of the town hall will be a hub for bus routes. Already an express bus runs from the town hall to down-town Sacramento. The Sacramento area has an expanding light-rail commuter system. It appears that commuter rail will not pass directly through Laguna West, but one line may pass within about a half-mile of the town center. Calthorpe believes well-timed feeder buses between the town center and the commuter rail station can give Laguna West residents convenient access to the light-rail system.

The town hall in an early stage of Laguna West's construction.

"I think what we've developed here," says Angelides, "is a place that will be transit-adaptable over time. Maybe 2 percent

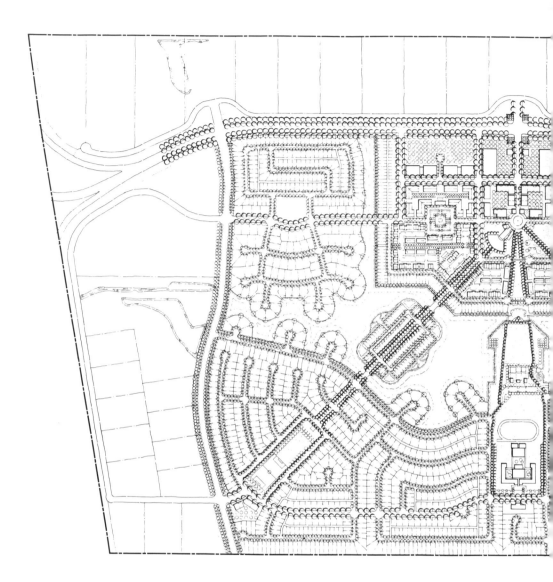

will use transit at first, then 5 percent, then more. In twenty to thirty years people are going to pay $3 to $4 a gallon for gasoline." When that time comes, he believes, people who work or live in Laguna West will be better prepared than people elsewhere.

Among those who want to reshape the suburbs, views differ on whether to accept the kinds of buildings that business has grown accustomed to or whether to insist on major changes. Calthorpe

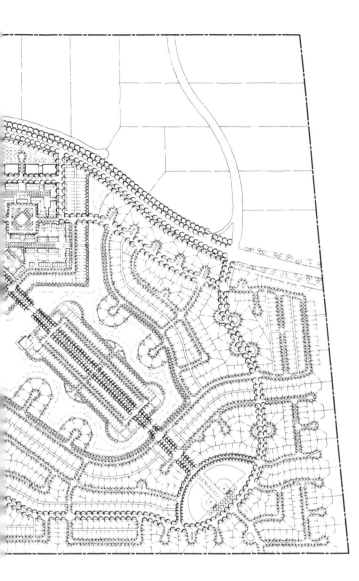

Plan of Laguna West. Streets radiate outward to connect the town center to lower-density residential neighborhoods.

believes that if American business insists on horizontal, large-square-footage industrial and office buildings, it's often futile to refuse them. He directs his efforts less toward redesigning such buildings than toward placing them where they will be close to mass transit and to walkable, diverse town centers. By contrast, Duany and Plater-Zyberk talk about the need to reject many conventional buildings and insist on smaller-scale buildings like those found in old cities and towns. Despite their occasional attempts to fit large supermarkets and shopping malls into traditional town layouts, the Miami architect-planners chiefly argue that businesses should use smaller buildings, which for centuries have composed walkable, varied, and attractive communities. The ideal Duany and Plater-Zyberk suburb would have most of its employment located in small buildings perhaps three stories high, facing tree-lined sidewalks and relatively narrow streets.

Some critics maintain that Duany and Plater-Zyberk's stance fails to come to grips with current economic realities, which favor big, horizontal buildings with extensive parking lots. McClendon of *Planning* magazine argues that Americans have shifted their buying from the corner store to the warehouse supermarket and from the little downtown dress shop to the megamall because in these large, automobile-accessible buildings they have found "vast selections of merchandise at lower prices—retail goals that are difficult to achieve in nineteenth-century retail buildings." In this view, economic realities brought about the Big Box and the commercial strip, and economic realities will prevent Americans from re-creating many of the compact business districts of yesteryear.

While economic forces indeed loom large, I would be wary of accepting the notion that the prevailing building patterns inevitably make economic sense and cannot be substantially altered. The fact that business has gravitated to particular sizes, shapes, and locations of buildings does not guarantee that those characteristics are either necessary or permanent. One need only look at suburban office construction to see how dubious common building formulas can be. Much suburban office construction has taken the form of large horizontal buildings. From this it is inferred that large horizontal buildings, with great numbers of workers all stationed on a single level, are the most efficient layouts for modern offices. But upon closer inspection, a large, open, horizontal layout does not seem to be essential at all. Many of the big businesses for which uninterrupted horizontal office space would seem to make the most sense are shrinking. The proportion of the American workforce employed by businesses with hundreds or thousands of employees has been falling. Just compare IBM's current employment with its employment ten years ago. The truth is, most American businesses are small, with fewer than twenty employees, and small businesses are now believed to the best long-term hope for expanding the American workforce. Small businesses do not require big, horizontal office buildings. Quite the contrary, anyone who visits suburban office buildings containing large floor areas will discover that to accommodate small firms (or to accommodate big firms that are organized into small departments), the big open interiors have more often than not been carved into a warren of many separate small offices.

A second example of how prevailing development practices can be out of touch with rational business needs is the vogue for building monolithic corporate headquarters on remote suburban or rural tracts. Some large headquarters buildings on isolated sites have turned almost overnight into corporate dinosaurs. In 1980 the Union Carbide Corporation erected a huge headquarters building on a hundred acres of woodland near Danbury, Connecticut. Within four years the company suffered the first of a series of major setbacks. As a result Union Carbide cut its workforce drastically. This left it with much more office space than it needed. But what company would want to share Union Carbide's isolated building? Burdened by the expensive empty space, the company invited outside tenants to occupy 30 percent of its gargantuan headquarters-in-the-woods. As of the end of 1992, not a single tenant had taken up the company's offer.

In the same spirit as Union Carbide, the American Can Company built a big headquarters in woodland in Greenwich, Connecticut, and occupied it in 1970. By the early 1980s the building no longer matched the needs of the company, which had decided to focus on different kinds of business and had changed its name to Primerica Corporation. The company moved out in 1984. As of the end of 1992 the complex still had not attracted a single tenant.

The *New York Times* reported that the suburban landscape of Fairfield County, Connecticut, "has become home to hundreds of vacant executive offices that analysts say are among the worst white elephants of American business." Experts cited "bad judgments in the design and location of the offices" for making it difficult to attract new tenants. The companies that commissioned these buildings were some of the most successful businesses in the nation; yet they failed miserably in selecting buildings and locations that would stand the test of time. So one should be careful about concluding that what business builds is what business actually needs. Businesses, like individuals, get caught up in fashions that turn out to be astonishingly shortsighted.

Wisdom sometimes demands that designers, planners, and the public resist prevailing development practices. It may be in the community's interest—and possibly in the interests of the affected businesses as well—to prod businesses to build in a more traditional manner. Florida planner Daniel M. Cary says some businesses could reap the benefit of enhanced flexibility if, say, they constructed several small buildings close to one another in a traditional town rather than constructing one big building off by itself. "You might have to spend a little more on construction," he concedes, "but you have the flexibility to lease out the space you don't need to other companies." Stores and services can be interspersed among small buildings more successfully than they can be made part of a single large building. In some instances, Cary says, housing can also be part of the mix. The result would be more interesting and convenient surroundings for the employees and for the community as a whole. If the surroundings are humanly satisfying, they may help the company retain valuable employees.

Princeton Forrestal Village on the outskirts of Princeton, New Jersey, is an attractive shopping place but lacks housing close by. One observer calls it "a town center without a town."

One model that Cary thinks is relevant to current business needs is a traditional campus plan in which a series of buildings are organized around a pleasant open area. Cary thinks the argument in favor of big, uninterrupted floor areas in office buildings

is weak, even for large corporations. "It's no better to have all your company's lawyers in 50,000 square feet on one floor than to have them in six buildings around a courtyard," Cary says. "They wouldn't necessarily have to walk any farther." The flexibility of groups of small buildings could be tremendously helpful in the long run. He observes: "IBM in Boca Raton is in one giant structure. They will live to regret the fact that they did this in one building."

Retailing, in many respects, is a tougher problem than employment. Developments like the Reston and Miami Lakes town centers consist of only a few blocks after years of planning and preparation. Elsewhere other attempts have been made to re-create business districts like those of the traditional small town; the conversion of a strip shopping center in Mashpee, Massachusetts, into a pedestrian-oriented multipurpose center is a good example. Off of U.S. 1 just north of Princeton, New Jersey, Sasaki Associates planned an interesting little center called Princeton Forrestal Village, where the stores are organized around streets rather than an internal mall. It has encountered economic problems, partly perhaps because it lacks a natural market; no one lives close by, and any customers must drive to it. Unlike the Reston and Miami Lakes town centers, there is no housing in the vicinity. Samuel M. Hamill, Jr., a New Jersey regional planner, calls Princeton Forrestal Village "a town center without a town."

"Retailing is the most intractable problem at this point," says Anne Tate, a Cambridge architect and professor at the Rhode Island School of Design. "Retailing is going into ever-bigger elements that nobody wants in their downtown but that everybody wants because of their discount prices." As this happens, most old downtowns and town centers in the United States are losing their vitality, and the competition faced by neighborhood-oriented merchants has become severe. Yet most people sense that with the decline of downtowns and neighborhood merchants, important sources of community life are lost. Harbor Town developer Henry Turley eloquently describes the delights of growing up forty years ago in a Memphis neighborhood that contained shops within walking distance of home. Here is what Turley says about the intersection of Bellevue and Lamar:

> A wondrous collection of stores was there: a hardware store;
> a bakery; a coffee shop; even a 5 & 10-cent store (imagine

that); and more—everything strange and exciting for a kid of six.

There were two drug stores crammed with delights like ice cream sodas. But they weren't within my economic reach. I could only look at them, as I did—furtively—the girlie magazines. The druggist, Dr. Garner, was given to calling my mother. "Henry's down here looking at those books again; what shall I do?"

"Send him right home . . . and watch him across that busy street; he's sure to be killed."

So right there in my neighborhood there seemed to be everything—a hint of all of life's possibilities mixed in with all kinds of people. And it was within walking distance. It was small—just my size—and they even knew my name.

That's what a neighborhood does, it seems to me. It takes the world—or at least a slice of the world—the more complete and varied the better, and makes it just our size—where our lives, with our neighbors, can be rich and meaningful and significant—where they know our names.

Turley describes a world that is increasingly foreign to today's Americans. It was a world with many humane, intimate connections that the force of economics has since snapped apart. It will not be easy to re-create communities in which such qualities abound. But it is well worth searching for ways to do so.

To conclude this chapter, let's turn to one other element of the suburban landscape—the roadside commercial strip. Commercial strips are some of the busiest places in any metropolitan area. They are also some of the most frustrating. As conduits of regional traffic, they perform poorly. Motorists who are trying to cover distance share the road uncomfortably with motorists interested in stopping at retail enterprises along the way. Vehicles entering and leaving the roadside commercial establishments slow down the through traffic unpredictably, causing congestion, annoyance, and accidents. As a place of travel, the roadside strip is inept.

In its other role, as a place of business, the roadside strip is equally awkward. Thrust upon each business is the job of attracting people who are in motion. No matter how restrained and tasteful a business might wish to be, it has to grab attention if it is to survive in such a ferocious setting. For every business that finds an agreeable way to make its presence known, many more resort to hackneyed or ugly means of achieving this end. Being almost wholly dependent on customers in private vehicles, businesses must invest heavily in land, which they proceed to pave over and paint stripes upon; business owners who think land is meant for higher purposes than parking are destined for insolvency should they act on such a conviction. A "rational" business buys much more land than is needed for its building and then covers most of the earth with asphalt.

On a roadside strip, sharing of parking by businesses with different peak hours is usually impractical, since most roadside buildings must be freestanding structures, widely dispersed. Customers go to the roadside strip because it contains the goods and services they want, but this is not to say they are happy about being there. To obtain goods and services, they must endure monotonous (or worse) surroundings as they drive from one enterprise to another. One-stop shopping on the strip is conspired against by its very dispersal. Rarely is the strip a place where a person simply enjoys the surroundings. Gardens, parks, and civic monuments are alien to the fume-laden corridor of commerce.

Jonathan Barnett blames the prolific development of roadside commercial strips partly on local governments' zoning, which has permitted low-density retailing to spread out along the roads. He argues that governments should make it their policy to discourage continuous strip development and to encourage business development in centers. Richard K. Untermann, a professor of landscape architecture at the University of Washington, has outlined how this might be carried out along one suburban road—Highway 99 north of Seattle. Untermann says most retail activity along Highway 99 should be "concentrated into several nodes called suburban centers—mixed-use places with shopping, work and housing all intertwined." The smallest center might occupy one corner of an intersection along the highway. The largest might occupy all four corners.

A network of sidewalks and streets leading from the center to residential neighborhoods would make it feasible for people to walk or bike between their homes and the closest center. Transportation shuttle systems could circulate between the center and the surrounding residential area, as is already done in some localities. In the suburban center, buses and other high-occupancy vehicles would stop to pick up or let off passengers. Ideally, Untermann says, the bus-stop areas would be "active, pleasant places offering such amenities as coffee vendors, newspaper stands, sundries, post office, dry cleaners, cash machine, and day care." Covered areas would be essential to protect pedestrians from rain, especially while waiting for transportation. Buildings in the suburban centers might have retailing on the ground floor and offices or apartments above. Parking lots would be kept small so that the entire center can be traversed on foot.

On Highway 99, Untermann says, the number of through lanes would narrow in the suburban centers, making room for on-street parking (perhaps diagonal parking). With fewer lanes of through traffic, the road would pose less of a threat to pedestrians. Stores in the suburban centers might face the highway, but if traffic is too heavy, an alternative is to have them face the calmer side streets. Essential services that pedestrians can use, such as grocery and drug stores, would be favored in the planning. Primarily automobile-oriented businesses, such as gas stations and repair shops, would be discouraged. Drive-through operations, such as fast-food restaurant take-out windows that are geared to customers in vehicles, would be prohibited in centers; they endanger pedestrians and make the area inconvenient for carrying out errands on foot.

Once much of the retailing that residents need on a regular basis is concentrated in walkable, mass-transit-oriented suburban centers, the rest of the highway would be able to carry vehicular traffic more smoothly. To help the highway perform better, Untermann believes governments must rezone much of the strip. Land along the road now zoned for strip-commercial development might be shifted to apartments and offices, which generate less traffic. Ideally, automobiles would enter and leave the apartments and offices via side streets or rear streets. The fewer the driveways that connect directly to the highway, the more relaxing and efficient it would be to travel the highway.

Some retail businesses that rely on access by automobile may profit from being clustered with others in related lines of trade. Spread out along part of Highway 99, Untermann notes, are a lumber company, a home improvement center, a plumbing shop, and several other do-it-yourself stores. They might function more effectively if they were gathered together, so that they were not only accessible to motor vehicles but also linked together by connecting streets and walkways, he says. The principle of clustering might be applied in many categories of retailing.

Changes of this sort require a public vision of what our communities should be. They necessitate greater coordination than has been common in American suburbs. Government, in particular, will have to approach its responsibilities differently. The following chapter looks in more detail at what government might do to pursue the vision I have been laying out.

EIGHT

What

Government

Can Do

D r. Thomas Scullen is superintendent of the Indian Prairie School District in Naperville and Aurora, Illinois. His district, approximately thirty-five miles west of Chicago's Loop, illustrates some of the practices that increasingly influence suburban planning decisions. In Dr. Scullen's forty-six-square-mile district, planning and zoning often is done with an eye to how it will affect local government and school finances. Public officials aim to approve developments that generate more in property taxes than they cost in public services. They try to discourage developments that may drain the public treasury. Among planners this practice is called fiscal zoning.

Dr. Scullen keeps a close watch on development being planned in Naperville and Aurora. He can describe the financial characteristics of every kind of development that's likely to be proposed in the district. Dr. Scullen says that apartments and townhouses with few bedrooms are a financial plus for the school district. The reason: They harbor few children. For Indian Prairie, which is trying to cope with rapid recent growth in school enrollment, this makes small apartments and small townhouses acceptable.

Mention inexpensive detached houses, and Dr. Scullen explains that they are a financial drain—usually they contain children who at the beginning of September will show up at school expecting to be supplied with books, buses, teachers, classrooms, and much else that costs the taxpayers money. Inexpensive detached houses will not generate enough property taxes to cover the expense of educating the youngsters living in them, according to Dr. Scullen. So the school district frowns on this form of housing. "Proposals for inexpensive single-family houses have been turned down by zoning in Naperville and Aurora," the superintendent observed. "If you build $65,000 to $75,000 houses, there are lots of kids, and the rest of the people pay the costs."

"What the governments have tried to do is get bigger lot sizes," Dr. Scullen said. "If you get bigger lots, the housing will be more expensive." Large, high-priced houses generate substantial tax revenues; equally important according to Dr. Scullen, they tend to contain few school-age children. Many couples who can afford very expensive houses are past the age of having children in elementary or secondary school. From the school district's perspective, this is a delectable demographic fact.

A few years ago Harold Moser, a longtime Naperville developer, proposed building a golf-course subdivision called White Eagle Club, where houses aimed at the business and professional elite would start at about $300,000, and some would sell for more than a million dollars. "We're absolutely not going to object to those," Dr. Scullen said. The superintendent noted that in addition to generating large tax revenues, "it's unlikely they'll have kids." Everyone knows, of course, about the best-laid plans of mice and men. White Eagle failed to live up to expectations— either the expectations of the developer or those of the school district. Moser's expensive house-lots sold slowly; in real estate circles, the development picked up the mocking nickname "White Elephant." And the development did not attract as many people in their forties, fifties, and sixties as the school district had expected. Heads of households in White Eagle turned out to have a relatively youthful average age of thirty-nine, placing them in the prime child-rearing years. Consequently White Eagle became home to many more children than the school district had hoped. White Eagle is a reminder that school districts and municipal governments sometimes calculate the effects of development incorrectly. But such failures do not deter them from trying to predict the impact of developments on public finances and to use those calculations to guide planning and zoning decisions. Quite the contrary. Indian Prairie goes on aggressively pursuing its concern about land-use decisions. The school district often discusses development with Naperville and Aurora public officials and lets the municipal officials know that if they make decisions that enlarge the school-age population without generating enough revenue, the school district will be forced to raise taxes. "We want everybody to know there's going to be a tax increase," Dr. Scullen said, "and know who's responsible for it."

Residential development is just one element in fiscal zoning.

Many suburbs in recent years have welcomed lavish houses like this one in the Chicago area. Housing for low- to moderate-income families has, by contrast, often encountered resistance or apathy from local governments.

Nonresidential development is another—planned for with at least equal and frequently even greater zeal. Increasingly suburbs vie with one another and with the central cities for office parks, shopping malls, light industrial facilities, and research and development complexes—clean, tax-generating nonresidential projects of many kinds. Naperville over the years has attracted numerous business facilities, including an Amoco research and development complex, a big AT&T research center, and many office parks. Dr. Scullen would like more of them. "You have to be very careful that you don't become a bedroom community because it will be very expensive for residents," he said. "If we can get enough commercial development, we get a tax base and we're much further ahead."

This is not to say that local governments are truly in charge of the quantity and quality of development that comes their way. In actuality, there are great economic and social forces that do much to shape development and influence its location—forces that a local government usually can affect only to a limited degree. The Naperville area is affluent enough to attract $300,000-and-up houses laid out along a golf course, but a blue-collar suburb would rarely get such lavish housing, no matter how skillfully it courted developers. Developers do not build top-of-the-line subdivisions in working-class areas. Nor do corporate headquarters complexes often arrive in towns at which the executives look askance. Decisions about what sort of development occurs in a community revolve more around market conditions (such as the wealth and social status of the locality) and regional transportation networks than around the policies and inducements of the local government.

Nonetheless, suburbs do compete, and often compete fiercely, to enhance their financial situation. Within the limits set by the market, geography, and transportation, they try to attract revenue-generating developments that might otherwise go to some other town. Combating this trend are a number of suburbs that encourage affordable housing. In Massachusetts more than half the municipalities have voluntarily formed "housing partnerships" that combine private initiative, state funds and authority, and local regulatory power to produce housing for people who would otherwise be shut out of the local market. But across the nation there are many more suburbs that, as Philip B. Herr observes, "don't really think about the housing cost or social class consequences of their actions but rather just regulate themselves so as to have new things not too different from old things, or so as to protect physical character or to avoid too-rapid growth or to avoid water-quality deterioration." Herr, a planning consultant in Newton, Massachusetts, says these municipalities' inattentiveness to the cost of housing and economic segregation "inadvertently limits the spectrum of households that can afford their housing. They are not intentionally mean; they simply don't think about it, which turns out to be mean."

In general, suburbs of above-average economic status succeed in capturing the region's most lucrative developments, while deflecting lower-income people to other municipalities. The competition among municipalities has grown so intense that some consider it a form of economic warfare—the affluent suburbs plucking economic assets that might once have settled in the cities, while refusing to accept the poorer people and less desirable development that have long been the cities' burden. Many people, including whole municipalities, come out losers. Inequities fester. The well-being of the metropolitan area as a whole is ignored. Mike Davis, in his caustic study of Los Angeles area development, writes that fiscal zoning "is often a municipal mini-imperialism by which 'have' communities aggressively redistribute resources from the 'have-nots.'" Ethan Seltzer of the Institute of Portland Metropolitan Studies takes a less denunciatory view of municipalities' intentions, yet he is equally critical of the results. "It's less a calculated approach of outdoing the

This is the kind of shopping environment usually created when suburbs lack a more demanding vision.

folks next door than of following a myopic strategy of what's good for the community," Seltzer says. "They don't start out trying to screw their neighbors. They *end up* screwing their neighbors." Even Dr. Scullen makes no claim that the policies pursued by Naperville, Aurora, and Indian Prairie are what's best for the Chicago area as a whole. "What's good for us," he said, "is not necessarily good for anyone else."

Ultimately, even an affluent suburb like Naperville is apt to reap a bitter harvest. No matter how independently Naperville may behave, it is tied to the social and economic health of the region. As economic vitality and social well-being wane in some of the older, lower-status municipalities in the Chicago area, a multitude of problems will likely worsen, making the region as a whole less livable. Balkanized government and land-use planning have the potential to damage the entire metropolis.

Municipalities caught up in fiscal zoning easily lose sight of the qualities that make a community a satisfying place to live and work. In excluding modest-priced housing, they make it difficult for police officers, firefighters, young teachers, and many other valuable members of the community to live there. They reduce the diversity upon which healthy communities are built. Suburbs heavily driven by the search for revenue have a hard time shaping themselves well. They welcome regional malls in developers' dull, formulaic arrangements, surrounded by mammoth parking lots and unconnected to residential neighborhoods except by automobile because the developer can always take his project to another town that's not so picky. They agree to office developments designed as conventional developers are accustomed to building them—unconnected to retailing, housing, and services. They agree to segregated forms of development, in part because they are focusing on financial benefits, not on whether the development is good in itself. A municipality fervently engaged in financial self-improvement doesn't have the luxury of asking itself a crucial question: What kind of development would make this community as satisfying as possible?

Herr tells of Bellingham, Massachusetts, an outer suburb of Boston, where Wal-Mart was interested in opening one of its big discount stores. The proposal made by the developer of the Wal-Mart site "was contrary to the letter and the spirit of local planning law," Herr said. The developer wanted to build an enormous parking area, twice as big as what the town's guidelines suggested was necessary. The developer wanted to put all of the parking in front of the store, contrary to a town planning policy that called for making parking areas visually unobtrusive. The developer skimped on tree-planting and objected to installing a sidewalk that would enable people to walk to the store from a nearby subdivision. The proposal fell well short of some of the planning standards that Bellingham had adopted as community goals. But the town, hungry for revenue, gave in to much of what the developer proposed. "The word came down," Herr said. "They wanted the taxes."

Communities caught up in the fiscal struggle can become blind to their true potential. Naperville allows new developments to adopt conventional, segregated, unwalkable layouts, even though every public official in town is familiar with an old section of Naperville that would make a superior model for new building. The old center of Naperville contains a pleasant downtown in which the buildings date as far back as the 1870s. Along a skewed grid of streets, most of them narrow enough for a person on foot to cross easily, are a sociable mixture of enterprises. Interspersed among the stores, many of them locally owned, are gathering places like the American Legion hall. A furniture factory covering two blocks of the downtown has been converted into luxury apartments, offices, and shops, making it possible for people to live and work downtown. Houses on pleasant tree-lined streets lie just beyond the business district. There is a station where commuters can board trains bound for downtown Chicago. Recreation and refreshment are integrated into the downtown environment; at one edge of the downtown is beautiful Central Park, where people listen to summer concerts in the amphitheater. Near it is the Riverwalk, built a dozen years ago almost entirely by volunteers; there people rent paddleboats and explore the DuPage River. The park, the Riverwalk, and the downtown collectively are Naperville's centerpiece. Real estate agents and corporate recruiters, recognizing its magnetic quality, love to show this part of Naperville to prospects from out of town.

Yet while downtown Naperville and its environs are frequently touted for their charm and amenity, they are treated if they were irrelevant to Naperville's planning needs. The impression given is that they are a kind of Disneyland on the DuPage—a place for an occasional escape. But in fact the downtown area could be much more than that—a living, functioning model of how to organize centers and mixed-use development in Naperville's newer areas. The traits that make downtown appealing could make new portions of Naperville more convenient, attractive, and distinctive. Naperville's municipal government has not been without accomplishments; it has limited strip development, and it has attempted to concentrate new retailing in clusters. But there is little mixture of uses and activities. Houses in the new parts of town are largely isolated from shopping, employment, transit, and gathering places. Naperville's new areas seem disjointed when

Pumpkin fields give way to subdivisions in Apple Valley, Minnesota.

compared to the old center of town. Local officials for the most part accept conventional development.

Few suburbs, when totally free to chart their own course, plan their development adequately. They lack the will or the capacity to do so. Suburban governments are typically small-time operations with limited staff and expertise. Especially at the outer edge of the metropolitan area, where decisions critical to the region's future are being made, local governments rarely have officials and staff members with a sophisticated long-range vision or with the experience to plan and negotiate well on large-scale development. Quite a few emerging suburbs are reluctant to surrender a semirural image of themselves; they are psychologically unprepared to develop an effective view of what they might become, as opposed to what they have been. They may, of course, have fragments of a vision. They may know, for instance, that they want their parking lots landscaped and their commercial thoroughfares free of billboards and flashing lights. But they rarely have a clear overall vision of what the community should be.

The weakness of suburbs is demonstrated by their caving in to pressure from real estate interests that challenge municipal decisions. Urban design consultant Jonathan Barnett says suburban governments are terrified of being sued by well-financed private interests. "The typical town government has as its counsel a lo-

cal attorney who works as a part-time consultant to the town," he says. The town attorney has to go up against a specialized law firm hired by a developer with deep pockets. "It's an uneven contest," Barnett says. Litigation can go on inconclusively for long periods of time; it becomes a contest less over the merits of the case than over who has the financial resources to persist longer. "Most of the big developers just keep the meter ticking," Barnett says. When a well-financed developer demands that a municipality back down from planning and zoning decisions, the odds are that the developer will win, even when his demands are neither legally well founded nor good for the community. The mere threat of a lawsuit is often enough to undo whatever strong planning the municipality has undertaken.

Local "independence" has often been extolled as an important principle of American government. But as fiscal zoning increases and as metropolitan development penetrates farther into the countryside, it becomes clear that local autonomy too often creates small, weak players incapable of producing well-planned, well-designed suburbs and unable to resist manipulation by real estate operators. The emerging suburb is nearly always unprepared to plan its long-range future. As suburban growth has exploded in recent years, the consequences have worsened. The great urban areas are undergoing a destructive fragmentation whose scale dwarfs the divisions of the past.

How might we begin to remedy the situation?

Part of the answer lies in restraining municipalities from grabbing lucrative development at the expense of neighboring communities. An example of how local governments have been brought into a more cooperative arrangement is found in Minnesota. Seven counties and approximately 190 municipalities in the Minneapolis–St. Paul area share some of their property tax revenues with one another. Forty percent of the growth in the commercial and industrial property tax base is redistributed among the governments of the region, and has been each year since 1975. Revenue-sharing guarantees a degree of fairness for residents of poorer communities. It also increases the likelihood that development will take place where it makes the most sense for the people of the whole region, not where it represents a windfall for a particular municipality. "I think it has made places more selective about development," says Gene Knaff, a research economist at the Metropolitan Council of the Twin Cities Area, which oversees revenue-sharing. Regional sharing of tax revenues does not guarantee that municipalities will make wise planning decisions—there is no institutional substitute for exercising intelligence and moral vision—but it creates conditions in which wise planning has a better chance of advancing.

Another part of the answer is to have a higher level of government, such as a state or regional government, exercise more power over certain kinds of planning and development decisions. A regional or state government has the potential to see a broader picture and represent the overall society, bringing greater fairness and a more coherent pattern of regional development.

The state might set general goals and require that local or regional governments act to meet those goals. Oregon is an example. In the 1970s Oregonians concluded that if urbanization continued without limit, many of the state's farms and forests would be threatened. To prevent the loss of forest and agricultural land, the state took a number of actions. One was to require local communities to adopt comprehensive plans. Included in the comprehensive planning was an "urban growth boundary." Within the boundary, urban development would be accommodated. Beyond the boundary, urban development would be discouraged.

The Portland area adopted an urban growth boundary in 1980. Modified since then, it now encompasses 362 square miles. Inside the boundary is a large supply of land available for building. Outside the boundary, governments discourage building by zoning agricultural areas for farm use only, by insisting on lot sizes that preclude much residential development, and by instituting policies such as refusing road improvements and sewer service. To help conserve land and generate affordable housing throughout the region, all Portland area municipalities have been required to enact plans allowing half their new housing to be apartments, townhouses, or other multifamily construction. The growth boundary and other regulations have significantly reduced suburban sprawl. The average size of a single-family lot has dropped from 13,200 to 8,700 square feet. By raising residential density the region has obtained the capacity to build as many as 310,000 houses and apartments inside its growth boundary— nearly double the number that could have been accommodated under previous planning and zoning.

Oregon has not done away with municipal governments. But the state has encouraged the emergence of a metropolitan government with the capacity to guide regional development and

The urban growth boundary of metropolitan Portland, Oregon, preserves farmland against encroaching suburban development.

encourage municipalities to live up to their regional responsibilities. Voters in the Portland area formed Metro, a regional government covering parts of three counties. The effectiveness of Metro has been enhanced by having its executive officer and legislators directly elected by the people.

As Portlanders have gotten accustomed to thinking in regional terms, they have gone beyond the initial goals of farm and forest preservation and have begun discussing additional objectives. They have started to think about how transportation systems can be better coordinated with residential, employment, and commercial growth, so that the region can maintain its good qualities—such as easy access to Portland's central city, one of the nation's healthiest downtowns. Thinking in the Portland area is moving in the direction of nurturing a number of large mixed-use centers containing offices, stores, housing, and parks. A series of dense, walkable developments connected to public transit would broaden suburbanites' choices of how to get around, Ethan Seltzer says. They would give people greater choices of environments to live in, work in, and turn to for recreation, culture, and leisure. Many jobs would be in locations accessible to suburbanites and city dwellers alike. Countryside would remain within reach of everyone, since suburban sprawl would be limited.

Oregon is further along than any other state in attempting to reform patterns of metropolitan development. About ten states, including Vermont, New Jersey, Florida, and Washington, have been trying various means of making metropolitan growth more orderly, cost-efficient, and compact. Florida has experimented with regional planning councils, which oversee "developments of regional impact"—developments that affect localities beyond the one in which they are located. In the New York area the Regional Plan Association, a voluntary organization, has been drawing up a program for the outward-spinning region, which spreads into three states, thirty-one counties, and approximately 2,000 units of government.

Jonathan Barnett suggests that if municipalities adopt planning and zoning that satisfy state standards, the state should offer to defend or indemnify the municipality if it is sued. Such state support could stiffen the backbone of many an irresolute municipality; it might make it more difficult for real estate interests to manipulate local governments. In New Jersey the state provides incentives for responsible planning; state money is given to governments that adhere to policies worked out in a state planning effort. Robert D. Yaro of the Regional Plan Association says states could set minimum standards for developments that affect the region. States, Yaro says, could control development at major highway interchanges and encourage dense development around commuter rail stations.

To shape a metropolitan area intelligently, it is essential to understand the whole region's assets. Among the most important of these are the region's natural systems, such as rivers and streams, public water supply watersheds, and agricultural valleys. Significant natural areas should be identified and preserved from development; networks of open space must be permanently set aside for public recreation and refreshment. The more land the metropolitan area covers, the more important it is to establish a network of natural or scenic areas—places where people can still experience the natural world and its beauty. State or regional action is a key to accomplishing this.

Along with identifying and protecting natural systems, efforts should be made to understand the region's infrastructure and its implications for future growth. The locations and capabilities of roads, rails, water lines, sewer lines, and other infrastructure will, in conjunction with natural systems, indicate where development should be accommodated and where it should be avoided. Highways, railroads, sewer lines, and the rest are extremely costly; the region's residents will be better off if construction of unnecessary, redundant new systems is avoided and if existing systems are put to good use, not wasted.

"There are classes of decisions that absolutely should be made at the regional level," says Herr. "Oregon illustrates these very well. They include the urban growth pattern, non-extension of infrastructure, and the idea of requiring minimum densities for development, rather than only establishing limits on maximum density and allowing development to be sparsely distributed."

But there is also—at least potentially—a less desirable side to placing decision-making power at higher levels of government. One of the dangers of regional, state, or federal control, Herr says, is that in such big governments there is an increase in the influence of specialists—administrators and experts who concentrate solely on transportation or the quality of the water supply or some other single topic across a broad range of communities, often at the expense of the overall well-being of individual communities. Community planning has suffered greatly from specialists and the rigid standards they impose. For instance, Herr says, regional, state, or federal concern over water quality has, in some locales, limited development to one dwelling per acre, "regardless of local preference and regardless of whether meeting that rule utterly precludes meeting other such sound planning intentions as avoiding sprawl." Experts on water quality have not concerned themselves with how their rules affect the community on balance. "Similarly," Herr says, "standards adopted for new streets too often are adopted to accommodate cars, snow plows, and trash trucks and consider little how well the standards serve pedestrians, bicyclists, or those who live in the social and visual environment created by such streets."

To the extent that regional approaches favor the rise of single-topic administrators and uncompromising, narrowly focused rules, good community planning is endangered. Herr points to Cape Cod, with its crowded and much loved old communities, as an example of how regional control threatens to produce some undesirable consequences, which could undermine the genuine benefits of regional management. The Cape Cod Commission was established in 1989 to oversee development in this increasingly suburbanized part of Massachusetts. Herr says that "despite the Commission's stated intention to promote compact village-centered development, under the Commission's rules new development like that which created Provincetown and other dense Cape Cod villages just isn't possible, not even in the areas contiguous to them."

Part of what's needed, Herr says, is a governmental structure that allows "place-responsive planning"—planning that takes into account the distinctive features of a community and allows communities to differ from one another. Often the regulations and requirements that come down from federal, state, and regional agencies make communities less distinctive; they make one town look and act just like hundreds of others. A better approach, Herr says, would entail "heightening rather than flattening the singularities that give the community a distinctive character and sense of place." That would imply imposing fewer rules with unyielding uniformity. Rather than requiring municipalities to meet uniform standards on water quality, air pollution, transportation, and other issues, an alternative would be to allow a municipality or a project to make trade-offs. Mediocre performance in one category would be allowed in return for outstanding achievement in another. A project or a municipality's performance might be judged on a point system; if the project scored high, let's say, on compactness and pedestrian access, it might be allowed to score below average on road capacity or water quality and still be approved. Some elements of this approach have been experimented with, to widespread praise, in Fort Collins, Colorado. A system of trade-offs that recognizes and encourages particular local virtues would indicate that something has been learned from America's older towns and neighborhoods. Old places often cannot meet many of today's government standards; yet in crucial respects they are often *superior* places to live. The penchant for uniform standards has had tragic effects on character in buildings, landscapes, and communities. We need to find more ways of allowing community distinctiveness to prevail.

It will take much effort to strike the right balance between regionalism and local power. Unfortunately, most local communities have not shown great wisdom when they have had opportunities to set standards on their own. Many municipalities, for example, have demanded that all new businesses provide parking on site. The result: freestanding buildings separated by parking lots, and a gradual disappearance of compact, traditional business districts. Many government standards become more stringent as years go by. Roads get wider lanes and broader shoulders. Requirements for off-street parking increase. And yet, in the face of higher and more expensive standards, the community becomes duller and less convenient. There is a connection here that has been too little examined. Governments at all levels need to evaluate the cumulative impact that their standards exert on the character of the community.

Municipal zoning needs to be overhauled. When most communities first adopted zoning, they had no idea that development would occur on the scale that it does today. In the early days of zoning, the 1920s, houses were built individually or a few at a time. Zoning was a method of dealing with small, incremental development. Now houses are built by the hundreds and in some places by the thousands. Hills and valleys in California are covered over in less time than it takes to declare a drought emergency. The quickening pace of development and its effect of making original zoning assumptions obsolete "sort of snuck up on people," Barnett says. In many communities, zoning has become a straitjacket that encourages monotonous collections of single-family houses here, equally monotonous apartments or townhouses there, and business and industry elsewhere. Zoning must be reformed so that it can foster the development of distinctive and well-rounded communities.

Barnett argues that the zoning code should contain an "environmental overlay." This overlay would prevent natural systems and distinctive landscapes from being mauled by development. The zoning code would specify that when a property has certain environmental characteristics, it can be built upon only at lower densities or subject to certain restrictions. In Barnett's judgment, wetlands or steep slopes should not be built upon at all. Building in mature woodlands should be restricted. It may be that such restrictions would spread development out. But a municipality could compensate by allowing higher densities in certain other areas, preferably areas that can eventually be served by mass transit. The result would be to save natural features—which were some of the most attractive attributes of suburbs in the first place—and to encourage town centers that could become crossroads for community life.

The current practice of zoning long stretches of highway frontage for commercial development should be brought under control. It has been sucking the vitality out of existing town centers, and its continuance will only make matters worse. Rather than spreading commercial development out mile after mile, communities should be concentrating more of it into centers. Anne Tate says one way to do this is to enact a zoning code that spurs certain kinds of buildings and activities to locate in town centers and does not allow them on the outskirts. For Norfolk, Massachusetts, Tate worked on a code that encourages small retail operations to open in the town center. Except for one grocery store that is allowed to occupy up to 30,000 square feet, no single use in the town center may occupy more than 8,000 square feet. Buildings must be taller than one story. Parking is mainly to be placed behind the buildings. "Uses that are good for a town center are prohibited by code from occupying highway sites," Tate says.

Sites that are to become town centers should not be chosen by developers, who often will choose land they happen to control rather than land in the most logical locations—close to a large population and able to be linked to mass transit. One of the chief defects of some of the otherwise admirable development plans drawn up by Andres Duany and Elizabeth Plater-Zyberk is that, in the absence of effective regional planning, the developers have sometimes chosen out-of-the-way land. "It is up to *communities* to choose the sites for town centers," Barnett says. A state or regional agency might review local decisions or set general goals; this may spur communities to make better decisions.

Some states, including California, authorize the municipality to draw up what's called a specific plan—a fairly detailed proposal on how to develop an area in which the municipal officials believe development should be strongly encouraged. The spe-

Rapid transit lines run through Shaker Square, a commercial center begun in 1929 to serve the Cleveland suburb of Shaker Heights. Transit adds to the center's vitality and makes for convenient commuting.

cific plan has the ability to show, in much greater detail than the usual planning and zoning document, the character that development should take. It may tell how tall the buildings will be, how the buildings will meet the street, what uses will be housed there, and so on. The specific plan lays out an urban design vision for the area. The properties covered by the plan need not be under a single ownership; they could belong to several owners who are to cooperate in bringing the plan to fruition.

For about a quarter-century, planners have shied away from developing a physical vision for communities. That is an additional reason for the accidental, uncoordinated look of commercial areas in the suburbs. Municipalities or regional or state governments need to pay greater attention to urban design. There needs to be a vision of how places will look and feel once development occurs.

Old communities are satisfying to walk or drive through in part because so many of the buildings face the streets and roads, making travelers feel they are *someplace,* not just in transit between destinations. Governments should try to infuse a sense of place into the roads along which residential subdivisions are planned. Instead of encouraging developers to build residential subdivisions with their backs to the arterial, why not encourage housing to be built *facing* the road? In old communities houses or apartment buildings often faced the crosstown roads, making those roads feel inhabited. Travelers felt they were in a community, not relegated to leftover space between subdivisions. If governments adopt a policy of building through roads at frequent intervals, traffic would distribute itself more evenly, and most of the through roads would not be unpleasant to live along. Construction of boulevards with trees and other landscaping in their median would create an attractive atmosphere on certain roads.

Where the traffic is so heavy that houses need to be placed more distant from the road, municipalities might encourage developers to use a design tactic that has been successful in portions of many old communities: Create a wide ribbon of grass and trees along the edge of the major road and then build a minor street with houses on its far side, facing the residential street, the landscape buffer, and the road. Roads built in this manner are enjoyable to travel. One of the county roads that passes through Kohler, Wisconsin, has a border of grass, shrubbery, flowers, and trees to one side. Beyond it lies a street with a row of houses and front lawns. This organization makes for a civilized driving experience. But developers will rarely build in this manner today unless they are encouraged or required to do so by governments; this is not an accepted part of modern development formulas. Even traditionalist developments like Kentlands do not address major roads on their perimeter as graciously as old communities often did. If we want transportation arteries—a major part of the public realm—to be inviting, local governments must take the initiative.

Because the building block of the community is the neighborhood, governments need to improve their attempts at creating balanced, satisfying neighborhoods. Duany and Plater-Zyberk have conceived five principles of neighborhood design that can serve as guide. The first principle is that the neighborhood have an identifiable neighborhood center and an identifiable edge. Second, the neighborhood should have a limited breadth, based on the distance a person can comfortably walk. Duany and Plater-Zyberk believe the ideal neighborhood has a quarter-mile radius, allowing a person to walk from the center to the edge in five minutes. Peter Calthorpe believes ten minutes is more realistic for today's development. Whatever figure is used, the neighborhood should be a place with a limited and walkable size. Third, there should be a mixture of uses and a mixture of different kinds of housing in close proximity to one another. Placing a hundred apartments next to two hundred detached houses will not suffice. There should be a much finer grain. Fourth, there should be a network of interconnected streets. Fifth, appropriate locations should be provided for "civic" buildings, by which the traditionalists mean schools, churches, post offices, meeting halls, day care centers, and other places where people gather, whether government-operated or not.

The five principles of neighborhood design have the potential to breathe new life into the ailing practice of suburban planning. A government that adheres to them will create neighborhoods where a greater number of daily needs can be fulfilled and where it is easier for people to develop ties with those living or working close by. Developers would no longer be granted free rein to create isolated subdivisions. New subdivisions would have to link their streets to the neighborhoods nearby. When new areas are developed, governments should insist that the additions compose complete neighborhoods, if not immediately, then as additional blocks are gradually added. Several neighborhoods together make up a town, which should have a town center.

This vision has a clear progression: The individual block is part of a complete neighborhood. The neighborhood is part of a well-balanced town. The town is part of the metropolitan region, which contains natural areas as well as man-made settings. As more places are built to these criteria and as the criteria themselves are further refined, the development of suburbs could begin to rise above the disappointing results of recent decades. This will no doubt be a long undertaking. It could also be an immensely rewarding one, for it involves nothing less than the creation of a satisfying human habitat.

NINE

**Repairing
the Existing
Suburbs**

Harvard professor Alex Krieger detects a habitual flaw in American efforts to improve the character of suburbs. Too often, Krieger says, designers and developers with strong ideas go out onto rural land and start all over again. They build brand-new developments on the metropolitan outskirts, hoping that the new communities will avoid the flaws of older places. The continual movement onto fresh land spreads out the population of the metropolitan area and diverts energy from the improvement of communities closer in. In some cases it hastens the older communities' decay. Krieger contends: "We need to change the pitch that a new development farther afield is always the answer. We shouldn't be going farther out, spreading out metropolitan development. We should work on existing urban areas. We should try to fill in and heighten the quality of the places that are already in existence."

Because the population of the United States is growing substantially, some new development at the metropolitan edge will continue to be necessary. But Krieger is right to draw attention to existing suburbs. They are where nearly half of America's population currently lives, and we should seize the potential for making them more satisfying. Suppose, then, that we accepted Kreiger's challenge and decided to "fill in and heighten the quality" of the existing suburbs. What would this entail?

To begin with, it would call for reinforcing old suburban downtowns, altering existing suburban shopping centers, and building new town centers in suburbs that lack them. Many old suburbs already have a downtown. Some of them were built during earlier suburban development. Others were the centers of outlying small towns that have since been brought within the orbit of an expanding metropolis. The old downtowns, eroded though

Carillon Point in Kirkland, Washington, contains two large office buildings, a hotel, shops, and eating places. Housing close by is part of the complex.

they may be, are places where future development ought to be encouraged. Some of these centers could become robust centers of business and community life.

To breathe vitality into an old center, a series of repairs and improvements may be necessary. Gaps in the streetscape may have to be filled with new buildings. Housing in the downtown or within walking distance may be needed to create a livelier atmosphere. Additional employment may be essential to provide downtown stores and restaurants with customers. Parking, pedestrian circulation, and transportation may have to be modified. A suburban downtown cannot be revived overnight, but over the long haul it's possible for it to improve greatly, even to the point of becoming more satisfying than it was in its heyday.

Kirkland, Washington, is one example of a suburb that has seized the potential for bolstering its old town center. A community of 42,000 people on the eastern shore of Lake Washington, Kirkland had its beginnings as an independent small town in the closing years of the nineteenth century. It was incorporated as a municipality in 1905, by which time Seattle, on the far side of Lake Washington, had already established itself as the region's dominant city. In recent years metropolitan Seattle's development has enveloped Kirkland and continued well beyond it, yet downtown Kirkland has managed to thrive, thanks to well-conceived public and private undertakings.

Numerous new office buildings two to six stories high have been erected in Kirkland's downtown area, especially in areas close to Lake Washington. Some, including a development called Carillon Point, have offices above ground-floor stores and restaurants. From the new offices it's a pleasant walk to Kirkland's small retail and service establishments, many of them occupying brick buildings that have stood along the principal business streets, Central Way and Lake Street South, for over fifty years. The office workers help to keep Kirkland's merchants in operation. Kirkland's policy of encouraging office growth close to the old town center, with retailing and other uses mixed in, is one that other suburbs should consider adopting.

A second Kirkland achievement that other suburbs should think of emulating is construction of dense new housing in and close to the downtown. Kirkland contains many three- and four-story apartment buildings with a density of about twenty-five housing units per acre. The residential population enhances the downtown's vigor. Another form of housing that can enhance a downtown is apartments above stores.

Third, Kirkland has paid careful attention to pedestrian circulation. In a few spots the streets have been narrowed to make it easier for pedestrians to cross. Sidewalks are everywhere, and they have been widened along some streets. Awnings or arcades along the fronts of some buildings shelter pedestrians from the weather. A few retailers have one customer entrance on the front, facing the street, and a second customer entrance on the rear, facing a parking area. These provide welcome, weather-protected shortcuts.

Fourth, Kirkland has provided parking in ways that do not make the downtown ugly or cause discomfort for people on foot. Kirkland has established small, discreet pockets of landscaped parking scattered throughout the downtown. Unlike the typical suburban strip, there are no parking lots situated between the stores and the streets; instead parking lots tend to be behind the stores, where they do not interfere with the ability of pedestrians to stroll along the sidewalks, look through the shops' display windows, and enter stores without the inconvenience of walking through a parking lot. Developers in Kirkland can satisfy their obligation for providing parking spaces by paying into a municipal fund rather than building out-of-character parking on individual lots.

Parking is allowed on all the streets—an unusual suburban

practice and one that makes Kirkland more comfortable for pedestrians. There is parallel parking on Central Way in front of the stores, and on two other streets diagonal parking has been created. Seattle landscape architect Richard Untermann notes that angled on-street parking—which was common in small towns until the 1950s, when federal highway standards hastened its disappearance—is used in some reviving Seattle neighborhood business districts. He urges other communities to adopt angled parking because of several virtues it possesses. It enables a larger number of people to park on the street in front of the stores they want to visit. It increases the buffer zone between pedestrians and moving traffic, making the sidewalks feel more protected. It brings more pleasing proportions to streets that may have been overly broad to begin with. It requires less skill of the driver than parallel parking. And it frees the driver from the danger of stepping out of the car into moving traffic. In some business districts with diagonal parking, the cars park with their rears toward the sidewalk and their fronts toward vehicular traffic, which eliminates the hazard of backing out into traffic.

Fifth, Kirkland has created parks and recreation areas linked to the other downtown attractions. Four waterfront parks have been built at intervals along Lake Washington. One of them, Marina Park, which has a beach, a children's play area, public toilets, a concert area, and a dance floor, is situated where the downtown abuts the lake. Municipal leaders had the foresight to realize that the closeness of the lake could provide opportunities for restaurants, art galleries, and other leisure- and culture-oriented establishments to prosper in the downtown, offsetting the departure of some traditional downtown retailers that have had a hard time competing with shopping malls.

A pedestrian walkway starts in Marina Park and heads eastward through the downtown. Its route passes a landscaped parking lot, stores, and a central park that contains a baseball field, a swimming pool, a public library, and a senior center. The walkway concludes at Park Place, a mixed-use development with small shops, a hardware store, a supermarket, and a six-screen movie theater on its ground floor and with several floors of offices above. Close by are office buildings and numerous apartments. Untermann says that as development continues in downtown Kirkland, pedestrian connections such as the one from Marina Park to Park Place will become increasingly useful. One other feature the pedestrian path passes is a major Metro transit

In good weather the benches along the pedestrian corridor in Kirkland, Washington, from a lakeside park to inland destinations, are well occupied.

center, a transfer point for several bus lines. Public transportation is a sixth ingredient in a successful downtown. It allows Kirkland to accommodate people without covering too much of its land with automobile parking.

Kirkland, then, has nurtured a prosperous and pleasurable downtown by paying attention to a whole series of attributes: employment close to retailing and services, dense housing, streets not overly wide, a scattering of parking both on and off the street, attractive public spaces, opportunities for recreational and cultural activities, interesting and direct pedestrian connections, and mass transit service. Much of the credit belongs to vigorous local control, Untermann says, observing, "For a long time people in Kirkland have paid a lot of attention to the community."

In a suburb that has no downtown, the local government may need to rezone land to allow mixed-use development. The land designated for such development should be in a location that many people will be able to reach, preferably not only by automobile but also on foot or bicycle and by public transportation. Such a mixed-use center may be easier to build if the land zoned for it is under a single owner or under several owners who are willing to cooperate with one another. Elizabeth Plater-Zyberk says many recently built suburbs contain a large tract under a single owner that could be developed into a town center.

Along with selecting the right site and giving it the zoning it needs, a community must arrive at a fairly detailed notion about the character the development should strive for. "You have to do what's called a *specific plan* or urban design," says Plater-Zyberk. "You have to specify the height of the buildings, how they meet the streets, and figure out what the uses might be." There should be a network of extensively connected streets, preferably with short blocks. There should be a fine-grained mixture of activities rather than, say, a big retailing complex here, a large expanse of housing development there, and a large collection of offices in yet another area. The town centers that are most enjoyable are sprinkled with variety throughout. The intimate mixture of uses generates liveliness and surprise and helps a center to become a community gathering place, something that conventional "mixed-use developments," with their several uses widely separated from one another, rarely succeed in doing.

"Most suburbs allow mixed-use development in business-zoned areas, but it doesn't happen because the real estate industry and financiers don't care for it," says planning consultant Philip Herr. "To get mixed-use development in the suburbs requires more than permission—it requires incentives, cajoling, or the good fortune to be dealing with the rare developer who understands it. Then it requires skillful design and management or it doesn't work."

Less than three miles south of Kirkland—also on the eastern shore of Lake Washington—is a suburb that had no downtown but decided to create one. That suburb is Bellevue, a community of 90,000 people. "Bellevue used all sorts of design tools to turn itself away from a suburban environment with no concentration of activity into a community with a downtown," says Mark Hinshaw, an urban designer who guided downtown growth through most of the 1980s. The city resolved in the late 1970s to build a downtown largely by offering economic incentives to developers. Developers were allowed to erect buildings of skyscraper height, concentrating much more office space on their properties, in exchange for making their buildings, parking areas, and open spaces more congenial to pedestrians. The city eliminated deep building setbacks from the streets and required instead that buildings come up to the sidewalks. Retailing in particular was directed to line the sidewalks. Parking lots in front of buildings were prohibited. The city cut in half the required ratio of parking space to building floor space. Bonuses were employed to encourage underground parking; virtually all recent development has taken advantage of that incentive. The city required numerous public spaces where people can relax or gather. In addition, the city constructed a formally designed seventeen-acre park as a focal point for the downtown.

Hinshaw paid attention to the details of everything from the design of street lights to the shadows cast by office towers. He championed the use of pleasing materials for pedestrian areas. Brick or stone exteriors are required on the ground floor of downtown buildings. Tall buildings must be set back as they rise so that areas frequented by pedestrians will catch as much of the Puget Sound area's scarce sunshine as possible. Dimensions of benches and drinking fountains were specified by the city. Hinshaw himself conceived a decorative design for light standards, with three-dimensional representations of apples, strawberries, and blueberries cast into their bases, reflecting Bellevue's history as a fruit-farming area.

Along a more than 2,000-foot-long stretch of Sixth Street the city decided to create a carless pedestrian area that would form a core for the downtown. Sixth Street, bordered in the late 1970s mostly by parking lots and undeveloped land, was envisioned as an intense, urbane place connecting major office towers to shopping, sidewalk cafes, and other gathering places. Stylistically, the goal was to achieve a character like that of grand old cities and to avoid the datedness that often befalls contemporary architecture. Planting tubs, tree grates, and paving bricks were selected for their classic qualities. The emphasis on historical ref-

Perhaps the grandest civic space in downtown Bellevue, Washington, is a new seventeen-acre park with a formal promenade.

erences and classic lines was echoed in a $5 million transit center that the regional transit authority, Metro, built in the center of downtown. Buses leave the transit center every half-hour for other Seattle area communities. Supplementing the investment in the transportation hub, a new freeway interchange will give buses and car pools a direct link to downtown. Businesses, in return for incentives such as permission to construct buildings exceeding the 300-foot downtown height limit, pay the costs of building and maintaining the pedestrian corridor. The trading of development bonuses for public amenities will allow the not-yet-finished pedestrian corridor to be built with practically no public funds.

The city government set the downtown development process in motion and gave it intelligent leadership, but this is not to say that business owners passively took orders from City Hall. Critical guidance for the planning came from the Bellevue Downtown Association, an organization of downtown business interests. Design guidelines were hammered out with the association in a consensus-building operation. Some proposed guidelines were abandoned when businesses refused to support them; this is perhaps regrettable, but it is offset by the fact that obtaining cooperation from property owners educated the owners in basic urban design considerations. In some instances the property owners then applied their new knowledge to other projects.

The refashioning of what is now downtown Bellevue has not been restricted solely to the pedestrian corridor. Bellevue's regional shopping mall, Bellevue Square, has also been rebuilt. Bellevue Square began as a one-story complex surrounded by parking. The only way to reach the stores was by going through the parking lot. In recent years, the center has added a second story and has expanded its concourses in four directions, with the result that people can now walk into the mall from streets on all four sides. The changes allow pedestrians to avoid trudging through a parking lot, and they make the downtown streets more lively. Four corners of the property have been developed into the mall's parking garages.

Parts of the 400-acre downtown are still not easy to traverse on foot. A visiting critic complained not long ago about wide streets with "such pedestrian-unfriendly features as the 'walk' lights that change to 'stop' in roughly six seconds or the eight-minute wait to cross the intersection to the new downtown park." Nonetheless, after a decade and a half of planning and building, Belle-

A popular outdoor gathering place has been added to the Bellevue Square shopping mall.

vue has made substantial progress toward creating a place that welcomes pedestrians. With its several million square feet of office towers and its ground-level pedestrian amenities, downtown Bellevue is a well-coordinated alternative to the usual suburban business area.

Not all suburban offices and retailing can be gathered into compact mixed-use areas like those in Bellevue and Kirkland. A large proportion of suburban business has already dispersed along suburban roads and will be there for years to come. A key to improving the existing suburbs therefore lies in making the roadside strips more attractive and inviting. Each strip needs to become more cohesive. Most strips, especially those built with minimal local design controls, are anything *but* cohesive; visually they are a mishmash. This problem can be addressed by requiring unifying elements along the strip—especially landscaping. If trees and other vegetation are planted consistently along the road's edges and, where possible, in the median as well, the road will be less harsh and more unified.

Trees and vegetation bring a calming influence to what is otherwise a discordant environment. Trees should be planted along the roads, either by property owners or by governments. Increasingly municipalities are adopting guidelines or regulations that require trees and other vegetation to soften parking areas. Preservation of mature trees often should be required. Large trees do wonders for the appearance of the strip. A love of nature was one of the original motivations for the migration to the suburbs; nature should be an integral part of today's suburban development.

Along with insisting on adequate planting, governments should control signs along the strip. With some exceptions, signs that tower against the sky usually make the environment feel crass and disorderly. A road generally feels more comfortable when businesses employ low, monument-style signs (signs whose bases rest entirely on the ground) or signs that are integrated into the buildings themselves. Local governments in most cases should encourage monument-style and integrated signs and discourage freestanding signs that reach into the sky.

Generally it is a good idea to encourage all the buildings in a shopping complex to harmonize by having some elements in common, such as colors, materials, proportions, and style. Freestanding buildings such as fast-food outlets occupying outlying sites in strip shopping center parking lots should adopt the same aesthetic as the strip center's main run of buildings. This will make the entire complex appear more unified to those driving past. Exceptions might be made for distinctive structures that act as landmarks.

Local governments might consider sharpening the distinctions between one road and another so that each travel corridor evolves its own identity. Mark Hinshaw now advises a number of governments on urban design. He believes communities can infuse character into their transportation corridors by formulating a vision of what each road should look like. For the city of Bozeman, Montana, Hinshaw drew up guidelines that reinforce the most prominent traits of several major road corridors. On one commercial strip, the guidelines encourage owners to use dramatic architectural forms such as bold building entrances, unique wall openings, and exaggerated parapets. Forceful architectural forms will make that particular strip more memorable, Hinshaw says. On another road, where much less commercial development has occurred, the guidelines take almost the opposite tack, calling for "very low-key building forms" which are to be subservient to plantings, such as trees native to the region; in this instance, the relatively limited extent of development suggests that a soothing, somewhat naturalistic atmosphere is the right choice. On a third road, which passes industrial buildings, the guidelines urge owners to seize the possibilities of industrial-style construction. Prefabricated metal industrial building systems, geometric forms, and bright accent colors will give that road a character much different from the others. And on one of the Bozeman area's more pastoral roads, where rows of trees frequently run perpendicular to the highway, creating a pattern of trees alternating with open spaces, the guidelines suggest planting additional rows of trees on property sidelines. The plantings will help the corridor retain its soft, semirural feeling. Bozeman's strategy could be followed in most suburban areas. A person with a trained eye can identify distinguishing traits of local roads and create something potentially artful.

Landscaping, sign control, a unified aesthetic within each building complex, and a distinctive character for each strip are four elements that can improve the strip's appearance. In addition, as construction continues on the strip, some buildings should be encouraged to extend closer to the road. It's more pleasurable to drive past buildings a few dozen feet from the road than to see them sitting hundreds of feet behind asphalt parking lots. Walls of buildings visible from the road should have windows in them, making them more interesting to look at. The local government might encourage some buildings to be built with only a small parking area in the front. Most of their parking would be to the side or rear. Such a design stratagem will make the strip seem more inhabited and appealing to passersby.

Local governments might also address material and construction quality. "The strip centers have always been among the cheapest buildings in the American city," writes architectural historian Robert Bruegmann, "but to everyone's amazement, continuous pressures for economy in the 1980s forced architects to find even cheaper substitutes for materials that were already thought to be about as ignoble as any ever used in construction." In Bruegmann's view, conditions began to change in some localities because of two factors. First, many municipalities enacted ordinances mandating higher-quality facade materials and other kinds of visual upgrading. (For example, Bozeman's guidelines say that walls facing streets should not be left blank; all sides of a building are encouraged to have interesting details and materials and to avoid presenting an ugly "back side" to neighbors.) Second, as strip centers saturated their markets, some developers voluntarily shifted to higher-grade materials and more distinctive styling to entice tenants.

Beyond the visual is the question of how to make the strip more physically accommodating for people once they get out of their cars. To make it easier and more comfortable for people to walk from one destination to another, communities should insist on improved pedestrian connections along the strip. Sidewalks should be built paralleling the road, separated from traffic by a planter strip or a row of parked cars or both. Clearly designated pedestrian walks should connect the sidewalks to the buildings' main entrances. The pedestrian walkways that hug the fronts of strip shopping centers should be improved.

Currently it's common for the walkway on a center's facade to be bordered by a "fire lane," a zone where parking is prohibited on the theory that someday the building will catch fire and when it does the fire trucks will need a guaranteed parking spot within ten feet of the smoking Radio Shack or the flame-emitting Safeway. This is public safety regulation carried to ridiculous excess. Traditional downtowns have no fire lanes in front of the buildings, yet firefighters manage to do their job perfectly well on the infrequent occasions when blazes break out. Fire lanes, besides not being needed at shopping centers, detract from the pleasure of being a pedestrian. Most of the time, the fire lanes are occupied by moving vehicles, so people walking in front of the stores always feel somewhat vulnerable—closer to moving traffic than they would like to be. It would be better to allow a row of parked cars to occupy the pavement between the pedestrian walkway and the vehicular traffic. The parked vehicles would buffer the pedestrians from traffic, making the walkways feel more protected and secure, like the sidewalks along traditional retail streets. Developers need to be reminded that as soon as people get out of their cars they become pedestrians and should benefit from an environment made for walking.

Hinshaw observes that people feel more comfortable with their surroundings when there are choices of things to see, things to do, people to interact with. Therefore strip shopping developments should be encouraged to provide opportunities beyond shopping. Of the suburban centers that I regularly shop at, the most enjoyable is the Hamden Plaza in Hamden, Connecticut. One of the plaza's owners, David Bermant, has installed sculptures and other artistic creations along an arcade in front of the stores. One of the art works is a collection of bells, which children test to discover what sort of music they can make. Another is drumlike metal seats, which people tap as they sit, creating musical sounds. Another installation is a transparent box six feet high. Inside the box is a whimsical mechanical contraption that slowly, constantly carries silver balls to the top of a convoluted

Time out from shopping at Hamden Plaza in Hamden, Connecticut.

series of chutes, after which each ball rolls downward—fast here, slow there, striking metal objects that reverberate with sound. It's a complex, brightly colored apparatus, and I often see adults and children pausing to watch and listen. These and other art works along the Hamden Plaza's arcade transport people into a realm of imagination. Unexpected pleasures have always been important ingredients in healthy cities; such pleasures could punctuate suburban routines if shopping centers were designed to be places to linger.

At Blackhawk, in Danville, California, the principal shopping center has an outdoor cafe under part of its arcade, near a supermarket that sells beverages and other take-out food. The cafe provides a social place for people from the surrounding residential areas. In Bozeman, Montana, the local government adopted guidelines that encourage restaurants, large retail stores, and large shopping centers to create usable outdoor spaces for public enjoyment in their vicinity. The guidelines recommend that these outdoor areas be landscaped and attractively paved and have movable seating. Outdoor public spaces are especially recommended near the main entrances of buildings. If vendors can be enticed to sell soft drinks or food in these locations, so much the better.

Retailers who are eager to establish a new store in a particular geographic area will usually make the building more congenial if the municipality insists upon it. In 1992 a developer announced plans to build a 125,000-square-foot Wal-Mart store on North

The Shops at Somerset Square in Glastonbury, Connecticut, were designed to give a town square to a town that never had one.

Seventh Avenue in Bozeman, Montana. The Arkansas-based discount chain intended to occupy a boxy, flat-roofed, gray cinderblock building with a horizontal red and blue band. Bozeman refused to approve the plans, saying the Wal-Mart design did not satisfy the road corridor guidelines the city had recently adopted. Wal-Mart, which builds a new store in the United States every other day, agreed to depart from its original design. The company substituted beige-painted split-face block for the flat gray block exterior it had first proposed. The company extended the building's entrance about twenty-five feet to make it more attractive. It added projections at intervals along the facade to give the wall additional visual relief. It added a parapet to hide mechanical equipment on the roof. It agreed to several improvements to the parking lot and other outdoor areas. A fourteen-foot-wide sidewalk with ten feet of planting on each side is to extend from the store's entrance to a public sidewalk on North Seventh Avenue. A bus stop is to be provided, and Wal-Mart has agreed to create a landscaped area with benches and a place for a hot dog vendor, so customers will have a pleasant spot for relaxing outdoors. Cottonwoods and other trees will be planted in many locations on the seventeen-acre site. All these improvements were agreed to by a company that is as economy-oriented as any retailer in America. Given such an experience in planning, local governments clearly should insist on upgraded standards for roadside development.

Roadside buildings undergo frequent alteration. Renovation and expansion should be viewed as opportunities to make the buildings more versatile, more accommodating to pedestrians, and more neighborhood-oriented. Governments could insist that, as time goes by, shopping centers add new buildings that reach the street. Shopping centers could be encouraged to add extra stories containing additional uses and activities. Sidewalks and in some instances streets could be extended to neighboring retail and office developments and to nearby residential areas, enabling people to reach shopping centers without aggravating congestion on the roads. Granted, some homeowners may initially voice apprehension about connections to shopping centers; fear of strangers and unpredictable behavior is one of the reasons why people move to suburbs. When the Southridge Mall was built in Greendale, Wisconsin, in 1969, the residents of the adjoining subdivision at first insisted that a fence should be put up to protect them from outsiders. Once the mall was in operation, however, the residents realized that what they wanted most was not an impenetrable fence but rather the ability to walk to the mall. A hole appeared underneath the fence. Finally, said village manager Donald Fieldstad, Jr., "some kid cut the fence open with a wire cutter." As a result, a gate was installed. Since then, residents have been able to take advantage of their proximity to shops, eating places, and entertainment.

Over the years, the buildings on the strip could acquire some of the congeniality and pedestrian convenience associated with traditional town centers. "I have seen strips change in my fifteen years here," Untermann says of the Seattle area, "and I think there is a natural urban development process that occurs with each public improvement or regulation."

"I think there's an enormous amount of potential in these places," says Cambridge architect Anne Tate. "The problem is lack of imagination. People see asphalt and think it's all built out." Some of the asphalt could be filled in with buildings, and links could be forged between separate developments.

There are increasing efforts to design new suburban shopping centers to achieve a comfortable balance of cars and pedestrians. Some of the new complexes attempt to learn from successful older shopping centers such as Market Square in Lake Forest, Illinois, and the Highland Park shopping center near Dallas. In Glastonbury, Connecticut, a suburb of Hartford, Robert Stern designed The Shops at Somerset Square with the goal of "giving a town square to a town which never had one." Stores are arranged around a landscaped oval area that contains a limited amount of parking. Occupying the middle of the oval is a two-story restaurant, a centerpiece that shoppers walk to from the sidewalks in front of the stores. Most parking is relegated to the perimeter of the complex.

Stern devised a similar layout for Wheaton Town Square, a two-story shopping center in Wheaton, Illinois. The hip-roofed, brick-clad Wheaton complex, reminiscent of Prairie School architecture, is organized around a central court. Cars drive through the court, but most of the parking is outside it, allowing the court to function as a pedestrian enclave, a refuge from the heavy traffic and noise of the suburban road along which Wheaton Town Square is situated. Bruegmann questions whether many stores can thrive in a courtyard, where motorists have trouble seeing them from the nearby arterial. Eye contact with tens of thousands of motorists is usually an important ingredient in retail success, he says. But not every store must be seen by motorists. Small stores in an enclosed shopping mall are not seen by motorists, yet they usually thrive because the mall and its anchor stores are a popular destination. Some courtyard-style centers on suburban arterials may similarly become destinations that attract people. Also, some retailers have an established clientele that seeks them out, so they do not need constant exposure to arterial traffic. Of the Wheaton Town Center, Bruegmann writes, "The view of shoppers sitting on the central court in fine weather, drinking Starbuck's espresso recalls the squares of the traditional European city center." Coming years may bring widespread experimentation in shopping center design.

Finally, existing suburbs need to look at ways of improving their residential neighborhoods. In municipalities that have some land yet to be developed, new subdivisions should link up with existing ones. Well-connected networks of streets should be the norm. To reduce the potential disturbance from through traffic, planning consultant Anton Nelessen says it's essential to plan for the use of "traffic-dampening" devices, such as planted circles in some of the intersections; these help to control the speed of traffic. Existing cul-de-sacs might be connected to each other, allowing pedestrians and bicyclists, if not vehicles, easier movement.

In the vicinity of places that residents would like to see develop into town centers, it is often a good idea to encourage higher density so that the nascent town center will have a large enough population to support it. In some large-lot suburban areas, Nelessen says, "we recommend that people be able to subdivide wide lots and put houses in there." As the number of houses or apartments increases, residents may wish to plant hedges and install low fences between buildings and sidewalks. By doing so, they can define semipublic spaces better and enable suburban areas to take on a more pedestrian-oriented, townlike character. Nelessen emphasizes that when increasing the density of a suburban residential area, it's critical to protect the privacy of the residents' rear yards.

Subdivision residents might study traditional landscape and community features—perhaps with help from a local historical society or planning agency—and try to reach a consensus on introducing some of those elements into their neighborhood. Street trees and indigenous vegetation might be planted. Fences appropriate for the area might be built. Networks of sidewalks might be installed or improved. More ambitious neighborhoods may wish to identify locations where public places and institutions, including parks, bus stops, child care centers, and small stores, ought to be established.

There are many opportunities in the suburbs, varying widely according to local circumstances. All that's needed is the energy and imagination to seize the untapped potential.

TEN

Prospects

for a

New

Vision

The main elements needed for better communities are clear. There should be a generously connected network of streets and sidewalks—a network that allows pedestrians, bicyclists, and motorists to move over many different routes, enjoying and learning from, not just tolerating, their surroundings. Streets should be conceived as outdoor "public rooms" that people will relish occupying—places pleasingly enclosed by the fronts of the buildings and other agreeable elements such as trees, hedges, and low fences. The character of the houses should enhance these public rooms. Garages should be relegated to rear alleys or to other inconspicuous locations so that the houses can display more engaging features—their entrances, windows, porches, architectural detailing, and landscaping. It is these elements that dignify the street and help to give it a congenial atmosphere.

Neighborhoods should contain housing in a mixture of sizes, prices, and types so that a variety of people and households can come together and rely upon one another. Varied housing makes it possible for a neighborhood to accommodate individuals in every stage of life, fostering ties between one age group or economic class and another. Communities should consider altering regulations that require large lots and large houses. Small to moderate-sized lots often make it easier for neighborhood spirit to arise and local institutions to flourish. Smaller houses also tend to lessen the financial strain on struggling homeowners.

Neighborhoods should be laid out so that in a few minutes residents can walk from their homes to parks, stores, services, and other amenities of daily life. By organizing the community on a pedestrian scale and making room for neighborhood stores, services, amd recreation areas, local gathering places will have a better chance of coming into being. Not every neighborhood

A Kentlands conversation in progress.

should be densely developed, but those that are concentrated and walkable will reap advantages unavailable to sparsely populated tracts. Moderate- to high-density neighborhoods are much more apt to obtain public transit service, which allows the young and the old to get around more readily and permits residents of all ages to reduce their dependence on private automobiles. The freedom to spend less on private vehicles is important since the median income of 80 percent of America's households, adjusted for inflation, has stagnated since 1973. Better-designed communities might relieve financial and emotional stresses, allowing people to live at lower expense and to gain the satisfaction of neighborhood involvement.

It will require years of effort to create the convenient, attrac-

237

Market Street in the Reston Town Center.

tive, affordable, and neighborly suburbs I have described. Even when no major obstacles stand in the way, good communities take a long time to come into being.

In the meantime, dangers loom ahead. One danger is that builders and developers will adopt only the most superficial aspects of this design approach. Builders may construct houses with front porches and old-fashioned decoration, claiming to recapture the virtues of a friendly, close-knit neighborhood, but they may place the houses in subdivisions riddled with all the defects of conventional community design. Front porches and traditional styling will not make much difference if the houses sit in subdivisions that lack a mixture of sizes and kinds of

Nursery Park, one of Harbor Town's neighborhood gathering places.

households, that lack a network of narrow streets and comfortable sidewalks, that lack closeness to shops, services, and gathering places, and that lack access to public transportation. Already some developments in the Washington, D.C., area have engaged in a kind of pseudo-traditionalism, advertising themselves as old-fashioned, friendly neighborhoods while disregarding most of the principles that give genuine old neighborhoods their convenience and vitality. Developments that falsely claim to have recaptured the virtues of older neighborhoods may lead many people to misunderstand what traditional community design entails. When stylizing masquerades as fundamental change, the task of applying the wisdom of old communities is impeded.

A second danger is that the proponents of reformed community design will make compromises that weaken their work's value. It's rare for designers to have full control over the projects on which they work. Andres Duany and Elizabeth Plater-Zyberk have designed some developments that possess exemplary plans for streets, parks, services, and neighborhood gathering places but that are in questionable locations on the metropolitan fringe, far from jobs, distant from mass transit. Such developments may be better than the suburban norm, but they will not deliver the full benefits available in better-chosen locations.

239

It will not be easy to bring this vision of suburban design to fruition. The idea of a compact, mixed, affordable, pedestrian-scale community has emerged at a time when there is still a great deal of wealth in the United States, especially in the top fifth of the population. Surplus wealth enables people to persist in building wasteful, inadequate communities and then compensate for the communities' failings by buying private vehicles and driving all over the metropolitan area in search of what ought to be available close to home. The satisfying community designs of earlier times were dictated to a considerable extent by scarce resources. People supported neighborhood stores, and relied on sidewalks to get to and from the stores, because they didn't have the money and cars that would allow them to shop at big stores dispersed along distant roads. People lived at higher densities—and enjoyed a robust neighborhood life—because they could not afford detached houses on large lots in subdivisions many miles from their place of work. People settled in compact, relatively self-sufficient communities because the economy permitted little extravagance. One complication for today's traditionalists, then, lies in advocating a more efficient, compact community before the economy has made it necessary for the nation as a whole to adopt such a thrifty outlook. Thus is it possible that most suburban development in the United States will continue for some time on the profligate course it has followed since the Second World War.

The damaging consequences of the post–Second World War mode of development are not equally distributed across the country. Some of the most troubling results are concentrated in the largest metropolitan areas, like southern California and the San Francisco Bay area. In those two regions frustrations associated with conventional development patterns—high costs, traffic congestion, long commutes, and the decay of community life—are helping to spawn a migration of families, employers, developers, and builders to other parts of the West. Large numbers of the discontented are moving to California's Central Valley and to the Las Vegas, Portland, and Seattle areas. Some of the areas receiving the migrations—Portland especially—are trying to plan intelligently to accommodate the influx. But there is a danger that many of the planning and development mistakes made in California's largest metropolitan areas will be repeated in other regions. The ease with which industries can relocate from a degenerating metropolis to an area that is less populated and not yet overburdened may allow conventional community development practices to continue for a long while before finally being recognized as the calamities they are.

Yet there is reason for hope. The United States is an open, self-critical society. Attitudes in this country can change dramatically in a relatively short period. As attitudes change, so does the behavior of governments, businesses, and many individuals. Americans have witnessed important transformations during the recent past—transformations that indicate that our approach to suburban development could similarly undergo a major change. One example of the country's shifting course is the growth of environmental consciousness in the past twenty-five years. Since the late 1960s the country has made great progress in identifying elements of the environment that need to be safeguarded and taking action to protect them. Environmental consciousness has become key to a number of government policies. It has the potential in coming years to buttress efforts to improve community design.

In particular, the desire for clean air indicates how the evolution of environmental consciousness could, in the not too distant future, improve community design. California is in the forefront of the battle against air pollution. Two California regulatory agencies—the South Coast Air Quality Management District in southern California and the California Air Resources Board—have, between them, targeted a large array of air pollution sources for remedial action. Regulations already adopted or proposed are aimed at forcing certain industries to change their manufacturing processes, requiring many employers to reduce the number of miles their workers commute on the highway, and forcing 2 percent of the new cars in the state in 1998 to be powered by electricity. The campaign against air pollution has already brought about restrictions on emissions from house paints, aerosol cleaning products, windshield wiper fluid, new lawn mowers, and deodorant spray. Even charcoal barbecue lighter fluid has had to be reformulated to reduce the vapors it gives off.

As the focus on air pollution sources has intensified, it has become clear that one of the important remedies for air pollution is a reduction in people's dependence on private transportation. If people can satisfy some of their daily needs without driving, or without driving such long distances, the air will be cleaner and people will be healthier. So the goal of reducing smog has focused attention on better community design. In 1993 the South

Coast Air Quality Management District adopted a handbook to guide local governments, developers, and planners in cutting air pollution. One of its recommendations is that services such as banks, day care centers, and eating places should be provided close to work so that employees will have less need to drive cars. Another recommendation is for establishing grocery stores, banks, restaurants, and other services "within a quarter-mile of residential subdivisions to encourage residents to walk or bicycle." The handbook is likely to be just the beginning of the impact that environmental consciousness will exert on community design. As time goes by, environmental thinking will increasingly prod large and polluted metropolitan areas to develop pedestrian-oriented, mixed-use neighborhoods.

Other problems that the country faces will probably add force to the movement for more well-balanced, walkable communities. One of these is transportation problems in major metropolitan areas. Building more and bigger highways is inordinately expensive in a period when governments at all levels are running short of money. Even if funds for big highway construction projects can be found, the new roads more often than not encourage more traffic, which clogs the system again. That conventional road-building schemes are not working was recognized by the federal government in 1991 with the adoption of the Intermodal Surface Transportation Efficiency Act. ISTEA (pronounced "ice tea") encourages cities and towns to consider alternatives to highway construction. "Those alternatives," *Planning* magazine reported, "may include not only mass transit but also bikeways, pedestrian walkways—even zoning changes that reduce the need for travel by increasing building density." Transportation thinking is changing. It is becoming obvious that one remedy for transportation problems is to build communities so that destinations are closer together, requiring less travel, especially less travel in private vehicles.

The need for affordable housing is another issue that may push governments toward embracing the principles of traditional community design. In the past, many programs subsidized housing for people of limited means. But few governments today have much money to spend on housing. The need for other approaches is becoming increasingly evident. These approaches could include production of more small dwellings, the mixing of different kinds of housing in a community, and development of towns and neighborhoods in which some residents can function with fewer cars or no cars at all. If people are freed from spending 20–30 percent of their incomes on private transportation, they would be better able to afford the housing they need.

There are signs that a convergence of thinking on a number of the country's major concerns is beginning to occur. Answers to issues of environmental quality, traffic congestion, and affordable housing all hinge to a considerable extent on changes in community design. Awareness of these problems suggests that public policy should encourage compact, pedestrian-scale development with shopping, services, and employment close to home. If we follow this course, many other benefits are likely to follow. Communities would be less fragmented. Parents would be less coerced to spend their leisure time as chauffeurs for their offspring. Children would have more opportunities to become self-reliant and to gain experiences that prepare them for a responsible adulthood. The elderly would find fewer obstacles to staying in their longtime neighborhoods. Neighborhoods might become more stable and vigorous, offering their inhabitants welcome relief from the increasing stresses of modern life.

Life need not be as expensive, disconnected, and pressured as it has become in many of the postwar suburbs. Lessons about how to build better communities can be extracted from the nation's successful older communities. Old suburbs and old urban neighborhoods embody a great deal of human experience and wisdom waiting to be rediscovered.

The United States has often changed course as it embraced new ideals or recommitted itself to old ideals that had fallen into neglect. Let us hope that a vision of a more lively and balanced community—a community with an appealing public environment and an appreciation of public responsibilities—is embraced with vigor and enthusiasm, and without delay. At stake is the future of our neighborhoods' vitality and of our country's civic spirit.

Notes

Many quotations in this book are from the author's interviews or correspondence and are therefore not cited below.

ONE America's Failing Suburbs

2   "Stress used to be noticeable" Elizabeth M. Fowler, "More Stress Found in the Workplace," *New York Times,* Sept. 12, 1989, p. D12.

4   Junior corporate managers Nicholas Lemann, "Stressed Out in Suburbia," *Atlantic Monthly,* Nov. 1989, p. 36.

5   Juliet Schor reports Juliet B. Schor, *The Overworked American: The Unexpected Decline of Leisure* (New York: Basic Books, 1991), p. 29.

6   "Around New York City, the new growth" John Herbers, "Now Even the Suburbs Have Suburbs," *New York Times,* May 5, 1985, p. 6E.

6   a new term—"the boomdocks" Rodney Ferguson and Eugene Carlson, "Distant Communities Promise Good Homes but Produce Malaise," *Wall Street Journal,* Oct. 25, 1990, p. A1.

6   the fastest-growing municipality William Fulton, "The Long Commute," *Planning,* July 1990, pp. 4–10.

7   The average freeway speed in southern California Figures for 1984 and 2010 are from Southern California Association of Governments, "Regional Mobility Plan (1988)," p. I-2. Robert H. Huddy, senior transportation planner for the association, estimated freeway speed for the mid-1970s.

7   "The Owl" Pauline Yoshihashi, "Remotely Affordable," *Wall Street Journal,* Feb. 19, 1989, p. R18.

9   Karen Palmer works Ferguson and Carlson, "Distant Communities," p. A1.

9   shopping was drudgery Trish Hall, "Shop? Many Say, Only If I Must," *New York Times,* Nov. 28, 1990, p. C8.

10   American Automobile Association calculates American Automobile Association, "Your Driving Costs, 1991 Edition" (AAA, Heathrow, Fla.).

15   "In Naperville" Lemann, "Stressed Out in Suburbia," p. 43.

15   *The Great Good Place* Ray Oldenburg, *The Great Good Place: Cafes, Coffee Shops, Community Centers, Beauty Parlors, General Stores, Bars, Hangouts and How They Get You Through the Day* (New York: Paragon House, 1991), pp. 3–42.

15   "sterilized and purified suburbs" Oldenburg, *Great Good Place,* p. 178.

19   Murray Bookchin argues   Murray Bookchin, *The Rise of Urbanization and the Decline of Citizenship* (San Francisco: Sierra Club Books, 1987), p. 10.

20   more medical complaints   Edward Shorter, *From Paralysis to Fatigue: A History of Psychosomatic Illness in the Modern Era* (New York: Free Press, 1991), pp. 320–23.

21   Social scientist Amitai Etzioni   Amitai Etzioni, *A Responsive Society: Collected Essays on Guiding Deliberate Social Change* (San Francisco: Jossey-Bass Publishers, 1991), p. 140.

21   "'make' one another"   Etzioni, *Responsive Society,* p. 139.

21   "not a community at all"   Jacqueline Weaver, "Shopping Malls No Bargain, Study Finds," *New York Times,* Apr. 22, 1990, Connecticut sec., p. 3.

23   a privilege Jane Jacobs identifies   Jane Jacobs, *The Death and Life of Great American Cities* (New York: Vintage Books, 1961), pp. 55–56.

24   "We humanize what is going on"   Hannah Arendt, *Men in Dark Times,* excerpted in *The Norton Book of Friendship,* ed. Eudora Welty and Ronald A. Sharp (New York: W. W. Norton, 1991), p. 524.

24   Loneliness soars   Jeff Meer, "Loneliness," *Psychology Today,* July 1985, pp. 31–32.

25   Suicides . . . quadrupled   *Atlantic Monthly,* Mar. 1992, p. 18.

TWO Streets and Where They Lead Us

31   One of the few professional studies   The study, by Walter Kulash, Joe Anglin, and David Marks, is "Traditional Neighborhood Development: Will the Traffic Work?" a paper prepared for American Society of Civil Engineers Conference "Successful Land Development: Quality and Profits," Mar. 1990. The analysis is repeated in a later report with the same title, solely by Walter Kulash presented in Oct. 1990 to the Eleventh Annual Pedestrian Conference, Bellevue, Wash. My citations are from the second report.

32   Northern and western communities   Orange County history is drawn from Rob Kling, Spencer Olin, and Mark Poster, eds., *Post-Suburban California: The Transformation of Orange County since World War II* (Berkeley: University of California Press, 1991), particularly pp. 1–22 and 57–67.

34   consider building mass transit   Martin J. Schiesl, "Designing the Model Community: The Irvine Company and Suburban Development," in *Post-Suburban California,* ed. Kling, Olin, and Poster, pp. 66–67.

35   how long the wait is   Kulash, "Traditional Neighborhood Development," p. 3–7.

36   few stores could survive   Douglas Pegues Harvey, "Escape from the Planet of the Modernists: Beyond the Growth Syndrome," *Texas Architect,* Sept.–Oct. 1988, pp. 36–41.

36   "gold-plated, irresistible invitation"   Kulash, "Traditional Neighborhood Development," p. 3–2.

36   visual preference studies   Kulash, "Traditional Neighborhood Development," p. 3–4 to 3–7.

38   "Rural cemeteries"   John W. Reps, *The Making of Urban America* (Princeton: Princeton University Press, 1965), pp. 325–48.

38   By the 1850s, curving roads   Robert A. M. Stern and John Montague Massengale, guest eds., *The Anglo-American Suburb,* published in *Architectural*

Design, Oct.–Nov. 1981, pp. 21–24; Spiro Kostof, *America by Design* (New York: Oxford University Press, 1987), pp. 27–28; and National Register of Historic Places, nomination form of Glendale, Ohio.

39 "leisure, contemplativeness, and happy tranquility" Olmsted, Vaux & Co., "Preliminary Report upon the Proposed Suburban Village at Riverside, near Chicago" (New York, 1868), p. 17.

41 Donald Appleyard found Donald Appleyard, with M. Sue Gerson and Mark Lintell, *Livable Streets* (Berkeley: University of California Press, 1981), pp. 20–24.

41 Radburn Clarence S. Stein, *Toward New Towns for America,* 3d ed. (Cambridge: MIT Press, 1966), pp. 37–73.

44 40 percent . . . shy Philip G. Zimbardo, *Shyness: What It Is, What to Do about It* (Reading, Mass.: Addison-Wesley Publishing, 1977), pp. 13–14.

44 rich possibility for movement Jacobs, *Death and Life,* pp. 178–86.

45 Levittown's most dissatisfied residents Herbert J. Gans, *The Levittowners: Ways of Life and Politics in a New Suburban Community* (New York: Pantheon Books, 1967), pp. 206–10.

46 "dark underside of suburbia" Carol Lawson, "A Writer Reveals the 'Dark Underside of Suburbia': Car Pools," *New York Times,* Sept. 12, 1991, p. C8.

49 "cul-de-sac smarts" Daniel Solomon, "Life on the Edge: Toward a New Suburbia," *Architectural Record,* Nov. 1988, p. 63.

49 "landmarks of my experience" Steve Coll, "Growing Up Suburban," *Washington Post Magazine,* June 10, 1990, pp. 27–29 and 52.

50 *All That Is Solid Melts* Marshall Berman, *All That is Solid Melts into Air: The Experience of Modernity* (New York: Simon and Schuster, 1982).

50 Oak Park is the older Information about Oak Park's history and development is drawn mainly from Carole Goodwin, *The Oak Park Strategy: Community Control of Racial Change* (Chicago: University of Chicago Press, 1979), pp. 29–45. For additional information, see Harold M. Mayer and Richard C. Wade, *Chicago: Growth of a Metropolis* (Chicago: University of Chicago Press, 1969), pp. 178–82 and 418.

53 third places Oldenburg, *Great Good Place,* pp. 14–16.

53 Upland, California Historical information on Upland and Euclid Avenue is drawn mainly from J. A. Alexander, *The Life of George Chaffey: A Story of Irrigation Beginnings in California and Australia* (Melbourne: Macmillan, 1928), pp. 48–59; Ruth Austen, *Ontario: The Model Colony* (Chatsworth, Calif.: Windsor Publications, 1990), pp. 8–43; and *Upland Yesterday* (Pomona: Pomona First Federal Savings and Loan Association, 1975), pp. 2–11.

THREE The Rise of Marketing and the Decline of Planning

67 "scenography" Rodney Friedman's comments on scenographic design are quoted in Charlie Haas, "The Great Condo Con," *Esquire,* Dec. 1981, pp. 33–44.

67 "an ESTATE or a SUBDIVISION?" This is the opening question in a brochure of Downing Thorpe James, an architecture and planning firm in Boulder, Colo., laying out what are called "planning criteria for a MARKETABLE DEVELOPMENT."

68 "Design Workshop" article "Gateways," *Builder,* Apr. 1987, pp. 86–89, by

William Devereaux of Berkus Group Architects and Deborah Woodcock, *Builder*'s new products editor.

70   "exciting, flexible, stimulating" Philip Langdon, "The American House," *Atlantic Monthly,* Sept. 1984, p. 50.

71   tract houses in the Bay Area Clare Cooper Marcus, Carolyn Francis, and Colette Meunier, "Mixed Messages in Suburbia: Reading the Suburban Model Home," *Places* 4, no. 1 (1987): 31.

71   lewd and lascivious conduct "Seen Having Sex in Window, 2 Are Charged," *New York Times,* July 20, 1991, p. L7.

74   an eternal adolescence Richard Sennett, *The Uses of Disorder: Personal Identity and City Life* (New York: Alfred A. Knopf, 1970), pp. 3–26 and 107–36.

76   "replenishes our beings" John Killinger, *The Loneliness of Children* (New York: Vanguard Press, 1980), p. 148.

76   "our most atomized communities" Gerald D. Suttles, *The Social Construction of Communities* (Chicago: University of Chicago Press, 1972), p. 15.

80   revisited a well-known community Rich Binsacca, "The New American Home: A Look Back," *Builder,* Jan. 1993, pp. 156–65; and June Fletcher, "Lessons from Long Island," *Builder,* Dec. 1988, pp. 72–77.

81   "Why I Won't Buy" June Fletcher, "Why I Won't Buy a New Home," *Builder,* March 1993, pp. 72–79.

81   felt like an insult J. Roger Glunt, "Seeing Red," *Builder,* May 1993, p. 74.

84   "sacrifice for the common good" James Lincoln Collier, *The Rise of Selfishness in America* (New York: Oxford University Press, 1991), p. 262.

FOUR Controlling the Neighborhood

86   "beige and off-beige" Stephanie Mansfield, "Guaranteed Expectations," *Washington Post Magazine,* Nov. 21, 1982, p. 21.

87   As of 1962 Community Associations Institute, "Community Associations Factbook" (Alexandria, Va.: Community Associations Institute, 1988), p. i.

87   More than thirty million "Government by the Nice, for the Nice," *Economist,* July 25, 1992, p. 25.

88   Evan McKenzie McKenzie's book *Privatopia* is to be published by Yale University Press.

88   properties maintained their value Byron R. Hanke and others, *The Homes Association Handbook* (Washington, D.C.: Urban Land Institute, 1964), p. 15.

90   "at least 50 percent of the market" Community Associations Institute, "Community Associations Factbook," p. i.

90   "Storm doors" Mark Grossman and Will Schermerhorn, "Door Color Controversy Storms: Burke Centre Board to Review Ruling," *Fairfax Journal,* Aug. 24, 1992, p. A1.

91   "white-stone discussions" Steve Twomey, "Pastel-Packing Lawmen Come Knocking," *Washington Post,* Aug. 31, 1992, p. D5.

92   A 1987 study in California William K. Stevens, "Condominium Owners Grapple with Governing Themselves," *New York Times,* Sept. 1, 1988, p. A18.

95   "linking house to house" J. Christopher Lang, *Building with Nantucket in Mind: Guidelines for Protecting the Historic Architecture and Landscape of*

Nantucket Island (Nantucket, Mass.: Nantucket Historic District Commission, 1978), p. 44. Much of this chapter's information about Nantucket's history is from this source.

96   "If you could trust"   Mansfield, "Guaranteed Expectations," p. 21.

97   "offenses against taste"   John Kennedy Toole, *A Confederacy of Dunces* (New York: Grove Weidenfeld, 1987), p. 13.

98   "Every exterior detail was approved"   *Builder,* Oct. 1989, p. 154.

100   "Soul yearns for attachment"   Thomas Moore, *Care of the Soul: A Guide for Cultivating Depth and Sacredness in Everyday Life* (New York: Harper-Collins, 1992), p. 92.

102   At Virginia Run   William F. Powers, "Community Covenants: Home Rules," *Washington Post,* Nov. 2, 1991, p. E1.

106   "joyful participation"   Robert Bly, *Iron John: A Book about Men* (Reading, Mass.: Addison-Wesley Publishing, 1990), p. 177.

106   At Village Homes   Michael N. Corbett, *A Better Place to Live: New Designs for Tomorrow's Communities* (Emmaus, Pa.: Rodale Press, 1981), pp. 46–55 and 94–97. See also Langdon, "American House," p. 51.

FIVE The Rediscovery of the Town

107   Florida's "redneck Riviera"   Portions of this chapter appeared in Philip Langdon, "A Good Place to Live," *Atlantic Monthly,* March 1988, pp. 39–60.

112   Davis wanted to develop   Daralice D. Boles, "Robert Davis: Small Town Entrepreneur," *Progressive Architecture,* July 1985, pp. 111–18.

112   Andres Duany and Elizabeth Plater-Zyberk   Most of this chapter's information about Duany and Plater-Zyberk is drawn from their public presentations and interviews with the author. Useful written sources include the following: Andres Duany and Elizabeth Plater-Zyberk, "The Second Coming of the American Small Town, *Wilson Quarterly,* Winter 1992, pp. 19–50; Alex Krieger, ed., with William Lennertz, *Andres Duany and Elizabeth Plater-Zyberk: Towns and Town-Making Principles* (Cambridge: Harvard University Graduate School of Design, 1991); Vincent Scully, "Back to the Future, with a Detour through Miami," *New York Times,* Jan. 27, 1991, p. 32; Joseph Giovannini, "Blueprint for the Future," *Esquire,* Dec. 1986, pp. 111–13; Eric Morgenthaler, "Old-Style Towns Where People Walk Have Modern Backers," *Wall Street Journal,* Feb. 1, 1993, pp. A1 and A12; and "Seaside and the Real World: A Debate on American Urbanism," *Architecture New York* (guest ed., David Mohney) 1, no. 1 (July–Aug. 1993).

116   Charleston Place   Susan Doubilet, "A Venerable Town Pattern Reemerges," *Progressive Architecture,* Aug. 1984, pp. 74–79.

119   the Gallup Organization   Duany and Plater-Zyberk, "Second Coming of the American Small Town," pp. 21–22.

122   "transit-oriented development"   Calthorpe's ideas are presented in the following works of his: *The Next American Metropolis: Ecology, Community, and the American Dream* (New York: Princeton Architectural Press, 1993); "Towns for All Seasons," *Architectural Record,* June 1991, pp. 44–45; and "The Post-Suburban Metropolis, *Whole Earth Review,* Winter 1991, pp. 44–51. See also Doug Kelbaugh, ed., *The Pedestrian Pocket Book: A New Suburban Design Strategy* (New York: Princeton Architectural Press, in association

with the University of Washington, 1989); and Michael Leccese, "Next Stop: Transit-Friendly Towns," *Landscape Architecture*, July 1990, pp. 47–53.

125 "blocks are bent, squeezed" Patrick Pinnell, "Organon," in *Andres Duany and Elizabeth Plater-Zyberk*, ed. Krieger, p. 106.

131 Mashpee, Massachusetts Mashpee Commons is discussed in Langdon, "Good Place to Live," p. 46; Paul M. Sachner, "Common Sense," *Architectural Record*, Mar. 1989, pp. 84–89; and Barbara Flanagan, "A Cape Cod Mall Is Disappeared," *New York Times*, Mar. 14, 1991, pp. C1 and C10.

133 In Kentlands, a church The initial planning of Kentlands in a weeklong charette is described in Patricia Leigh Brown, "In Seven Days, Designing a New Traditional Town," *New York Times*, June 9, 1988, pp. C1 and C6.

139 Mariemont P. M. Sexton, *Mariemont: A Brief Chronicle of Its Origin and Development* (Mariemont, Ohio: Village of Mariemont, 1966); Warren Wright Parks, *The Mariemont Story: "A National Exemplar in Town Planning"* (Cincinnati: Creative Writers & Publishers, 1967); and John Nolen, "Modern City Planning Principles Applied to a Small Community," *National Real Estate Journal*, Mar. 26, 1923, pp. 1–7.

142 they [greenbelts] say to residents How to demarcate neighborhoods without closing them off from one another is thoughtfully discussed in Christopher Alexander, Sara Ishikawa, and Murray Silverstein, *A Pattern Language: Towns, Buildings, Construction* (New York: Oxford University Press, 1977), pp. 80–90.

143 "belonging to Oak Park" Carole Goodwin, *The Oak Park Strategy: Community Control of Racial Change* (Chicago: University of Chicago Press, 1979), p. 31.

146 features . . . at their borders Richard Hedman, "Suburban Sketchbook," *Planning*, Dec. 1989, pp. 18–19.

SIX Turning Around the American House

148 Family rooms Philip Langdon, "The Family Room and How It Has Changed," *New York Times*, Jan. 6, 1983, p. C10.

148 "energy-consuming appliances" Marcus, Francis, and Meunier, "Mixed Messages in Suburbia," p. 30.

149 ever-increasing number of vehicles Federal Highway Administration, "Summary of Travel Trends: 1990 Nationwide Personal Transportation Survey," Mar. 1992, pp. 6–24.

150 "wall-to-wall garage doors" Wentling's observations in this chapter are drawn mainly from a draft of his manuscript, "A Place Called Home: Designing New Homes and Communities," to be published in 1994.

151 "Driving to the kitchen" Daniel Solomon and Susan Haviland, "Emerald City," *Oz* (Kansas State University College of Architecture & Design) 11 (1989): 42.

152 "the laws of convenience" Jesse Jackson, quoted in *New York Times*, Mar. 29, 1984, p. B9.

152 "information is no longer controllable" Neil Postman, *Technopoly: The Surrender of Culture to Technology* (New York: Alfred A. Knopf, 1992), pp. 72–73.

153 "That man is richest" Henry David Thoreau, *The Journal of Henry D. Thor-*

eau (1906; reprint, New York: Dover Publications, 1962, ed. Bradford Torrey and Francis H. Allen), 8: 981, entry for Mar. 11, 1856.

153   The poet Horace   *The Works of Horace,* trans. with a life and notes by Sir Theodore Martin, K.C.B. (Edinburgh: William Blackwood and Sons, 1888), 1:128.

153   "The cultivation of needs"   E. F. Schumacher, *Small Is Beautiful: Economics As If People Mattered* (New York: Harper & Row, 1973), p. 31.

154   Median household income   Louis Uchitelle, "Trapped in the Impoverished Middle Class," *New York Times,* Nov. 17, 1991, sec. 3, p. 1.

155   "No architect is skillful enough"   Duany and Plater-Zyberk, "Second Coming of the American Small Town," p. 38.

155   many ways to make garages less obtrusive   Philip Langdon, "Planning a Garage," *Home,* Feb. 1991, pp. 102–3.

163   Laguna West   Flaws are found in Laguna West in Eve M. Kahn's "Critic-at-Large" article "Laguna West: Suburbia's Future?" *Landscape Architecture,* July 1993, pp. 34–35.

166   nearby mixed-use town center   Calthorpe, *Next American Metropolis,* pp. 42, 58, and 64.

SEVEN Work, Shopping, and Transportation

173   Chicago's western and northern suburbs   Illinois Department of Employment Security, "Where Workers Work in the Chicago Metro Area, 1990: A Summary of Employment Covered under the Illinois Unemployment Insurance Act," pp. 5–16.

173   In 1972 more than half   Illinois Department of Employment Security, "Where Workers Work," pp. 26–62.

175   Gurnee Mills, a gigantic outlet mall   Robert Bruegmann reports incisively on retailing trends in metropolitan Chicago in "Vox Populi," *Inland Architect,* Nov.–Dec. 1992, pp. 53–61.

175   Texas Transportation Institute   Anthony Downs, *Stuck in Traffic: Coping with Peak-Hour Traffic Congestion* (Washington, D.C.: Brookings Institution, and Cambridge, Mass.: Lincoln Institute of Land Policy, 1992), pp. 11–12.

176   "peak-hour congestion is so bad"   Downs, *Stuck in Traffic,* p. 138.

177   "times should get worse"   Phone interview with Alan Pisarski. *Commuting in America* was published by Eno Foundation for Transportation (Westport, Conn., 1987).

177   "Traffic congestion on Saturdays"   George James, "The New Rush Hours: All Day Saturday," *New York Times,* Dec. 2, 1989, p. 29.

178   Miami Lakes Town Center   Miami Lakes is discussed in June Fletcher, "Mastering Planned Communities," *Builder,* Nov. 1987, pp. 72–83, and an interview with Lester Collins, p. 128.

179   Reston Town Center   Reston and Miami Lakes town centers are discussed in Philip Langdon, "Pumping Up Suburban Downtowns," *Planning,* July 1990, pp. 22–28. Reston Town Center is also examined in Nancy McKeon, "City of Lite," *Washington Post Magazine,* Aug. 23, 1992, pp. 12–16; and Andrea Oppenheimer Dean, "New Town Downtown," *Architecture,* Dec. 1991, pp. 56–61.

183   Jonathan Barnett   Barnett discusses shared parking in "Accidental Cities:

The Deadly Grip of Outmoded Zoning," *Architectural Record,* Feb. 1992, pp. 94–101.

184   designs for Avalon Park   Krieger, *Andres Duany and Elizabeth Plater-Zyberk,* pp. 88–94.

185   a regional shopping mall   Philip Langdon, "Beyond the Cul-de-sac," *Landscape Architecture,* Oct. 1989, pp. 72–73.

187   transit-oriented design   Calthorpe, *Next American Metropolis,* pp. 41–67.

188   Laguna West   Laguna West is discussed in Gary Delsohn, "The First Pedestrian Pocket," *Planning,* Dec. 1989, pp. 20–22.

193   "worst white elephants"   Thomas J. Lueck, "Vacated Corporate Headquarters Scatter the Suburban Landscape," *New York Times,* Dec. 7, 1992, p. A1.

197   Highway 99 north of Seattle   Richard K. Untermann, "Linking Land Use and Transportation: Design Strategies to Serve HOV's and Pedestrians," a report for the Washington State Department of Transportation, June 1991, pp. 1–51.

EIGHT What Government Can Do

202   Naperville . . . business facilities   Lemann, "Stressed Out in Suburbia," pp. 34–48; and collection of Naperville articles, *Crain's Chicago Business,* Oct. 31, 1988, pp. T1–T10.

203   "municipal mini-imperialism"   Mike Davis, *City of Quartz: Excavating the Future in Los Angeles* (New York: Verso, 1990), p. 215.

209   The Portland area   Philip Langdon, "How Portland Does It," *Atlantic Monthly,* Nov. 1992, pp. 134–41.

211   the region's natural systems   A classic argument for planning in accordance with natural systems is Benton MacKaye's *New Exploration: A Philosophy of Regional Planning* (1928; reprint, Urbana: University of Illinois Press, 1962).

212   "standards adopted for new streets"   Philip B. Herr, "The Case of the Northeastern Village," *Historic Preservation Forum* 6, no. 5 (Sept.–Oct. 1992): 22.

214   zoning has become a straitjacket   See Barnett, "Accidental Cities," pp. 94–101.

NINE Repairing the Existing Suburbs

224   "Bellevue used . . . design tools"   Terry Jill Lassar, *Carrots and Sticks: New Zoning Downtown* (Washington, D.C.: Urban Land Institute, 1989), pp. 124–26, 148–51, 164, and 172.

226   "pedestrian-unfriendly features"   Jane Holtz Kay, "Building a *There There,*" *Planning,* Jan. 1991, p. 4.

228   a vision of . . . each road   Ruth Eckdish Knack, "Park and Shop: Some Guidelines," *Planning,* May 1992, pp. 18–21; and Mark L. Hinshaw, "Design Objectives Plan: Entryway Corridors, Bozeman, Montana" (1991), pp. 1–95.

229   "even cheaper substitutes"   Bruegmann, "Vox Populi," p. 58.

234   Wheaton Town Center   Bruegmann, "Vox Populi," pp. 59–61.

TEN Prospects for a New Vision

242   ISTEA   F. K. Plous, Jr., "Refreshing ISTEA," *Planning,* Feb. 1993, pp. 9–12.

Books

Alexander, Christopher, Sara Ishikawa, and Murray Silverstein. *A Pattern Language: Towns, Buildings, Construction.* New York: Oxford University Press, 1977.

Altman, Irwin, and Ervin H. Zube, eds. *Public Places and Spaces.* New York: Plenum Press, 1989.

Altshuler, Alan A., and José Gómez-Ibáñez, with Arnold M. Howitt. *Regulation for Revenue: The Political Economy of Land Use Exactions.* Washington, D.C.: Brookings Institution, and Cambridge, Mass.: Lincoln Institute of Land Policy, 1993.

Anderson, Stanford, ed. *On Streets.* Cambridge: MIT Press, 1978.

Appleyard, Donald, with M. Sue Gerson and Mark Lintell. *Livable Streets.* Berkeley: University of California Press, 1981.

Austen, Ruth. *Ontario: The Model Colony.* Chatsworth, Calif.: Windsor Publications, 1990.

Bishir, Catherine W., and Lawrence S. Earley, eds. *Early Twentieth-Century Suburbs in North Carolina: Essays on History, Architecture, and Planning.* North Carolina Department of Cultural Resources, 1985.

Bookchin, Murray. *The Rise of Urbanization and the Decline of Citizenship.* San Francisco: Sierra Club Books, 1987.

Buder, Stanley. *Visionaries and Planners: The Garden City Movement and the Modern Community.* New York: Oxford University Press, 1990.

Bunting, Bainbridge. *Houses of Boston's Back Bay: An Architectural History, 1840–1917.* Cambridge, Mass.: Belknap Press, 1967.

Calthorpe, Peter. *The Next American Metropolis: Ecology, Community, and the American Dream.* New York: Princeton Architectural Press, 1993.

Cervero, Robert. *Suburban Gridlock.* Piscataway, N.J.: Center for Urban Policy Research, 1986.

Collins, George R., and Christiane Craseman Collins. *Camillo Sitte: The Birth of Modern City Planning.* New York: Rizzoli, 1986.

Corbett, Michael N. *A Better Place to Live: New Designs for Tomorrow's Communities.* Emmaus, Pa.: Rodale Press, 1981.

Creese, Walter L., ed. *The Legacy of Raymond Unwin: A Human Pattern for Planning.* Cambridge: MIT Press, 1967.

Darley, Gillian. *Villages of Vision.* London: Architectural Press, 1975.

Davis, Mike. *City of Quartz: Excavating the Future in Los Angeles.* New York: Verso, 1990.

Downs, Anthony. *Stuck in Traffic: Coping with Peak-Hour Traffic Congestion.* Washington, D.C.: Brookings Institution, and Cambridge, Mass.: Lincoln Institute of Land Policy, 1992.

Easterling, Keller. *American Town Plans: A Comparative Time Line.* New York: Princeton Architectural Press, 1993.

Ebner, Michael H. *Creating Chicago's North Shore: A Suburban History.* Chicago: University of Chicago Press, 1988.

Etzioni, Amitai. *A Responsive Society: Collected Essays on Guiding Deliberate Social Change.* San Francisco: Jossey-Bass Publishers, 1991.

Fishman, Robert. *Bourgeois Utopias: The Rise and Fall of Suburbia.* New York: Basic Books, 1987.

———. *Urban Utopias in the Twentieth Century: Ebenezer Howard, Frank Lloyd Wright, and Le Corbusier.* Cambridge: MIT Press, 1982.

Gans, Herbert J. *The Levittowners: Ways of Life and Politics in a New Suburban Community.* New York: Pantheon Books, 1967.

Garreau, Joel. *Edge City: Life on the New Frontier.* New York: Doubleday, 1991.

Goodwin, Carole. *The Oak Park Strategy: Community Control of Racial Change.* Chicago: University of Chicago Press, 1979.

Gottdiener, Mark. *Planned Sprawl: Private and Public Interests in Suburbia.* Beverly Hills, Calif.: Sage Library of Social Research, 1977.

Hall, Peter. *Cities of Tomorrow: An Intellectual History of Urban Planning and Design in the Twentieth Century.* Cambridge: Basil Blackwell, 1990.

Hayden, Dolores. *Redesigning the American Dream: The Future of Housing, Work, and Family Life.* New York: W. W. Norton, 1986.

Hiss, Tony. *The Experience of Place.* New York: Alfred A. Knopf, 1990.

Hough, Michael. *Out of Place: Restoring Identity to the Regional Landscape.* New Haven: Yale University Press, 1990.

Jackson, Kenneth T. *Crabgrass Frontier: The Suburbanization of the United States.* New York: Oxford University Press, 1985.

Jacobs, Allan B. *Great Streets.* Cambridge: MIT Press, 1993.

Jacobs, Jane. *The Death and Life of Great American Cities.* New York: Vintage Books, 1961.

Kelbaugh, Doug, ed. *The Pedestrian Pocket Book: A New Suburban Design Strategy.* New York: Princeton Architectural Press, in association with the University of Washington, 1989.

Kling, Rob, Spencer Olin, and Mark Poster, eds. *Post-Suburban California: The Transformation of Orange County since World War II.* Berkeley: University of California Press, 1991.

Krieger, Alex, ed., with William Lennertz. *Andres Duany and Elizabeth Plater-Zyberk: Towns and Town-Making Principles.* Cambridge: Harvard University Graduate School of Design, 1991.

Lang, J. Christopher. *Building with Nantucket in Mind: Guidelines for Protecting the Historic Architecture and Landscape of Nantucket Island.* Nantucket, Mass.: Nantucket Historic District Commission, 1978.

Langdon, Philip. *American Houses.* New York: Stewart, Tabori & Chang, 1987.

Lassar, Terry Jill. *Carrots and Sticks: New Zoning Downtown.* Washington, D.C.: Urban Land Institute, 1989.

Linden-Ward, Blanche. *A Silent City on a Hill: Landscapes of Memory and Boston's Mount Auburn Cemetery.* Columbus: Ohio State University Press, 1989.

Louv, Richard. *America II.* Los Angeles: Jeremy P. Tarcher, 1983.

MacKaye, Benton. *The New Exploration: A Philosophy of Regional Planning.* 1928. Reprint. Urbana: University of Illinois Press, 1962.

Mackin, Anne, and Alex Krieger. *A Design Primer for Cities and Towns.* Massachusetts Council on the Arts and Humanities, 1989.

Mohney, David, and Keller Easterling, eds. *Seaside: Making a Town in America.* New York: Princeton Architectural Press, 1991.

Morris, A. E. J. *History of Urban Form: Before the Industrial Revolutions.* 2d ed. New York: John Wiley & Sons, 1979.

Moudon, Anne Vernez, ed. *Public Streets for Public Use.* New York: Van Nostrand Reinhold, 1987.

Muller, Peter O. *Contemporary Suburban America.* Englewood Cliffs, N.J.: Prentice-Hall, 1981.

Newton, Norman T. *Design on the Land: The Development of Landscape Architecture.* Cambridge: Harvard University Press, 1971.

Oldenburg, Ray. *The Great Good Place: Cafes, Coffee Shops, Community Centers. Beauty Parlors, General Stores, Bars, Hangouts and How They Get You Through the Day.* New York: Paragon House, 1991.

Parks, Warren Wright. *The Mariemont Story: "A National Exemplar in Town Planning."* Cincinnati: Creative Writers & Publishers, 1967.

Peets, Elbert. *On the Art of Designing Cities: Selected Essays of Elbert Peets.* Edited by Paul D. Spreiregen. Cambridge: MIT Press, 1968.

Pisarski, Alan. *Commuting in America: A National Report on Commuting Patterns and Trends.* Westport, Conn.: Eno Foundation for Transportation, 1987.

Reps, John W. *The Making of Urban America.* Princeton: Princeton University Press, 1965.

Rowe, Peter G. *Making a Middle Landscape.* Cambridge: MIT Press, 1991.

Rudofsky, Bernard. *Streets for People: A Primer for Americans.* Garden City, N.Y.: Doubleday, 1969.

Schor, Juliet B. *The Overworked American: The Unexpected Decline of Leisure.* New York: Basic Books, 1991.

Sennett, Richard. *The Uses of Disorder: Personal Identity and City Life.* New York: Alfred A. Knopf, 1970.

Sexton, P. M. *Mariemont: A Brief Chronicle of Its Origin and Development.* Mariemont, Ohio: Village of Mariemont, 1966.

Solomon, Daniel. *ReBuilding.* New York: Princeton Architectural Press, 1992.

Stein, Clarence S. *Toward New Towns for America.* 3d ed. Cambridge: MIT Press, 1966.

Stern, Robert A. M., and John Montague Massengale, guest eds. *The Anglo-American Suburb. Architectural Design* (London) 51 (Oct.–Nov. 1981).

Stilgoe, John R. *Borderland: Origins of the American Suburb, 1820–1939.* New Haven: Yale University Press, 1988.

Suttles, Gerald D. *The Social Construction of Communities.* Chicago: University of Chicago Press, 1972.

Untermann, Richard K. *Accommodating the Pedestrian: Adapting Towns and Neighborhoods for Walking and Bicycles.* New York: Van Nostrand Reinhold, 1984.

Unwin, Raymond. *Town Planning in Practice: An Introduction to the Art of Designing Cities and Suburbs.* 1909. Reprint. New York: Benjamin Blom, 1971.

Warner, Sam Bass, Jr. *Streetcar Suburbs: The Process of Growth in Boston, 1870–1890.* 2d ed. Cambridge: Harvard University Press, 1978.

Weiss, Marc A. *The Rise of the Community Builders: The American Real Estate Industry and Urban Land Planning.* New York: Columbia University Press, 1987.

Weiss, Michael J. *The Clustering of America.* New York: Tilden Press, 1988.

Whyte, William H. *The Organization Man.* Garden City, N.Y.: Doubleday Anchor, 1956.

Worley, William S. *J. C. Nichols and the Shaping of Kansas City: Innovation in Planned Residential Communities.* Columbia: University of Missouri Press, 1990.

Yaro, Robert D., Randall G. Arendt, Harry L. Dodson, and Elizabeth A. Brabec. *Dealing with Change in the Connecticut River Valley: A Design Manual for Conservation and Development.* Cambridge: Lincoln Institute of Land Policy and the Environmental Law Foundation, 1989.

Zucker, Paul. *Town and Square from the Agora to the Village Green.* New York: Columbia University Press, 1959.

Articles and Reports

Barnett, Jonathan. "Accidental Cities: The Deadly Grip of Outmoded Zoning." *Architectural Record,* Feb. 1992, pp. 94–101.

Calthorpe, Peter. "The Post-Suburban Metropolis." *Whole Earth Review,* Winter 1991, pp. 44–51.

——. "Towns for All Seasons." *Architectural Record,* June 1991, pp. 44–45.

Cannell, Mike. "Brave [New] World." *Metropolis,* May 1988, pp. 62–67 and 95–97.

Coll, Steve. "Growing Up Suburban." *Washington Post Magazine,* June 10, 1990, pp. 27–29 and 52.

Delsohn, Gary. "The First Pedestrian Pocket." *Planning,* Dec. 1989, pp. 20–22.

Doubilet, Susan. "A Venerable Town Pattern Reemerges." *Progressive Architecture,* Aug. 1984, pp. 74–79.

Duany, Andres, and Elizabeth Plater-Zyberk. "The Second Coming of the American Small Town." *Wilson Quarterly,* Winter 1992, pp. 19–50.

Fishman, Robert. "America's New City." *Wilson Quarterly,* Winter 1990, pp. 24–45.

Haas, Charlie. "The Great Condo Con." *Esquire,* Dec. 1981, pp. 33–44.

Harvey, Douglas Pegues. "Escape from the Planet of the Modernists: Beyond the Growth Syndrome." *Texas Architect,* Sept.–Oct. 1988, pp. 36–41.

Hedman, Richard. "Suburban Sketchbook." *Planning,* Dec. 1989, pp. 18–19.

Herr, Philip B. "The Case of the Northeastern Village." *Historic Preservation Forum* 6, no. 5 (1992): 20–28.

Hinshaw, Mark L. "Design Objectives Plan: Entryway Corridors, Bozeman, Montana." Report for the Bozeman City Commission, 1991.

Kahn, Eve M. "Critic-at-Large. Laguna West: Suburbia's Future?" *Landscape Architecture,* July 1993, pp. 34–35.

Kay, Jane Holtz. "Building a There There." *Planning,* Jan. 1991, pp. 4–8.

Knack, Ruth Eckdish. "Park and Shop: Some Guidelines." *Planning,* May 1992, pp. 18–21.

——. "Selling Cluster." *Planning,* Sept. 1990, pp. 4–10.

——. "Tony Nelessen's Do-It-Yourself Neotraditionalism." *Planning,* Dec. 1991, pp. 18–22.

Kulash, Walter [of Glatting Jackson Lopez Kercher Anglin Lopez Rinehart, Orlando, Fla.]. "Traditional Neighborhood Development: Will the Traffic Work?" Report for the Eleventh Annual Pedestrian Conference, Bellevue, Wash., Oct. 1990.

Langdon, Philip. "Beyond the Cul-de-Sac." *Landscape Architecture,* Oct. 1989, pp. 72–73.

——. "A Good Place to Live." *Atlantic Monthly,* Mar. 1988, pp. 39–60.

——. "How Portland Does It." *Atlantic Monthly,* Nov. 1992, pp. 134–41.

——. "Pumping Up Suburban Downtowns." *Planning,* July 1990, pp. 22–28.

Leccese, Michael. "Next Stop: Transit-Friendly Towns." *Landscape Architecture,* July 1990, pp. 47–53.

Lemann, Nicholas. "Stressed Out in Suburbia." *Atlantic Monthly,* Nov. 1989, pp. 34–48.

Marcus, Clare Cooper, Carolyn Francis, and Colette Meunier. "Mixed Messages in Suburbia: Reading the Suburban Model Home." *Places* 4, no. 1 (1987): 24–37.

Mohney, David, guest ed. "Seaside and the Real World: A Debate on American Urbanism," *Architecture New York* 1, no. 1 (July–Aug. 1993): 6–53.

Rabinowitz, Harvey, Edward Beimborn, Charles Mrotek, Shuming Yan, and Peter Gugliotta. "The New Suburb: An Examination and Analysis of Recent Proposals." a Report by the Center for Urban Transportation Studies and the School of Architecture and Urban Planning, University of Wisconsin-Milwaukee, for the United States Urban Mass Transportation Administration, July 1991.

Teska Associates Inc. "Guidelines for Diversified Regional Centers." Report for the Northeastern Illinois Planning Commission, Chicago, May 28, 1991.

Untermann, Richard K. "Linking Land Use and Transportation: Design Strategies to Serve HOV's and Pedestrians." Report for the Washington State Department of Transportation, June 1991.

Illustration Credits

All photos and drawings are by Philip Langdon, except as noted.
Frontispiece: ii–iii: Max MacKenzie, courtesy of Sasaki Associates, Inc.

Chapter 1 Page 5: Dan Weiner, courtesy Sandra Weiner; 9: California Department of Transportation; 16: French Government Tourist Office; 17: Christopher Faust, Suburban Documentation Project, St. Paul, Minn.

Chapter 2 Page 29: Glatting Jackson Kercher Anglin Lopez Rinehart, Community Planning, Orlando, Fla.; 30: Duany and Plater-Zyberk, Architects; 33: The Irvine Company; 35: Glatting Jackson Kercher Anglin Lopez Rinehart, Community Planning; 38: *Left,* Mount Auburn Cemetery, and *right, American Magazine of Useful Knowledge,* June 1835, both courtesy Mount Auburn Cemetery; 40: Prepared by Ed Straka, Riverside, Ill.; 51: James F. Quinn Photography; 54: Ontario City Library, Model Colony Room'Collection.

Chapter 3 Page 64: Markborough Florida, Inc.; 80: Chicago Historical Society; 82: Courtesy David Yamashita

Chapter 4 Page 101: Elm Research Institute, Harrisville, N.H.

Chapter 5 Pages 108, 109, 117: Courtesy Duany and Plater-Zyberk, Architects; 125: RTKL Associates, Baltimore, Md.; 126: Courtesy Duany and Plater-Zyberk, Architects; 127: Robert Llewellyn, photographer; 130: Courtesy Mashpee Commons; 131: Nick Wheeler, © Wheeler Photographics; 132: Mick Hales, photographer, courtesy Orr & Taylor, Architects; 134: Robert Llewellyn, photographer; 138: Harry Connolly

Chapter 6 Page 150: Anton C. Nelessen; 155: Christopher Faust, Suburban Documentation Project, St. Paul, Minn.; 157: Calthorpe Associates; 158: John O'Hagen; 159: Jeffrey Jacobs, Mims Studio, courtesy Looney Ricks Kiss Architects, Inc., Memphis, Tenn.; 160: Courtesy Duany and Plater-Zyberk, Architects; 162: Jeffrey Jacobs, Mims Studio, courtesy Looney Ricks Kiss Architects, Inc., Memphis, Tenn.; 163, 165: Calthorpe Associates; 168: Jeffrey Jacobs, Mims Studio, courtesy Looney Ricks Kiss Architects, Inc., Memphis, Tenn.; 169: Looney Ricks Kiss Architects, Inc., Memphis, Tenn.

Chapter 7 Page 176–77: Christopher Faust, Suburban Documentation Project, St. Paul, Minn.; 180: Max MacKenzie, courtesy Sasaki Associates, Inc.;

185, 186: Courtesy Duany and Plater-Zyberk, Architects; 188, 189, 190–91: Calthorpe Associates; 194: Peter Aaron/Esto, courtesy Sasaki Associates, Inc.

Chapter 8   Page 204: Glatting Jackson Kercher Anglin Lopez Rinehart, Community Planning, Orlando, Fla.; 206–7: Christopher Faust, Suburban Documentation Project, St. Paul, Minn.; 210: Oregon Department of Land Conservation and Development

Chapter 9   Page 220: Rich K. Untermann; 225, 227: Mark L. Hinshaw; 231: Nicholas Walster Photography; 232, 233: Copyright Peter Aaron/Esto Photographs

Chapter 10   Page 237: Robert Llewellyn, photographer; 238: Reston Town Center Associates; 239: Jeffrey Jacobs, Mims Studio, Memphis, Tenn., 1993

Index

street hierarchy and, 27–29
suburban commercial development and, 175–77, 189
time spent, 176–77
Compromises, 164–66, 239
Congress for the New Urbanism, 121
Connection. *See also* Fragmentation, sense of
cul-de-sacs and, 36, 44–45, 235
market segmentation and, 72–73
neighborhood life and, 135–41,
   152–53
between neighborhoods, 141–47
between residential and shopping
   areas, 233
street networks and, 53, 60, 182
traditionalist approach and, 123,
   135–41
Consistency/variety balance. *See*
   Harmony, and variety
Construction quality, ix–x, 163–66,
   229
Contact, wanted vs. unwanted, 43
Courtyards, 118, 234–35
Cranbury, New Jersey, 150
Crofton, Maryland, 17–19
Crosstown streets, 57–59, 76, 143–
   45. *See also* Boulevards; Street
   networks
Cul-de-sacs, 41–49, 130, 235
Curving roads, 37–40

Danbury, Connecticut, 193
Danville, California. *See* Blackhawk
Davis, Andrew Jackson, 39
Davis, Mike, 203
Davis, Robert S., 110–12
Deakin, Elizabeth, 10
de Bretteville, Peter, 120
"Dendritic" system, 181
Developers
boulevards and, 59
government policy and, 216–18
harmony controls and, 161–63
in late 1970s, 115
local control and, 231–32
marketing and, 63, 71
mixture of housing types and,
   166–67
prevailing practices and, 192–94
sources of ideas and, 83–84
trade magazines and, 79–83
Distinctiveness, 100–101, 228–29
Diversity, 73–76, 136, 140, 204

Dodd, Christine, 46
Dodd, Michael, 46
Downs, Anthony, 175–76
Duany, Andres, 12, 105, 182. *See
   also* Duany & Plater-Zyberk
Duany & Plater-Zyberk. *See also* Duany, Andres; Plater-Zyberk,
   Elizabeth
Avalon Park and, 184–86
business buildings and, 191–92
Charleston Place and, 116–18
connection between neighborhoods and, 141–42
diversity and, 136
garages and, 155
harmony and, 160–61
Kentlands and, 125–27, 134–35
orientation of, 123
principles of community design
   and, 217
projects of, 118, 239
Seaside, Florida, and, 111–16,
   118
street networks and, 124–27

East Aurora, New York, xi
Economic factors, 50, 192, 202–3,
   240
Education, 48–49, 133–35
Edward Scissorhands (movie), 42
Elderly persons, xii, 44, 47–48, 96–
   97, 243
Employment
character of suburbs and, 174
job growth in suburbs and, 172–
   74
length of workweek and, 4–6
women and, 6
Enclave developments, 65–71
Entrances
in enclave developments, 68–69
to houses, 70, 156–57
Environmental concerns, 121, 241–
   42. *See also* Natural systems
Environmental Design Research Association, 83–84
Etzioni, Amitai, 21
Euclid Avenue, Upland, California,
   53–58
Existing suburbs, repair of
roadside strips and, 227–35
town centers and, 219–27
Expensive houses, 164–66, 201–
   2